United States
Department of
Agriculture

**Forest
Service**

**North Central
Research Station**

**General Technical
Report NC-242**

# RPA Data Wiz Users Guide, Version 1.0

Scott A. Pugh

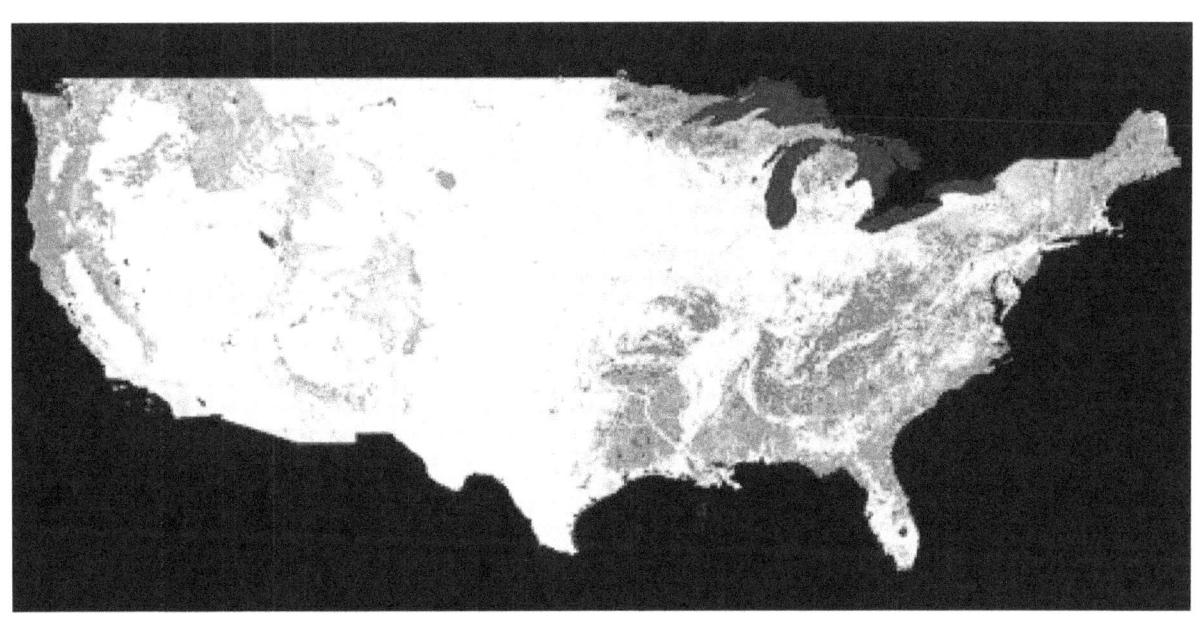

## MISSION STATEMENT

We believe the good life has its roots in clean air, sparkling water, rich soil, healthy economies and a diverse living landscape. Maintaining the good life for generations to come begins with everyday choices about natural resources. The North Central Research Station provides the knowledge and the tools to help people make informed choices. That's how the science we do enhances the quality of people's lives.

For further information contact:

North Central
Research Station
USDA Forest Service
1992 Folwell Ave., St. Paul, MN 55108

# SUMMARY

RPA Data Wiz is a computer desktop application that allows users to customize summaries of Resource Planning Act (RPA) Assessment forest information. Summary tables, graphs, and choropleth maps can be produced with this software. A number of variables can be analyzed. Volumes for growing stock, live cull, dead salvable, netgrowth, and mortality can be estimated. Acreage, biomass, and tree count estimates are also available. Currently, removals are not available in this software. RPA Data Wiz is available in English and metric versions. This software was developed using Microsoft Visual Basic 6.0 (SP5), Microsoft ADO, Microsoft ADOX, Microsoft Windows Common Controls 6.0 (SP5), Microsoft Hierarchical FlexGrid Control 6.0 (SP4), Microsoft Common Dialog Control 6.0, Microsoft Chart Control 6.0 (SP4 OLEDB), ESRI MapObjects LT 2.0 (2000), a Microsoft Access 2000 database, several ESRI ArcView shapefiles, and a number of other minor components.

# TABLE OF CONTENTS

# Chapter 1
# Before You Begin

The RPA Data Wiz Users Guide contains detailed information about querying Resource Planning Act (RPA) Assessment forest data to produce summary tables, graphs, and maps. A number of variables can be analyzed (appendix A, B, C). Volumes for growing stock, live cull, dead salvable, netgrowth, and mortality can be estimated. Acreage, biomass, and tree count estimates are also available. Currently, removals are not available in this software. RPA Data Wiz is available in English and metric versions. This software was developed using Microsoft Visual Basic 6.0 (SP5), Microsoft ADO, Microsoft ADOX, Microsoft Windows Common Controls 6.0 (SP5), Microsoft Hierarchical FlexGrid Control 6.0 (SP4), Microsoft Common Dialog Control 6.0, Microsoft Chart Control 6.0 (SP4 OLEDB), ESRI MapObjects LT 2.0 (2000), Microsoft Access 2000 databases, several ESRI ArcView shapefiles, and a number of other minor components. RPA Data Wiz is available on CD by request from the North Central Research Station, St. Paul, MN (http://www.ncrs.fs.fed.us/4801/tools-data/mapping-tools/rpa-data-wiz.asp).

This version of RPA Data Wiz uses the 2002 RPA Assessment. Most of the data comes from the Forest Inventory and Analysis (FIA) program (http://www.fia.fs.fed.us/, http://www.ncrs.fs.fed.us/4801/tools-data/data; *The Forest Inventory and Analysis Database: Database Description and Users Manual Version 1.0*, Miles *et al.* 2001) Other parts of the data come from lands administered by the National Forest System in California, Colorado, Idaho, Nevada, Oregon, Washington, and Wyoming. RPA Data Wiz has no information for Hawaii or interior Alaska. In addition to the information provided in this users guide, a description of the 2002 RPA data can be found in *The 2002 RPA Plot Summary Database Users Manual Version 1.0* (Miles and Vissage, In prep.).

The users guide begins with instructions for installing and removing RPA Data Wiz. Next, it provides some general guidance for running RPA Data Wiz (Chapter 2). Chapters 3 through 5 cover the fine details of running each part of the application. A tutorial chapter follows. You may wish to skip Chapters 3 through 5 and proceed to Chapter 6. Finally, several appendices define selection and output variables in RPA Data Wiz.

**Author**

**Scott A. Pugh**, Information Technology Specialist, North Central Research Station, 410 MacInnes Drive, Houghton, MI 49931-1199.

RPA Data Wiz is available on CD by request from the North Central Research Station, St. Paul, MN (http://www.ncrs.fs.fed.us/4801/tools-data/mapping-tools/rpa-data-wiz.asp).

## Typographic Protocol

Most of the time this manual presents information in paragraph form. It tries to thoroughly cover important aspects of each topic. Otherwise, bullets or numbered steps are used to present the information. When reading this manual, keep in mind the following typographic protocol:

| Example | Description |
|---------|-------------|
| Start \ Programs \ RPA Data Wiz | Bold words should be chosen, typed, or acknowledged. A backslash between bold words indicates a series of choices should be made. |
| *multiple variable sums table* | Italicized words indicate a defined item or term. |
| CTRL + S | Capitalized letters usually indicate keyboard keys. The + sign indicates multiple keys should be pressed at the same time. |
| Tables and Graphs | Capitalized words indicate the name of a menu, dialog, button, or other object in Windows or RPA Data Wiz. |
| "Installation" | Words in quotation marks may be a reference to a specific section in the RPA Data Wiz Users Guide. |

## System Requirements

Your computer must have one of the following operating systems:

- Windows 95
- Windows 98
- Windows NT 4.0 (need system administrator privileges to install)
- Windows 2000 (need system administrator privileges to install)
- Windows XP (need system administrator privileges to install)

Your computer must have the following:

- CD-ROM or DVD-ROM drive
- Microsoft Internet Explorer Version 5.0 or higher
- Total minimum of 848 MB of disk space for one version (1,030 MB for both versions)
  - Minimum of 318 MB of hard disk space before installation (500 MB to install English and metric versions)
  - Minimum of 530 MB of hard disk to run RPA Data Wiz after installation

The following items are recommendations, but are not essential:

- Minimum of 200 MB of virtual memory
- Minimum of 512 MB of RAM
- Minimum of a Pentium III processor
- Minimum of a 14-inch computer monitor

As previously mentioned, there is an English and a metric version of RPA Data Wiz. Each employs a different Microsoft Access database. The English version uses RPADb2002.mdb, which occupies approximately 183 MB; the metric version uses RPADb2002met.mdb, which occupies approximately 166 MB. The installation package allows you to install one or both of these versions. In addition to the databases, other support files are installed. If both versions are installed, the total package will require approximately 500 MB of storage space (approximately 318 MB of space for one database). Temporary files are created while running RPA Data Wiz. Theoretically, the temporary files could occupy about 530 MB of additional space. RPA Data Wiz will run more efficiently when sufficient virtual memory is allocated. We recommend that the maximum amount of virtual memory be set to at least 200 MB. This amount is set in Control Panel \ System Properties \ Virtual Memory. We recommend at least 512 MB of RAM and a Pentium III or faster processor. More RAM and faster processors will decrease the processing time of RPA Data Wiz. These are only recommendations and RPA Data Wiz will run on slower computers. Remember that a slower computer could take hours to produce a complicated table using all the RPA data available for the United States (there is a Stop button available).

Sometimes headings in the output tables, graphs, and maps can be quite long. On smaller computer monitors (e.g., 12 or 14 inches), some headings can be cut off if you are using a coarse monitor resolution (e.g., 640 X 480 or 800 X 600). If this is a problem, increase the resolution of the computer monitor.

1. Select **Start \ Settings \ Control Panel**.
2. Choose **Display**.
3. Select **Settings** in the Display Properties dialog.
4. Increase the resolution of the monitor to 1,024 X 768 or higher.
5. Select **Apply** and accept the settings.
6. Close the **Display Properties** dialog and the **Control Panel** form.

## Installation

If you do not have Windows XP, you should read "Installation – Discussion and Notes" before executing the following general installation instructions (focus on reading the notes that pertain to your operating system). Follow these steps after you have covered the previous material or have determined that you have Windows XP. Use **system administrator privileges** while loading in Windows NT 4.0, Windows 2000, or Windows XP. Make sure programs like anti-virus software are not running. In general, insert the RPA Data Wiz CD into your CD-ROM drive and execute the setup application, setup.exe. If the installation program does not automatically start, then you will have to run setup.exe manually. Here is one way to run setup.exe.

1. On the desktop, double-click **My Computer**.
2. Double-click the icon for the CD-ROM drive.
3. Double-click **setup.exe** (computer icon is usually associated with this file).

Here is a second way to run setup.exe.

1. Select **Start \ Run**.
2. In the Open input box, type the path to the setup.exe file on your CD-ROM drive plus "setup.exe" (e.g., D:\setup.exe).
3. Click **OK**.

After the setup program starts, follow the directions.

1. Make sure other programs like anti-virus software are not running. Click **OK** to accept the message.
2. Keep the default installation directory or click **Change Directory** to place RPA Data Wiz in an alternate location. Remember that the directory for output from RPA Data Wiz will be in a directory, temp, within the directory specified here. Click the computer icon to install RPA Data Wiz in the specified directory.

3

3.  Click the option indicating your choice of database(s). Click **Done Selecting Databases(s)**.
4.  Choose a group name or create a new one. We recommend using the default group name "RPA Data Wiz." If the default is chosen, then RPA Data Wiz will show up in Start \ Programs. We do not recommend chosing Startup, because this will start RPA Data Wiz every time the computer boots up. Click **Continue**.
5.  The components will be installed.

If you are installing as system administrator, you may want to create a shortcut to RPA Data Wiz for other login accounts.

1.  Select **Start \ Settings**.
2.  Choose **Taskbar & Start Menu… \ Advanced \ Add**.
3.  Now **Browse** to the RPA Data Wiz application file, RPA_Data_Wiz.exe. The file is in the installation directory you chose earlier, usually in C:\ProgramFiles\RPA Data Wiz\. Click **RPA_Data_Wiz.exe**.
4.  Click **Next** and the location where you wish the shortcut to appear. Click **Next \ Finish**. Finally, click **OK** on the Taskbar and Start Menu Properties dialog.

## Installation - Discussion and Notes

Either Microsoft Windows 95, Windows 98, Windows NT 4.0, Windows 2000, or Windows XP with the appropriate updates and Microsoft Internet Explorer version 5.0 or higher are required to run RPA Data Wiz. RPA Data Wiz is not supported in Windows 3.1, Windows NT 3.51, or older systems. Windows ME is not supported. Most computers will have the necessary components to install and run this application. However, there is wide variability among the Windows operating systems present on computers. Some users will have to install updates to their operating systems. The setup program installs Microsoft Data Access Components (MDAC) 2.5 SP2 (2.52.6019.2) on Windows 95, 98, and NT 4.0. The setup program cannot install MDAC on Windows 2000 machines. Windows 2000 service pack 2 or newer is required to install MDAC on a Windows 2000 operating system. Windows XP already has the necessary MDAC. MDAC includes Microsoft Jet 4.0 (SP5). The MDAC End-User License Agreement (EULA) is found on the installation CD in the Windows_Support directory. The setup program installs other Microsoft support files, MapObjects LT 2.0 (ESRI 2000) components, Microsoft Access database files, map layers as ArcView shapefiles, the RPA Data Wiz application file, and supporting documentation. In rare instances, the installation process may require a reboot after some system files are updated. If necessary, the setup program will indicate the required reboot. If a reboot is required to update system files, then the RPA Data Wiz setup program must be run a second time. The following list contains information critical to installing RPA Data Wiz in specific Windows operating systems:

The most recent version of DCOM for Windows 95 may be found at http://www.microsoft.com/com/resources/downloads.asp.

### *Microsoft Windows 95*

The Distributed Component Object Model (DCOM) must be installed on Windows 95 operating systems. A number of applications (e.g., Microsoft Internet Explorer 4.01 and 5.0) install DCOM automatically, so it may be present on your machine. DCOM can be detected on your system if a search of the registry keys contains {bdc67890-4fc0-11d0-a805-00aa006d2eaf4}. This does not mean you have the latest version of DCOM. The latest version at the time of this writing is DCOM95 version 1.3. This can be found on the installation CD in the Windows_Support directory of this application as dcom95.exe. The DCOM95 version 1.3 EULA can also be found on the CD. The most recent version of DCOM for Windows 95 may be found at http://www.microsoft.com/com/resources/downloads.asp. We recommend you do not work with the registry. If DCOM is not installed, the RPA Data Wiz application will issue an error and fail to run. This is the easiest way to determine if DCOM is not installed. If the RPA Data Wiz installation fails, then install DCOM (copy **dcom95.exe** from the Windows_Support\dcom95 directory of the installation CD to your machine and execute the file). You will have to reinstall RPA Data Wiz, but first uninstall the previous RPA Data Wiz installation (see "Uninstalling RPA Data Wiz" later in this chapter).

MDAC 2.5 service pack 2 installs with the RPA Data Wiz setup program. MDAC 2.5 service pack 2 will not install if a newer version of MDAC exists on your machine. Although it's unlikely, a previous user could have installed a newer version of MDAC like 2.6 or 2.7. These versions do not come with the Jet 4.0 components required by RPA Data Wiz. More than likely, some other program has already installed the Jet components on your machine. However, if they do not exist, then RPA Data Wiz will not connect to the required Microsoft Access database. In this case, RPA Data Wiz will give errors indicating that it cannot connect to the database. You will have to install Jet 4.0 service pack 3.0 (http://www.microsoft.com/data/download.htm) at a minimum. Jet 4.0 service pack 3.0 is also available on the CD in the Windows_Support directory. After installing Jet 4.0 service pack 3.0, you have the option to upgrade to the latest service pack.

## Microsoft Windows 98

The Distributed Component Object Model (DCOM) must be installed on Windows 98 operating systems. DCOM comes on Windows 98 Second Edition. A number of applications (e.g., Microsoft Internet Explorer 5.0, Microsoft Visual Studio 6.0, Microsoft Office 2000) install DCOM automatically, so it may be present on your machine. DCOM can be detected on your system if a search of the registry keys contains {bdc67890-4fc0-11d0-a805-00aa006d2eaf4}. This does not mean you have the latest version of DCOM. The latest version at the time of this writing is DCOM98 version 1.3. The most recent version of DCOM for Windows 98 may be found at http://www.microsoft.com/com/resources/downloads.asp. Microsoft does not allow redistribution of DCOM98 so it is not available on the installation CD. We recommend you do not work with the registry. If DCOM is not installed, the RPA Data Wiz application will issue an error and fail to run. This is the easiest way to determine if DCOM is not installed. If the RPA Data Wiz installation fails, then install DCOM (double-click the DCOM file). You will have to reinstall RPA Data Wiz, but first uninstall the previous RPA Data Wiz installation (see "Uninstalling RPA Data Wiz" later in this chapter).

The most recent version of DCOM for Windows 98 may be found at http://www.microsoft.com/com/resources/downloads.asp.

MDAC 2.5 service pack 2 installs with the RPA Data Wiz setup program. MDAC 2.5 service pack 2 will not install if a newer version of MDAC exists on your machine. Although it's unlikely, a previous user could have installed a newer version of MDAC like 2.6 or 2.7. These versions do not come with the Jet 4.0 components required by RPA Data Wiz. More than likely, some other program has already installed the Jet components on your machine. However, if they do not exist, then the RPA Data Wiz will not be able to connect the Microsoft Access database. In this case, RPA Data Wiz will give errors indicating that it cannot connect to the database. You will have to install Jet 4.0 service pack 3.0 (http://www.microsoft.com/data/download.htm) at a minimum. Jet 4.0 service pack 3.0 is available on the installation CD in the Windows_Support directory. After installing Jet 4.0 service pack 3.0, you have the option to upgrade to the latest service pack.

## Microsoft Windows NT 4.0

DCOM is already installed on Windows NT 4.0. Run the RPA Data Wiz setup program. If system files are updated, then a reboot and a second run of the setup program will be required.

MDAC 2.5 service pack 2 installs with the RPA Data Wiz setup program. MDAC 2.5 service pack 2 will not install if a newer version of MDAC exists on your machine. Although it's unlikely, a previous user could have installed a newer version of MDAC like 2.6 or 2.7. These versions do not come with the Jet 4.0 components required by RPA Data Wiz. More than likely, some other program has already installed the Jet components on your machine. However, if they do not exist, then RPA Data Wiz will not connect to the required Microsoft Access database. In this case, RPA Data Wiz will give errors indicating that it cannot connect to the database. You will have to install Jet 4.0 service pack 3.0 (http://www.microsoft.com/data/download.htm) at a minimum. Jet 4.0 service pack 3.0 is also available on the installation CD in the Windows_Support directory. After installing Jet 4.0 service pack 3.0, you have the option to upgrade to the latest service pack.

### Microsoft Windows 2000

DCOM is already installed on Windows 2000. The Windows 2000 operating system must have service pack 2 or newer. Service packs may be found at http://www.microsoft.com/windows2000/downloads/servicepacks/default.asp. Check the service pack on your system in **My Computer \ Properties**. Click the **General** tab and look under **System**. After verifying that service pack 2 or newer is installed, run the RPA Data Wiz setup program. System files cannot be updated on this operating system without installing service packs or other Microsoft software updates. Run the RPA Data Wiz setup program. If you try installing and get a message indicating that some of your system files are out of date, then you do not have service pack 2 or newer installed.

### Microsoft Windows XP

Windows XP has the necessary system files for the RPA Data Wiz setup program. Run the RPA Data Wiz setup program.

## Uninstalling RPA Data Wiz

You may want to uninstall RPA Data Wiz. If you run into trouble and RPA Data Wiz does not install correctly, the safest thing to do is uninstall the application. RPA Data Wiz can be installed again later. When uninstalling RPA Data Wiz we recommend you do not remove shared files. Here are the steps for uninstalling RPA Data Wiz.

1. Select **Start \ Settings \ Control Panel**.
2. Choose **Add/Remove Programs**.
3. Look for and select **RPA Data Wiz**.
4. Select **Change/Remove**.
5. Select **Yes** to remove the application.
6. If you are asked to remove shared files, we highly recommend you do not remove them.

## References

A number of references are associated with map layers in RPA Data Wiz. Some of the map layers were created by manipulating other original map layers. The references directory of the installation CD has the references for the original map layers. See **readme.txt** in the references directory for further information. The RPA Data Wiz application directory (usually C:\Program Files\RPA Data Wiz\) has the reference information or metadata for each of the final map layers used in RPA Data Wiz. These files have "met" extensions and can be read in a text editor. The references directory on the installation CD also has the original references for the rural urban continuum and Baileys' ecological subregion codes.

# Chapter 2
# Getting Started with RPA Data Wiz

RPA Data Wiz allows users to create tables, graphs, and maps of the forest information from the 2002 RPA Assessment database without having to know the structure of the database and without having to know computer programming or *Structured Query Language* (SQL is a standard ANSI / NCITS language for querying and manipulating databases). Pointing and clicking in the graphical user interface works to achieve most results. A user performs the following basic steps:

1. Pick one or more RPA subregions to work in. All RPA plot information is initially chosen for the subregions you pick.
2. Narrow your selection of RPA plot information by picking variables and their respective values of interest. For example, you could choose only to work with oak forest types on timberland.
3. Make summary tables, graphs, and maps on the resulting information.
4. Save your tables, graphs, and maps in a number of formats to use in other applications.
5. Repeatedly add to or select from your existing RPA plot information and create more output.

## Answering Questions

You can answer many questions with RPA Data Wiz—a small sample is included below. Not all of these questions are answered directly in this users guide, but the guide presents methods that allow you to answer these questions and more. In the examples below, geographic units can be RPA assessment regions or subregions, States, counties, Baileys' Ecosections, 107th or 108th Congressional Districts, USGS Hydrological Accounting Units, or U.S. National Forest System lands. Volumes can be for growing stock, live cull, dead salvable, netgrowth, or mortality.

- What is the biomass, volume, or number of trees on a per area basis?
- What is the ratio of mortality to netgrowth?
- What is the ratio of softwood to hardwood?
- What is the ratio of large trees to all trees?
- What is the ratio of forest land or timberland to all land by geographic unit?
- What is the ratio of National Forest System timberland to private timberland (derive indirectly using output from RPA Data Wiz in a spreadsheet)?
- What is the ratio of productive reserved forest land to productive nonreserved forest land by forest type and age class (derive indirectly using output from RPA Data Wiz in a spreadsheet)?
- What geographic units have overstocked forest stands and how much biomass is present in these areas (may indicate fire hazard)?
- What is the volume, biomass, or number of trees in highly productive black walnut stands?
- What is the volume, biomass, or number of trees by owner and stand-diameter class?
- What is the volume, biomass, or number of trees by age and stand-size class?
- What is the volume, biomass, or number of trees in planted versus natural forest stands?
- How much stand conversion, clearcutting, or other type of treatment has occurred in each geographic unit?
- What is the volume, biomass, or number of trees associated with counties that have various levels of rural/urban continuums (levels of metropolitan or urban development)?
- What geographic units have potentially favorable habitat for a particular animal species of interest?

## Important Points

Before covering specific methods and examples of output, there are several important points to remember when using RPA Data Wiz.

- Many times throughout this application, multiple selections are allowed. Unless noted otherwise, hold SHIFT and click over a range of choices or hold CTRL and click on multiple individual choices. One of these noted exceptions occurs when creating tables and picking grouping variables.

- Remember that choices in menus or dialogs are only enabled or available when they appear in text that contrasts with the background (e.g., black text on the gray menu).

- The abbreviations "SW" and "HW" represent softwood and hardwood respectively throughout RPA Data Wiz.

- "AEF" occurs in the output tables and represents area (appendices B and C).

- Make sure your form sizes are maximized to see the graphs well (click on the box in upper right-hand corner of each form to maximize the size).

- Since the data were acquired from a number of sources using various sampling techniques, there is no easy way to present sampling errors. The number of plots or records associated with a query is the only measure of accuracy provided. Most of the data in the 2002 RPA Assessment do come from the FIA program. A description of the FIA sampling and accuracy standards can be found in *The Forest Inventory and Analysis Database: Database Description and Users Manual Version 1.0* (Miles *et al.* 2001).

- Area is the only attribute information that can be output for nonforest and water plots. Otherwise, all the output information in RPA Data Wiz is associated with some type of forest land. Therefore, you will usually limit your selections to some type of forest land (see Land Cover Class and Forested Land Code in appendix A).

- Time series analysis is not part of RPA Data Wiz. The database is a "snapshot" of the most up-to-date information. A small amount of this latest information is decades old. Source Date (appendix A) indicates the year of the information.

- Information on individual tree species is not part of RPA Data Wiz. Forest Type Group and Local Forest Type are available (appendix A).

- Number of trees and board-foot volume (appendix B) are only available for timberland (see Forested Land Code in appendix A). In addition, board-foot volume is only available in the English version of RPA Data Wiz.

- Finally, the structure of this application is very autonomous, allowing users a great degree of freedom to pick specific RPA information and present it in many ways. Take care to make selections and create output in ways that make sense. As an aide, we recommend looking over the definitions of the selection and output variables in the appendices.

## Starting RPA Data Wiz

There are a number of ways to start RPA Data Wiz, depending upon how you installed the application. If the defaults were selected during installation, then RPA Data Wiz will show up in Start \ Programs. Select **Start \ Programs \ RPA Data Wiz**. You may have created a shortcut to the application. If this is the case, double-click the shortcut. Otherwise, go to the installation directory and double-click the RPA Data Wiz application file, **RPA_Data_Wiz.exe**.

After starting the application, a splash screen will appear. Click in the gray area of this screen to proceed. If you installed the English and metric databases, then you will have to decide whether to work with the English or metric version of RPA Data Wiz.

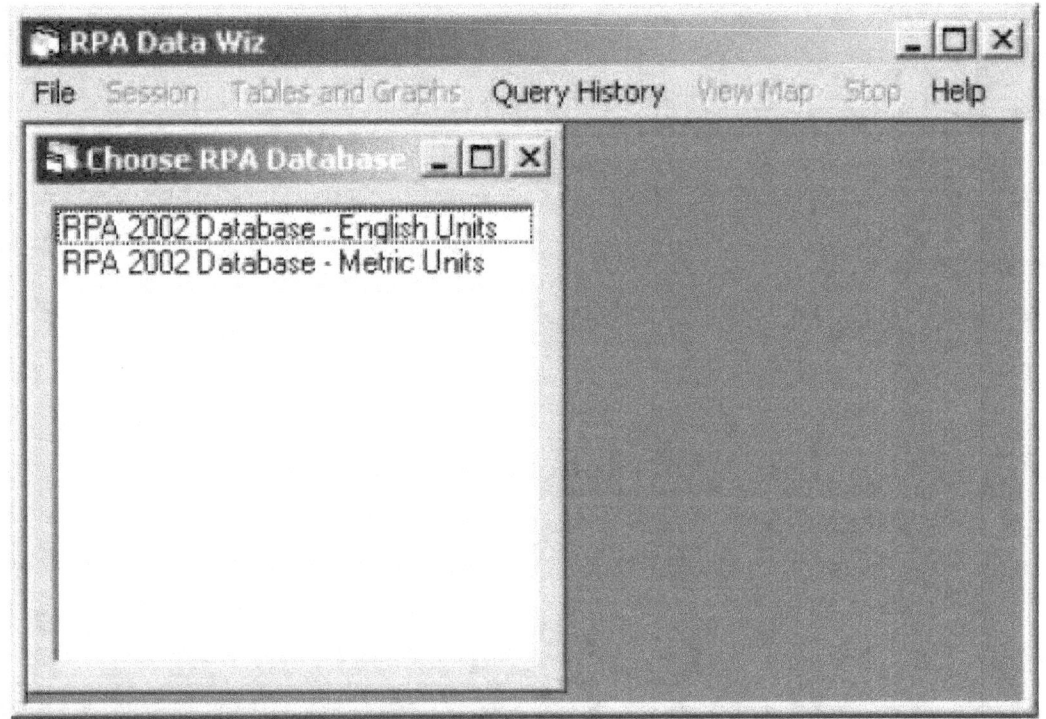

Any future updates to RPA Data Wiz will be located at http://www.ncrs.fs.fed.us/4801/tools-data/mapping-tools/rpa-data-wiz.asp.

## Help

Select Help \ RPA Data Wiz Info to display reference information on RPA Data Wiz. Select Help \ Help and you will be referred to the RPA Data Wiz Users Guide. In this version, there is no help section built into the program. However, tool tips appear for a number of objects in RPA Data Wiz. Momentarily place the cursor over an object to see if a tool tip is available. Most menus do not have tool tips. Just click on the menu to see what is available. Any future updates to RPA Data Wiz will be located at http://www.ncrs.fs.fed.us/4801/tools-data/mapping-tools/rpa-data-wiz.asp.

# Chapter 3
# Working with Sessions

## New Session

You can start a new session in many different stages throughout the application. Right after starting RPA Data Wiz, you have to start a new session. Start a new session by clicking **Session \ New Session**.

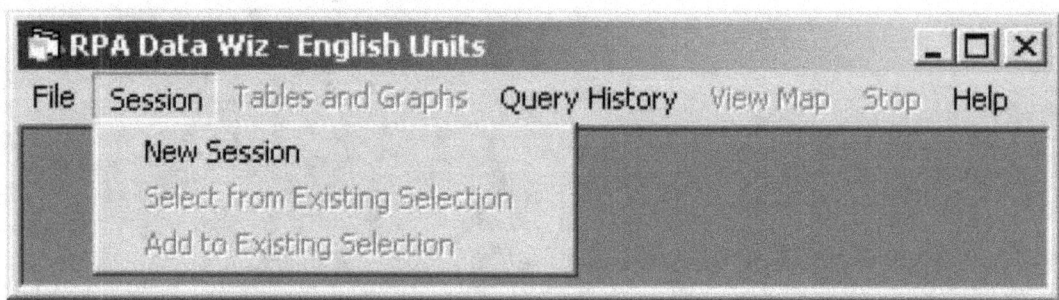

After creating a new session, you have to choose one or more RPA subregions. After making your choice, click **Done Selecting RPA Subregion(s)**.

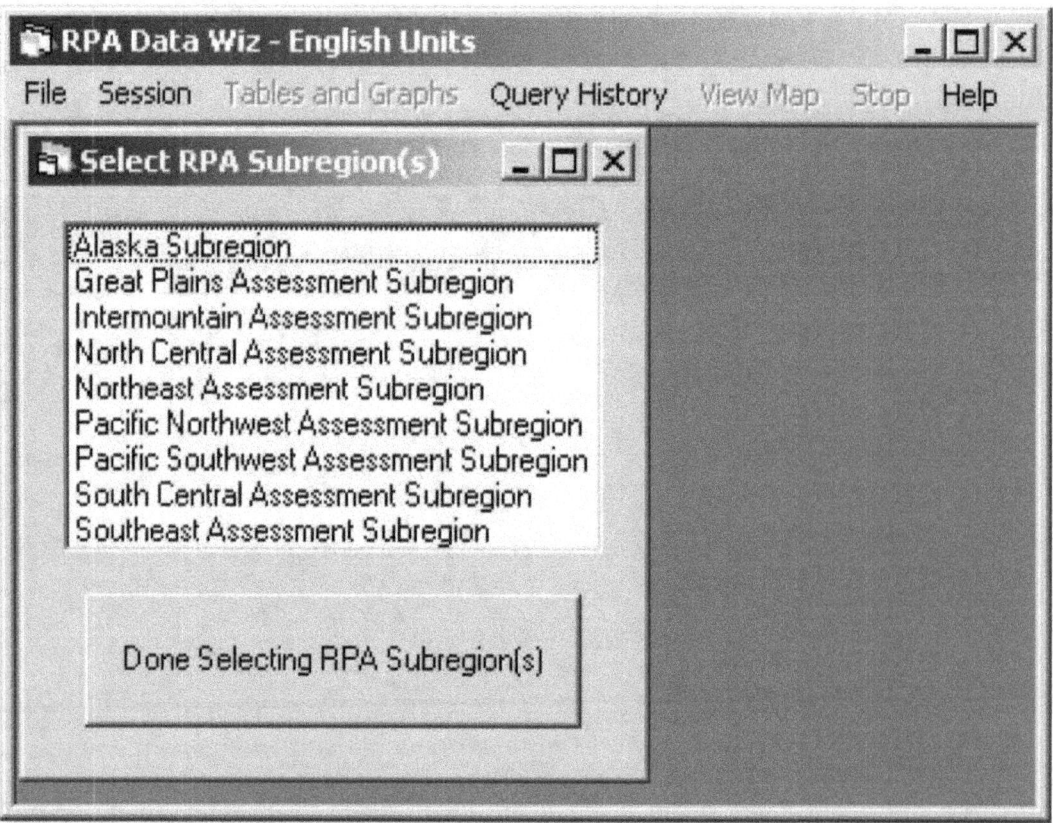

Next, the RPA Variable Selection dialog appears. Select a single variable. The Select Field Value(s) dialog appears with all the available values for the previously chosen variable. Choose any number of these values for the variable. Click Done Selecting Field Value(s). Repeat this process as many times as necessary to reduce the selection of database records. Normally, you would include a selection here for some type of forest land (Forest Land as the value for Land Cover Class or a specific forest land type for Forested Land Code). Area is the only output variable associated with nonforest and water. Press Done Selecting to keep the selection criteria or choose Skip Selecting – Use All Current Records to use all the current records in future analyses.

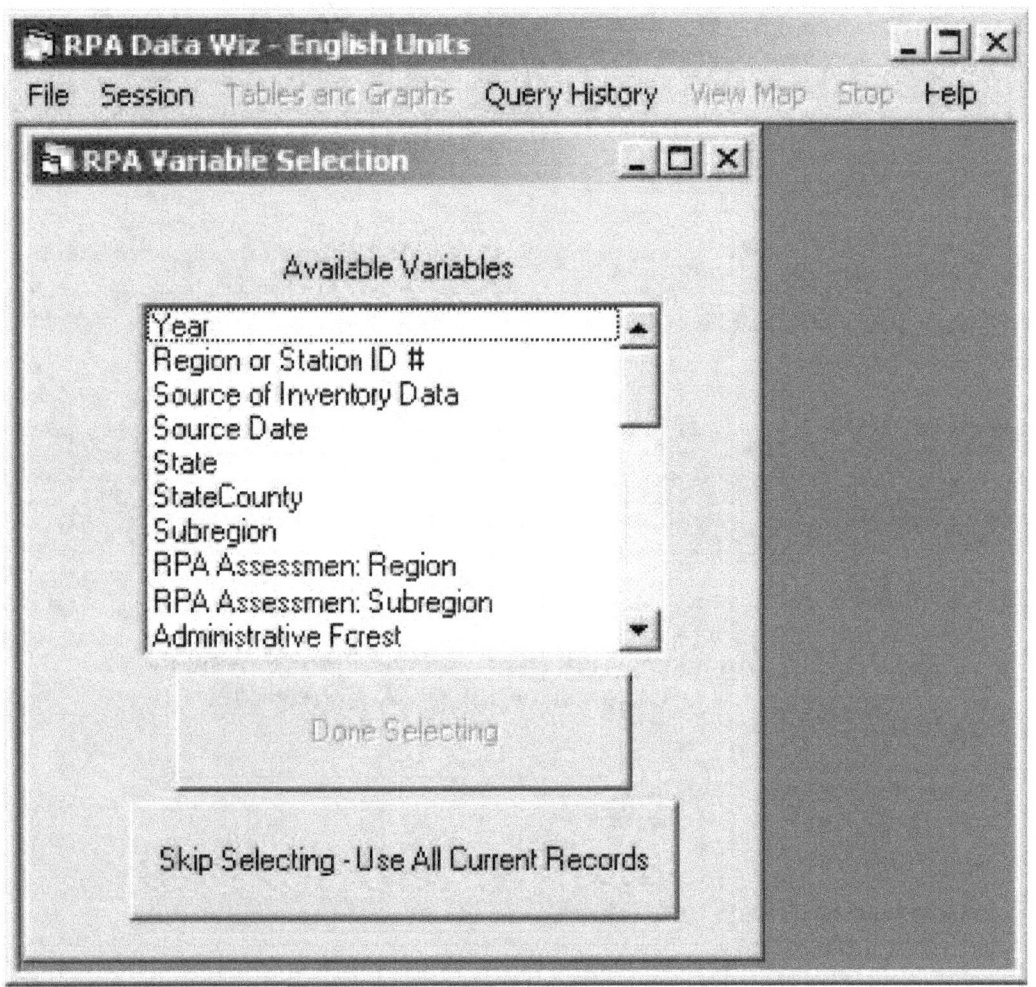

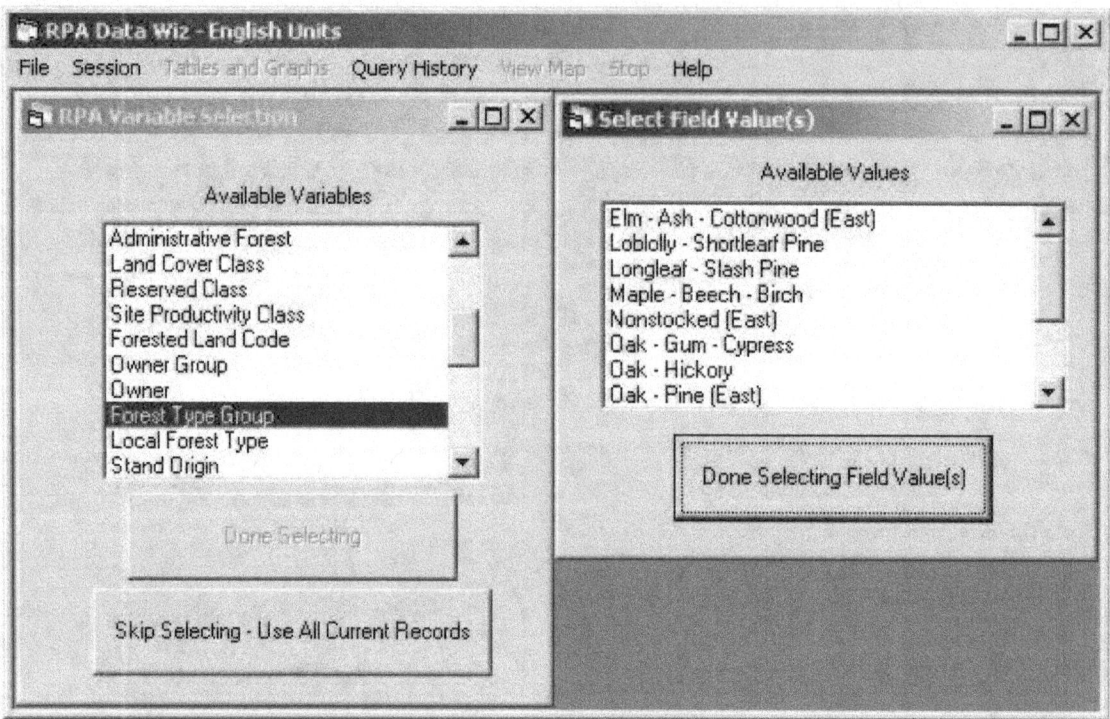

If desired, choose Query History to show a simplified version of the selection code. Field names and codes appear as they are in the RPA Data Wiz database. Note that sometimes the length of the selection queries can become longer than is allowed. If this is the case, the query will fail and a new query will have to be chosen with fewer selection criteria. Some field value code definitions are listed in Query History; however, all of them are listed in appendix A.

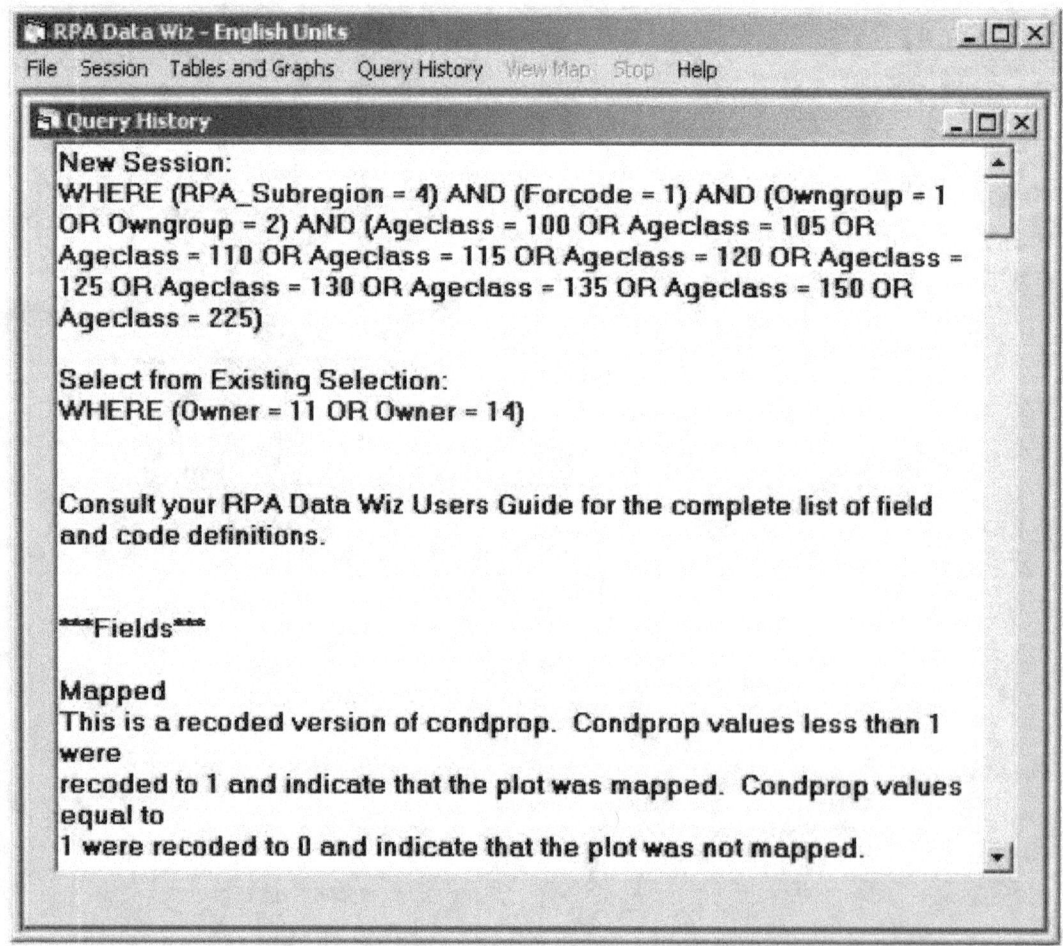

## Select from Existing Selection

After you have completed creating a new session, you can go back and narrow that selection further. Using the existing records selected from New Session, click Session \ Select from Existing Selection to allow further reselection of records with the RPA Variable Selection and Select Field Value(s) dialogs as previously described. Any time Select from Existing Selection is enabled, you can use it to narrow your selection of records. Normally some output (like tables or graphs) is created that results in more questions about the resource. Then you can further narrow the selection of records using the previous techniques to produce more output on the reselected records.

## Add to Existing Selection

After you have narrowed a selection (applied New Session or Select from Existing Selection techniques), you can go back and add more records. Select Session \ Add to Existing Selection. All records (even those you already have selected) from the most recent selection of RPA subregions are available for addition to the latest selection of records. The information is made available for addition through the RPA Variable Selection and Select Field Value(s) dialogs using the steps previously described. Since all the information from the most recent selection of RPA subregions is provided for addition, some additions may not add any new records. To prevent duplicate information, RPA Data Wiz will not add records if they already exist in the latest selection. If necessary, choose Query History to review previous selection criteria.

## Exiting RPA Data Wiz

If Exit (under File) is enabled, then it is safe to shutdown RPA Data Wiz. When you are ready, select File \ Exit to quit RPA Data Wiz.

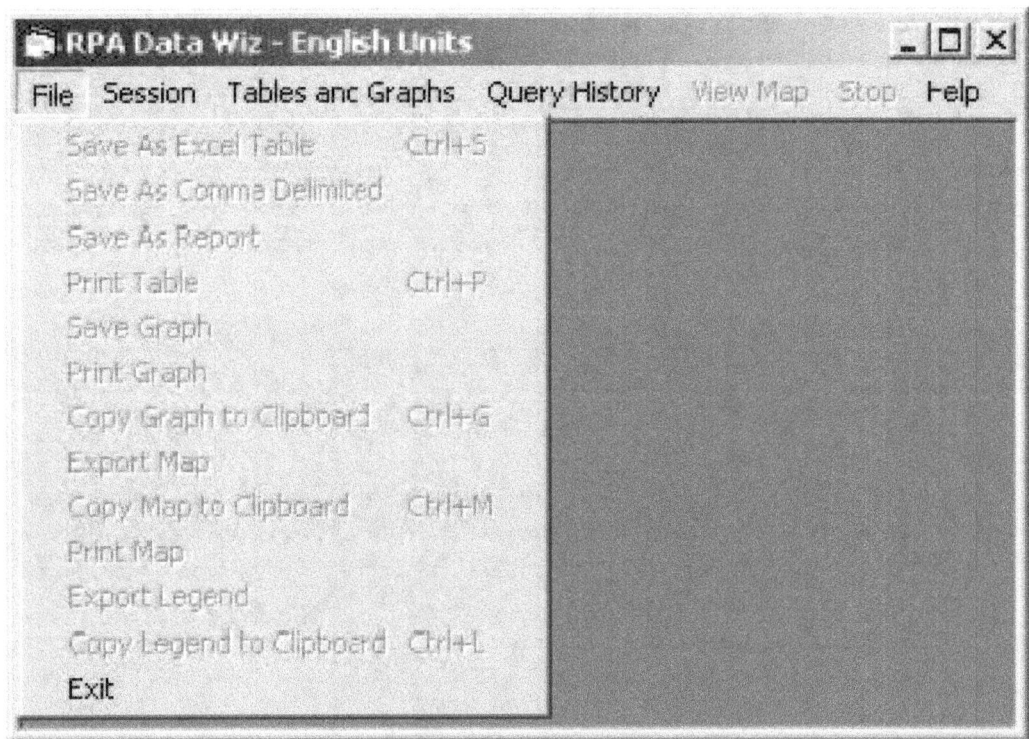

# Chapter 4
# Working with Tables and Graphs

All of the output tables in RPA Data Wiz are two-way tables made of rows, columns, and cells. You choose the variables that define the row and column headings and the variable(s) represented in the cells. The tables can report sums or ratios. As presented below, you can create two variations of the two-way table in RPA Data Wiz.

RPA Data Wiz produces two-dimensional bar graphs. Stacking bar graphs are produced when working with sums and nonstacking bar graphs are produced with ratios.

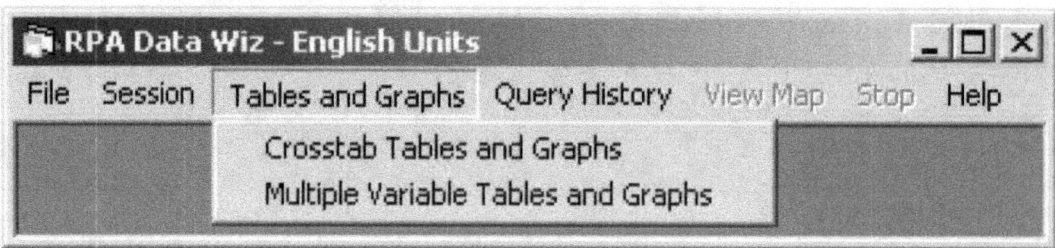

## Crosstab Table and Graph Generator
Choose **Tables and Graphs \ Crosstab Tables and Graphs** to display the Crosstab Table and Graph Generator.

### Creating a Table
In general a *crosstab* is a table of sums, averages, or some other calculation for a continuous variable grouped by two or more discrete variables. Each discrete variable can be composed of multiple divisions or classes. For example, forest type is composed of many classes, such as red pine and sugar maple.

In RPA Data Wiz, the continuous variable is a sum, so it is called the *sum variable*. Only one sum variable can be selected. Sums are grouped by up to four variables on the left side of the table (*grouping variables* defining row headings) and one variable (*pivot variable* defining column headings) across the top of the table. This type of table is commonly created in spreadsheets.

1. Choose one to four **grouping variables** in the Crosstab Table and Graph Generator. In this case, the CTRL and SHIFT keys do not add flexibility in selecting multiple variables. Just point and click the variables you wish to use as grouping variables. If you decide that you do not want a variable already selected, then click on the variable again. It will be deselected. The order in which you choose the grouping variables dictates the order in which they appear in the table. The example table below shows that Owner Group was chosen first, followed by Stand Size Class.

2. Choose one **pivot variable** to determine the column headings. In this case Forest Type Group was chosen as the pivot variable.

3. Choose the **sum variable** to occupy the cells of the table. SW Netgrowth was chosen in this example.

4. Click **Add number of samples as extra column** to include the number of RPA plots or records as an option. This is the sum of the samples associated with each row heading. This is meant to add a

measure of accuracy to the estimates displayed in the table. The numbers in the rows with thousands of associated RPA plots are more reliable than those in the rows with hundreds of associated plots.

5. Finally, click **Create Summary Table** to produce a table similar to the example below

Rarely, the number of column headings exceeds the allowable limit and the table is not created. If this happens, switch the pivot variable with a grouping variable to achieve the same information in a different output format. This will work in most situations where there is only one grouping variable of interest.

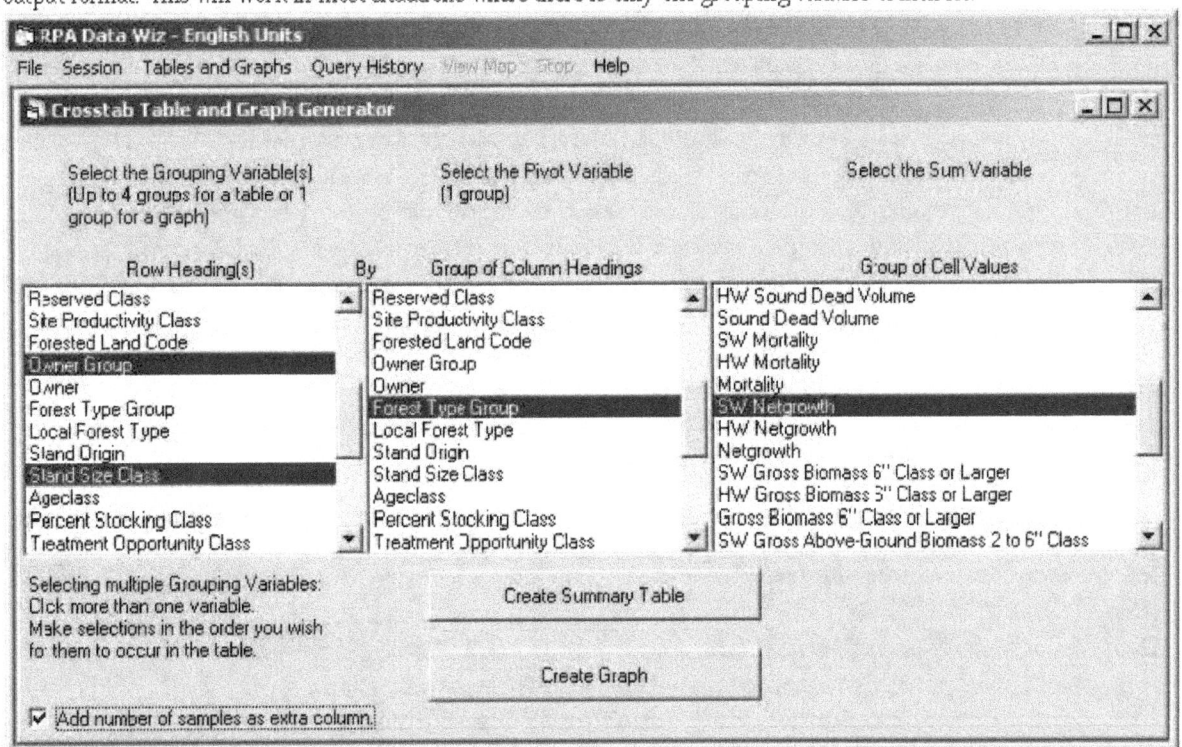

| Owner Group | Stand Size Class | Number of Plots | Unknown | White - Red - Jack Pine | Spruce - |
|---|---|---|---|---|---|
| | Missing | 110 | 21,000 | 0 | |
| | Nonstocked | 23 | 0 | 0 | |
| National Forest | Small Diameter | 1,002 | 0 | 4,451,310 | |
| | Medium Diameter | 1,407 | 26,400 | 16,522,000 | |
| | Large Diameter | 1,295 | 0 | 22,971,996 | |
| | Missing | 216 | -800 | 0 | |
| | Nonstocked | 126 | 107,500 | 0 | |
| Other Public | Small Diameter | 3,417 | 72,800 | 5,031,326 | |
| | Medium Diameter | 3,557 | 93,700 | 28,822,203 | |
| | Large Diameter | 2,841 | 81,400 | 23,447,400 | |
| | Missing | 128 | 182,500 | 0 | |
| | Nonstocked | 157 | 27,800 | 0 | |
| Private | Small Diameter | 4,767 | 259,200 | 8,230,500 | |
| | Medium Diameter | 5,787 | 320,800 | 44,743,851 | |
| | Large Diameter | 6,898 | 276,600 | 37,266,910 | |
| Total | | 76,105 | 1,468,900 | 191,487,496 | |

Total acreage (sum of AEF) is 159,454,921. This is the acreage represented by all plots in this session.
Possible Units: Volume in cubic feet, Biomass in pounds, Area in acres

## Creating a Graph

In the Crosstab Table and Graph Generator, choose variables of interest as you would when making a table (see "Creating a Table") except only choose one grouping variable. Click Create Graph. A two-dimensional stacking bar graph is created. The classes or divisions of the grouping variable are the series and the classes or divisions of the pivot variable are the bar categories.

The example below shows the classes of stand-size class as being the bar categories. The series comprise the divisions of age class. The example shows the 15-year age class as being selected. Select a series with a click of the mouse in the graph or in the legend, then the corresponding row in the table is also highlighted. This allows you to see the exact numbers associated with the selected series.

There is another way to clarify and depict the information associated with a single series. You can change the graph to show only a selected series. While holding the SHIFT key down, click on a series in the graph or legend. A new graph appears for the selected series. The second example below shows the graph for the 15-year age class series. The scale bar changes to provide more detail in many cases. Click outside the graph outline (outside the dotted line) to restore the display to the original graph with all the series. Clicking in the table does nothing. When a selected series is displayed in a new graph, the series is still highlighted on the graph and displays with annoying selection brackets. Click within the dotted line but off from the bars or legend to remove these selection brackets from the display.

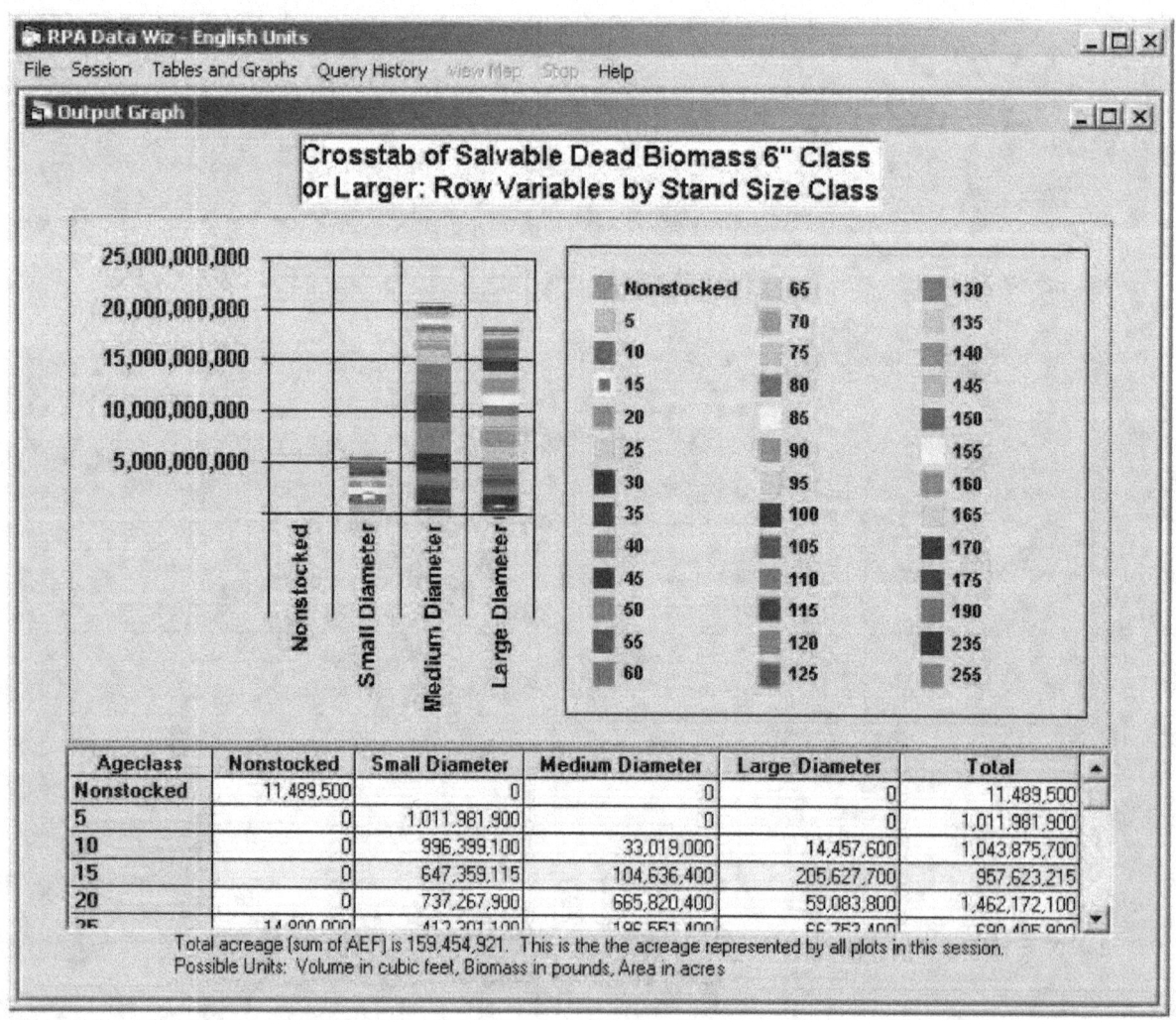

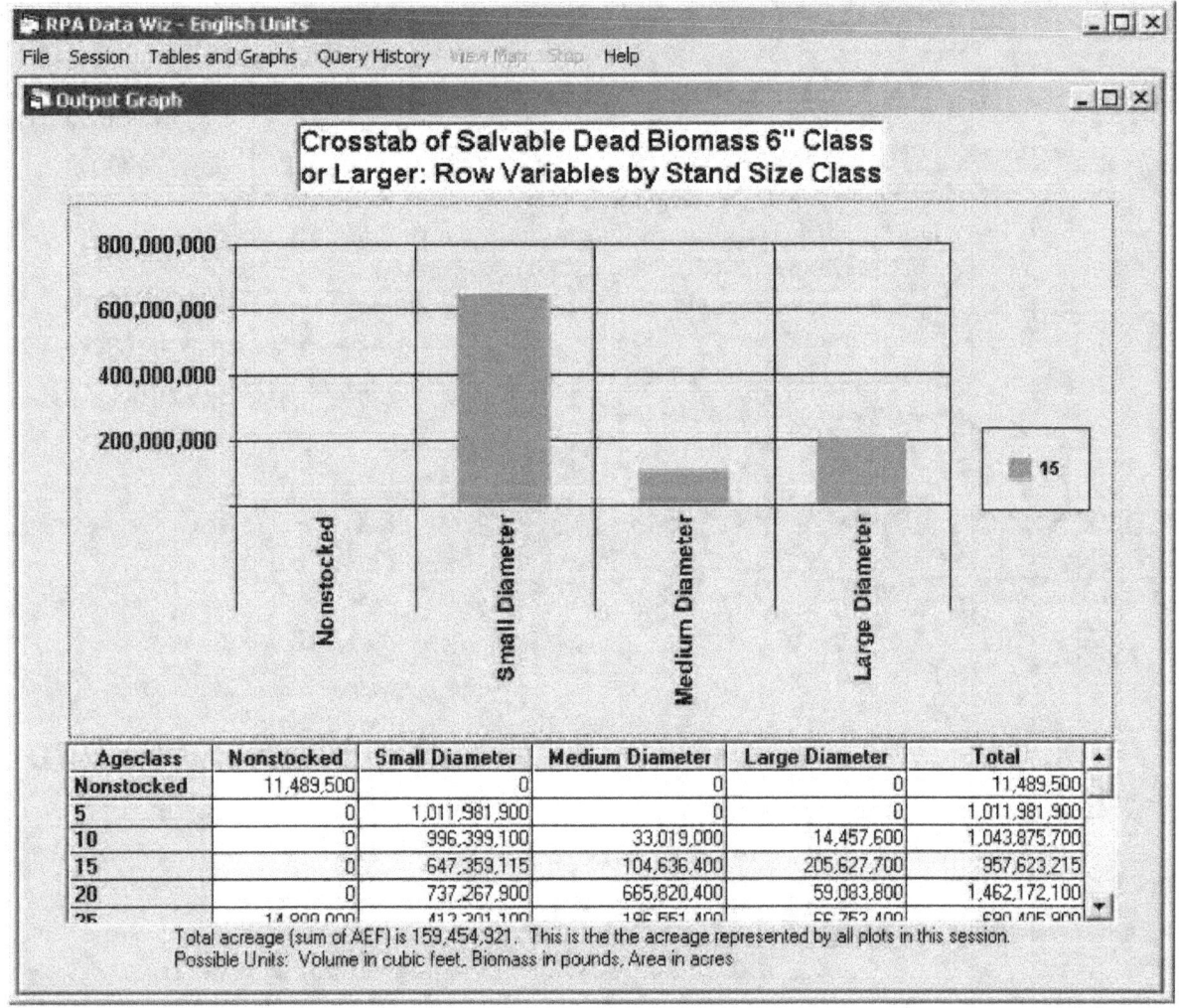

| Ageclass | Nonstocked | Small Diameter | Medium Diameter | Large Diameter | Total |
|---|---|---|---|---|---|
| Nonstocked | 11,489,500 | 0 | 0 | 0 | 11,489,500 |
| 5 | 0 | 1,011,981,900 | 0 | 0 | 1,011,981,900 |
| 10 | 0 | 996,399,100 | 33,019,000 | 14,457,600 | 1,043,875,700 |
| 15 | 0 | 647,359,115 | 104,636,400 | 205,627,700 | 957,623,215 |
| 20 | 0 | 737,267,900 | 665,820,400 | 59,083,800 | 1,462,172,100 |
| 25 | 14,800,000 | 412,301,100 | 196,551,400 | 66,753,400 | 690,405,900 |

Total acreage (sum of AEF) is 159,454,921. This is the the acreage represented by all plots in this session.
Possible Units: Volume in cubic feet, Biomass in pounds, Area in acres

## Multiple Variable Sums Table and Graph Generator

Choose Tables and Graphs \ Multiple Variable Tables and Graphs to display the Multiple Variable Sums Table and Graph Generator.

### Creating a Table

*Multiple variable sums table* is a name created for tables in RPA Data Wiz that report sums for one or more continuous variables (*sum variables* defining column headings) indicated across the top of the table and grouped by up to four discrete variables (*grouping variables* defining row headings) on the left side of the table. The continuous variable(s) can be any number of sum variables listed.

If an optional continuous variable (only for ratios of sums) is chosen, then each sum variable total is divided by the sum of this optional variable for each unique grouping in the table. The result of this division, the quotient, will be identified as "undefined" if the sum of the optional variable (the denominator) equals zero. This is useful in a number of ways. Dividing by area results in per acre or per hectare estimates. Also, you can look at things like the ratio of mortality to netgrowth or the ratio of softwood to hardwood for the selected plots. Follow these steps.

1. Choose one to four grouping variables in the Multiple Variable Sums Table and Graph Generator. In this case, the CTRL and SHIFT keys do not add flexibility in selecting grouping variables but do work when selecting sum variables. Point and click the variables you wish to use as grouping variables. If you decide that you do not want a variable already selected, then click on the variable again. It will be deselected. The order in which you choose the grouping variables dictates the order in which they appear in the table. The example table below shows that StateCounty was chosen first, followed by Administrative Forest.

2. Choose one or more sum variables. The example below shows that the variables SW Mortality through Netgrowth were chosen. The order of column headings in the output table always follows the order in which sum variables are displayed in this dialog.

3. You may choose an optional ratio variable to divide the sum variable totals. This example shows that Area was chosen. The result is a table with mortality and netgrowth per acre. Remember that this is only for the records that were chosen in the session so these numbers may not represent all the plots in each StateCounty-Administrative forest combination. For example, the user may have only picked forest stands designated with the large stand-size class.

4. Click **Add number of samples as extra column** to include the number of RPA plots or records as an option. This is the sum of the samples associated with each row heading. For tables in this dialog, this column appears at the end or far right of the table. This is meant to add a measure of accuracy to the estimates displayed in the table.

5. Finally, click **Create Summary Table** to produce a table similar to the example below.

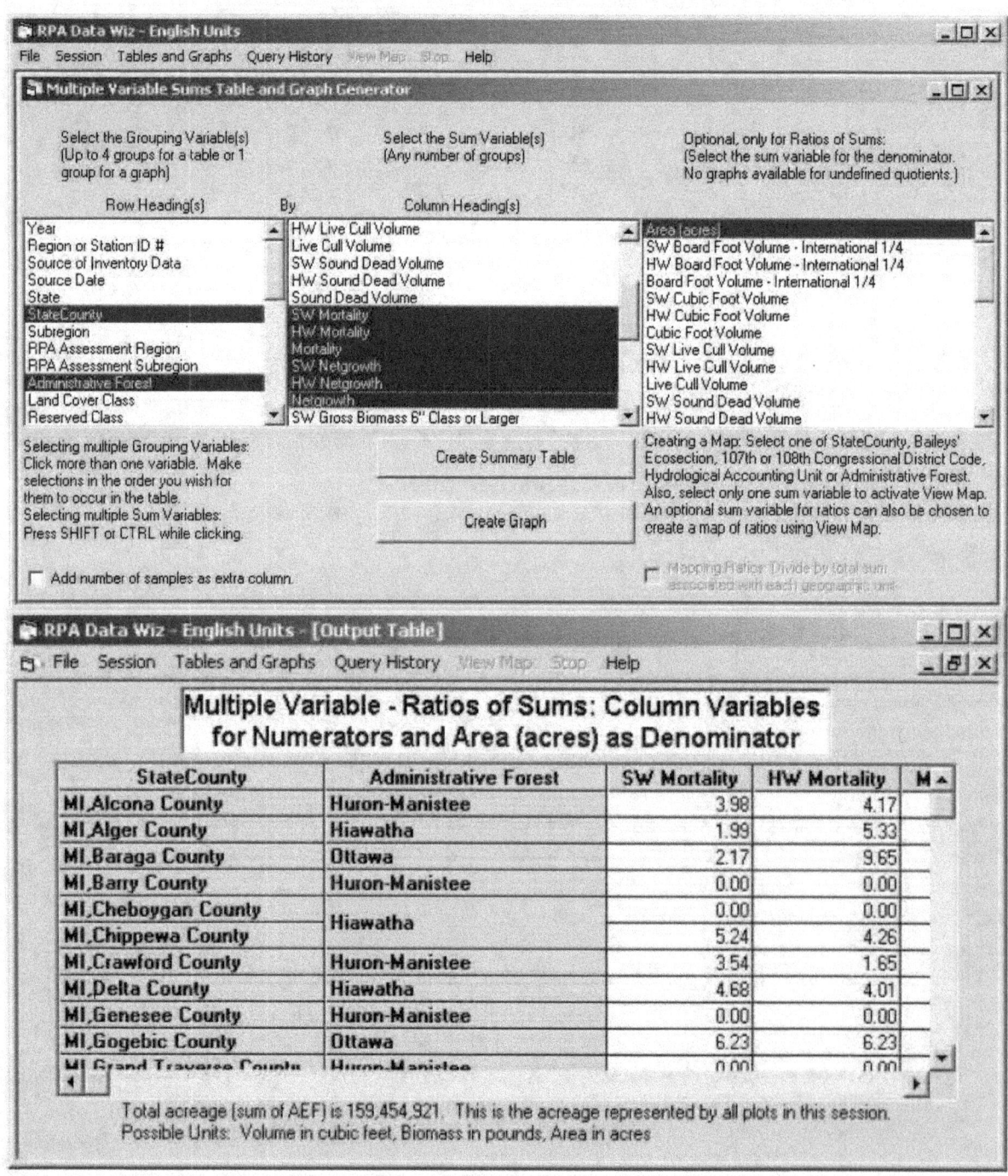

A second optional ratio can be produced when working with grouping variables associated with maps in RPA Data Wiz. The Mapping Ratios checkbox is available when one mapping, grouping variable (StateCounty, Baileys' Ecosection, 107th or 108th Congressional District Code, Hydrological Accounting Unit, or Administrative Forest); one sum variable; and one variable in Optional, only for Ratios of Sums are chosen. If this checkbox is chosen, then a ratio of the sum variable total to the optional variable total in each geographic unit populates the table. The key is that the optional variable total is the total for all plots in the geographic unit, even when the records involved with the sum variable totals may only involve a subset of the plots in the geographic unit. For instance, the user may have only picked forest stands designated with the large stand-size class but the optional variable total will involve all plots regardless of stand size. The results would represent the ratio of large stand-size class plots to all stand-size class plots. Another common output from using this technique would be to produce the ratio of timberland to all land for each county.

## Creating a Graph

In the Multiple Variable Sums Table and Graph Generator, choose variables of interest as you would when making a table (see "Creating a Table"), except only choose one grouping variable. Click **Create Graph**. If no optional ratio variable is chosen then a two-dimensional stacking bar graph is created. The classes or divisions of the grouping variable are the series, and the sum variables are the bar categories.

The example below shows SW Gross Biomass 6" Class or Larger and HW Gross Biomass 6" Class or Larger as being the bar categories. The series make up the Forest Type Group. The example shows the Elm-Ash-Cottonwood (East) series as selected. Select a series with a click of the mouse in the graph or in the legend, then the corresponding row in the table is also highlighted. This allows you to see the exact numbers associated with the selected series.

As with graphs associated with crosstabs, there is another way to clarify and depict the information associated with a single series. You can change the graph to show only a selected series. While holding the SHIFT key down, click on a series in the graph or legend. A new graph appears for the selected series. The second example below shows the graph for the Elm-Ash-Cottonwood (East) series. The scale bar changes to provide more detail in many cases. Click outside the graph outline (outside the dotted line) to restore the display to the original graph with all the series. Clicking in the table does nothing. When a selected series is displayed in a new graph, the series is still highlighted on the graph and displays with annoying selection brackets. Click within the dotted line but off from the bars or legend to remove these selection brackets from the display.

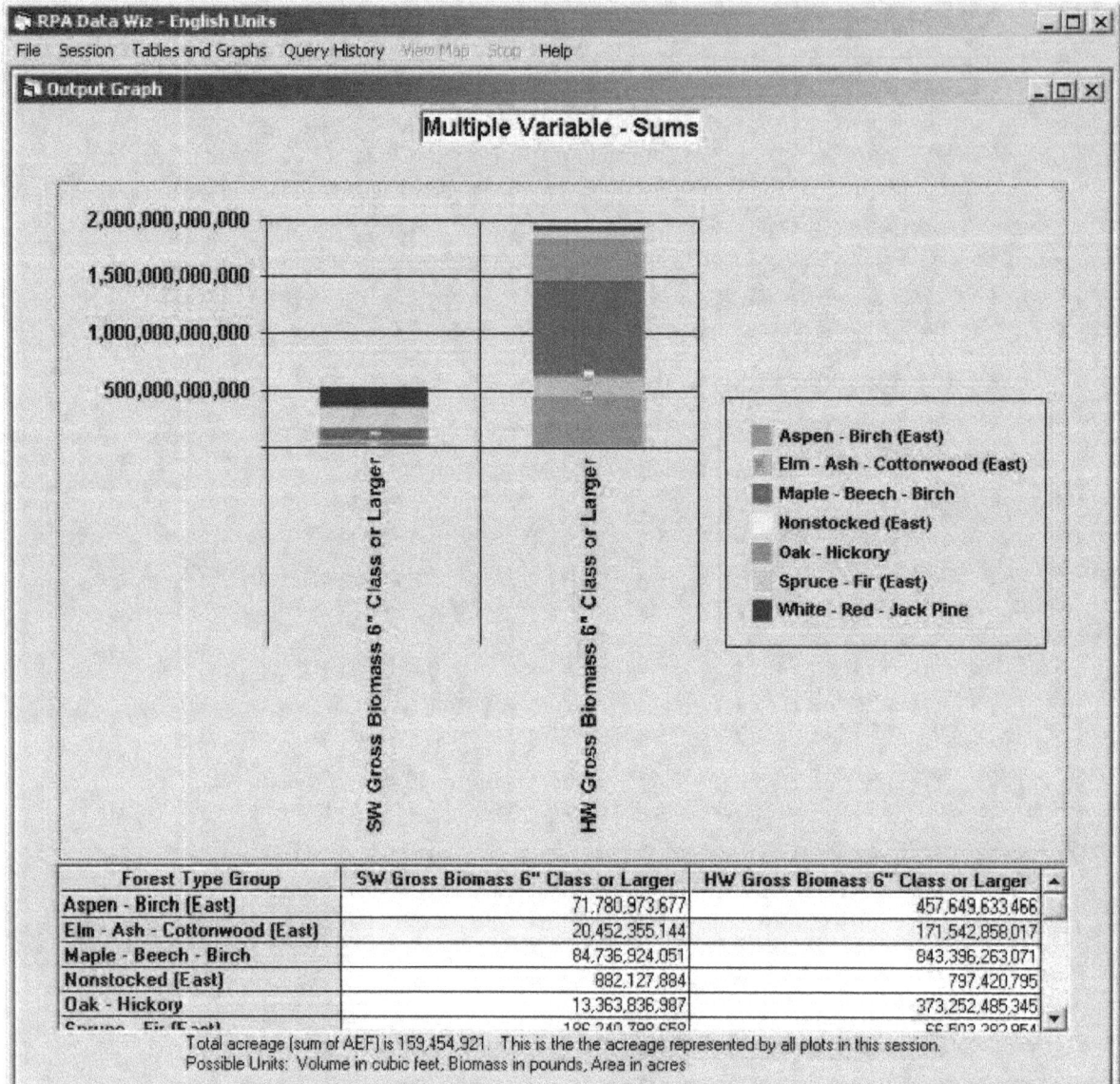

| Forest Type Group | SW Gross Biomass 6" Class or Larger | HW Gross Biomass 6" Class or Larger |
|---|---|---|
| Aspen - Birch (East) | 71,780,973,677 | 457,649,633,466 |
| Elm - Ash - Cottonwood (East) | 20,452,355,144 | 171,542,858,017 |
| Maple - Beech - Birch | 84,736,924,051 | 843,396,263,071 |
| Nonstocked (East) | 882,127,884 | 797,420,795 |
| Oak - Hickory | 13,363,836,987 | 373,252,485,345 |
| Spruce - Fir (East) | 196,240,799,659 | 56,503,393,954 |

Total acreage (sum of AEF) is 159,454,921. This is the the acreage represented by all plots in this session.
Possible Units: Volume in cubic feet, Biomass in pounds, Area in acres

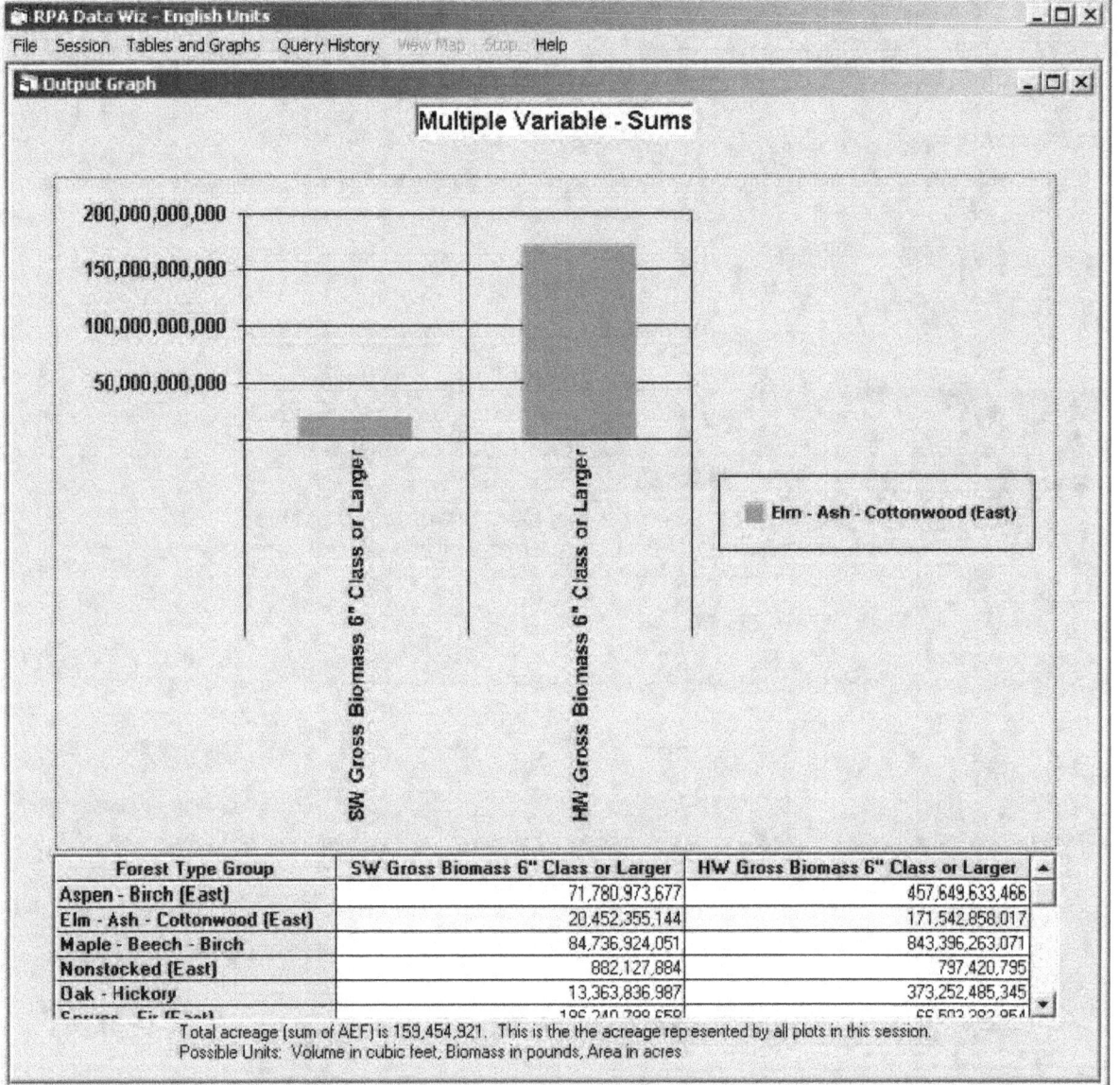

File   Session   Tables and Graphs   Query History   View Map   Stop   Help

**Output Graph**

## Multiple Variable - Sums

| Forest Type Group | SW Gross Biomass 6" Class or Larger | HW Gross Biomass 6" Class or Larger |
|---|---|---|
| Aspen - Birch (East) | 71,780,973,677 | 457,649,633,466 |
| Elm - Ash - Cottonwood (East) | 20,452,355,144 | 171,542,858,017 |
| Maple - Beech - Birch | 84,736,924,051 | 843,396,263,071 |
| Nonstocked (East) | 882,127,884 | 797,420,795 |
| Oak - Hickory | 13,363,836,987 | 373,252,485,345 |
| Spruce - Fir (East) | 196,240,798,658 | 66,593,292,954 |

Total acreage (sum of AEF) is 159,454,921. This is the the acreage represented by all plots in this session.
Possible Units: Volume in cubic feet, Biomass in pounds, Area in acres

21

There is a difference in the type of graph displayed if an optional ratio variable is chosen in the Multiple Variable Sums Table and Graph Generator. Instead of a stacking bar graph, a nonstacking bar graph is created (see example below). In a stacking bar graph, the top of the bar represents the total sum for the bar category. This is useful when showing sums; on the other hand, it makes no sense to show ratios as stacking when the total sum of the ratios for a bar category does not represent the overall ratio. Notice in the example below that the overall ratio of SW Cubic Foot Volume to HW Cubic Foot Volume is 0.38 (Total row of the associated table). As explained in the first section of "Creating a Graph," you can highlight individual series and display graphs of individual series.

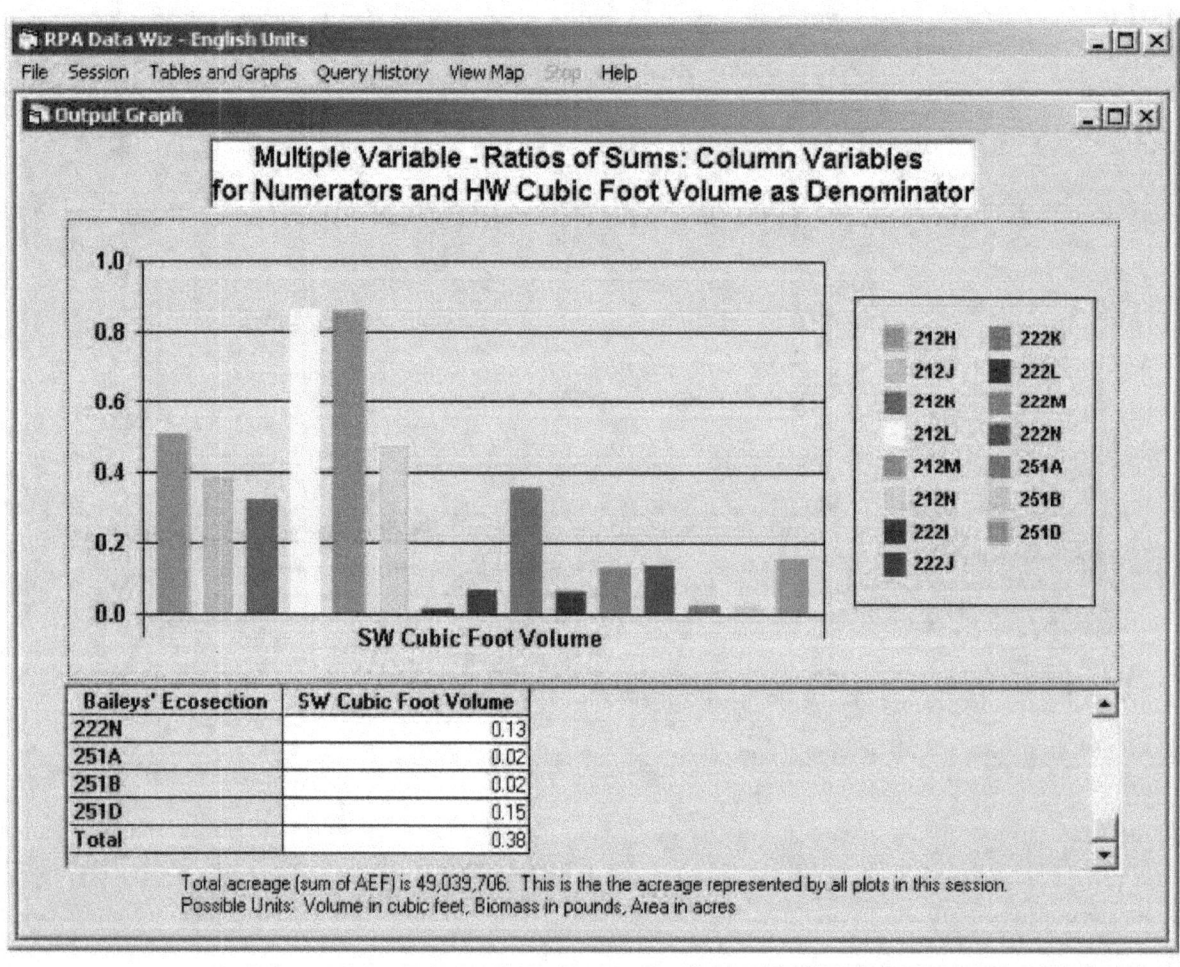

## Warning Message

If a resulting crosstab or multiple variable table is large, you may see a warning like the one below. What you do next depends on the speed and memory of your computer. On a 1.8 GHz machine with 1 GB of memory (a fast computer), the operation below (4,556 records) took 8 minutes.

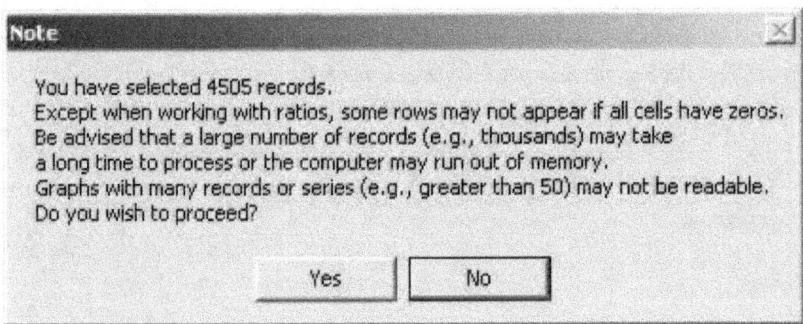

We recommend trying to create some of the bigger tables and pressing the Stop button on the main menu if the operation takes too long. After awhile you will gain a sense of how long it takes to create various size tables on your computer. Keep in mind that given the same number of rows in a table, it takes longer when more grouping variables are involved.

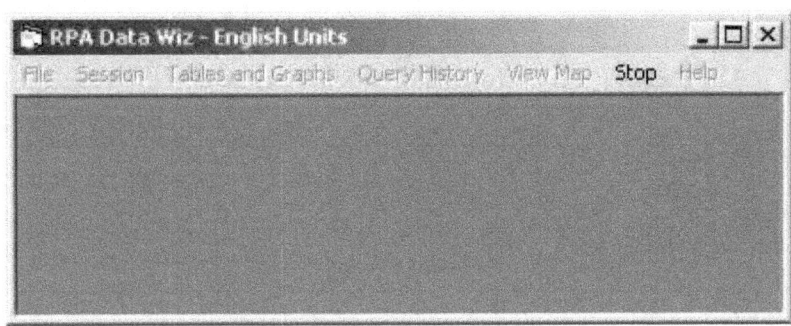

## Problem: Record Headings Filling the Screen?

Sometimes when working with small computer screens and multiple grouping variables (define row headings), the row headings fill the screen and the rest of the table cells appear to be unavailable. First, make sure your form sizes are maximized (click on the box in the upper right-hand corner of each form to maximize the size). If there is still a problem, you will need to narrow the column width for some of the row headings. Place the cursor on the division line between column headings. Next, click and drag with the mouse to decrease column width. This should allow you to scroll through the rest of the table.

## File Menu and Table Output Options

There are many options for table output from the File menu in RPA Data Wiz. A Save / Print dialog will appear for each of the formats and you can choose where to save the file. The default is in the temporary directory, temp, of the RPA Data Wiz application directory.

If you have Microsoft Excel installed on your computer, then you can save the table in Excel format. Choose Save As Excel Table or press CTRL + S to save the table in your version of Excel. This option will not work if you do not have Excel or if your Excel version is older than Excel 95. The column and row headings are automatically fixed and appear in bold font when opened in Excel.

The next two output formats are text. Pick Save As Comma Delimited to save the output with table headings and values separated with commas ("csv" file extension). This format can be imported into many software applications. Choose Save As Report to save the table in a report format ("txt" file extension).

Finally, select Print Table or press CTRL + P to print the table to a printer using the Print dialog. The recommendation is to choose landscape for the orientation (the default). Note that you can also save output tables associated with graphs.

## File Menu and Graph Output Options

Like the table output options, there are several options for graph output from the File menu in RPA Data Wiz. A graph heading does not output with the graph image. This allows you the freedom to make your own title in a final product using another software package like Microsoft PowerPoint. You can easily import or copy and paste the graph into another software package.

Choose Save Graph to save the graph in bitmap format. The Save / Print dialog displays and allows you to save the file in a location of your choice. The default is in the temporary directory, temp, of the RPA Data Wiz application directory. You can now import the graph into another software package. If you are working in PowerPoint, select Insert \ Picture \ From File and then choose the file.

Choose Copy Graph to Clipboard or press CTRL + G to copy the graph as a Windows metafile to the Windows clipboard. The data in the graph is also pasted into memory. The clipboard holds copied objects in memory and not as files. Consequently, you are not asked to save to a file. Depending upon where and how you perform a paste, the data or the image of the graph is pasted. If you are working in Excel, then select Edit \ Paste to paste the number data in the spreadsheet. Note that the row heading may not paste with the rest of the data. This appears to be a Microsoft bug in the software. To paste an image of the graph into the spreadsheet, choose Edit \ Paste Special… and select the Bitmap type. If you are working in Microsoft PowerPoint, then the image of the graph will paste into the document. We recommend that you choose Edit \ Paste Special… and select Device Independent Bitmap; otherwise, the graph may not paste correctly. You may try pasting in a number of different formats to see what works best for you. Usually, the bitmap option works well for this situation.

Whether you are opening the image from a saved bitmap or pasting from the clipboard, you may need to resize the graph to fit your area of interest. This is usually done by selecting the pasted bitmap image and then changing the size properties of the image or by clicking on a corner of the image and dragging it. In PowerPoint, select Format \ Picture \ Size and change the size.

Finally, choose Print Table to print the table using the Print dialog. We recommend choosing landscape for the orientation (the default). Note that you can also save output tables associated with graphs (see "File Menu and Table Output Options").

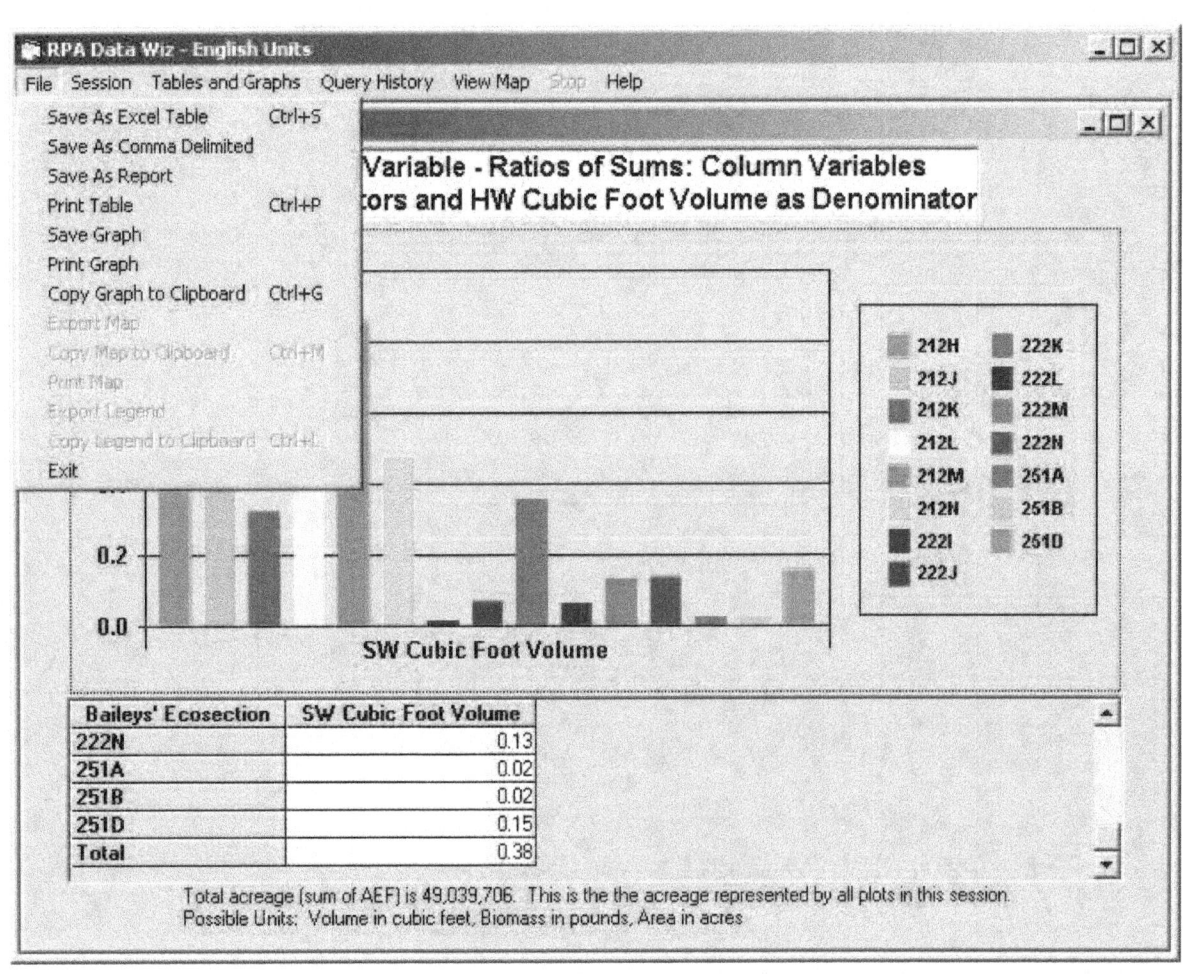

## Working with Multiple Output Tables in a Spreadsheet

Except when working with ratios, any row containing all zeros will not appear. Likewise, these rows are not part of the output from RPA Data Wiz. Some large tables result in thousands of rows and many total to 0. By not displaying or including these rows in output, computer resources are saved and tables are easier to read. This is important to remember. The disadvantage is that it can cause problems when working with multiple output tables in one spreadsheet. You may try working with multiple output tables in one Excel sheet and expect the rows from the tables to match up. Holding everything else constant, output tables with ratios may have more rows than output tables that report sums. In future versions of RPA Data Wiz, the option to include rows that total to 0 in any table will probably be added.

# Chapter 5
# Working with Maps

## Preparing to View Map

Before creating a map, you must first create a table or graph in the Multiple Variable Sums Table and Graph Generator (see Chapter 4). Here are the extra requirements for making a map. While creating the table or graph, select only one mapping, grouping variable and only one sum variable. Any of the other options in the dialog may also be chosen. The mapping, grouping variables are StateCounty, Baileys' Ecosection, 107th or 108th Congressional District Code, Hydrological Accounting Unit, and Administrative Forest.

Make a table using the Multiple Variable Sums Table and Graph Generator and the restrictions mentioned. Afterwards, select **View Map** and the appropriate map choice is enabled. The example below shows the 108th Congressional District Code as the grouping variable of choice. Consequently, a 108th Congressional District map will be developed. Area is the choice for the sum variable and the optional ratio variable. Both optional boxes are checked. The number of samples associated with each congressional district will be displayed in the table. Including the number of samples in the table never affects the map. The optional Mapping Ratios checkbox will result in a different kind of ratio (see "Multiple Variable Sums Table and Graph Generator" in Chapter 4). During the creation of the initial session (see Chapter 3), timberland only occurring on public land was chosen for MI, WI, and MN. In this case, checking the Mapping Ratios checkbox will result in a ratio of public timberland to all land for each congressional district. Consequently, the result will be a 108th Congressional District map of public timberland to all land. The congressional district code is defined in appendix A.

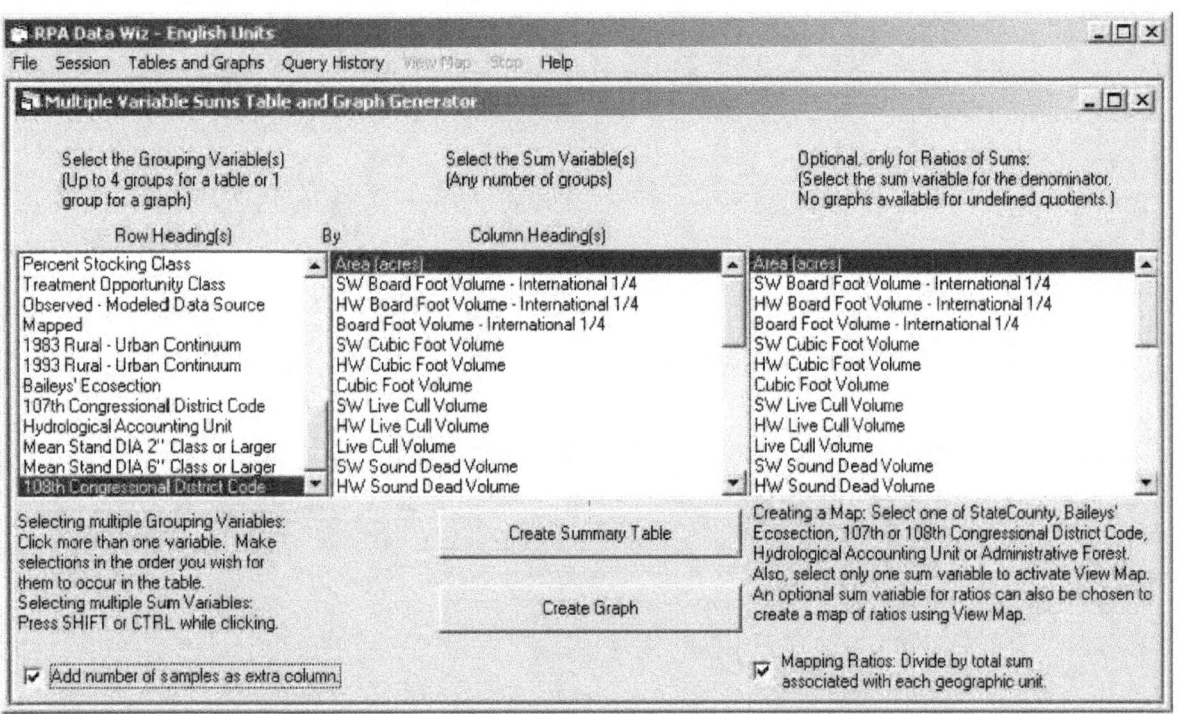

## View Map

All maps in RPA Data Wiz are *classification* or *choropleth* maps, which group the values of the sum variable or ratios into discrete ranges and represent each range with a different color. Follow the steps below to create several different types of choropleth maps.

## Equal Interval Map

1. Select **View Map** and the enabled map. The Map form appears. The map view is automatically zoomed in on the polygons involved. The area of the map displayed is called the *map extent*.
2. Choose *Equal Interval Classes* to display a map where the classes have an equal range of values.
3. Change the number of classes by typing in a different number for **Number of Classes**.
4. *Ramp* the colors; in other words, change the colors of the classes using a graduated scheme by selecting the **Start Color** and **End Color**.
5. Choose **Polygon Labels** to display the names of the geographic units.
6. Change the size (points) of the polygon labels by adjusting the number for **Label Size**. Click **Polygon Labels** for the change to take effect.

The example below is the 108th Congressional District map of public timberland acreage to all land acreage using five equal interval classes. The congressional district labels are also displayed. Notice that the titles on the maps in RPA Data Wiz are generic, only identifying the variables involved in the output and not including information indicating any choices made while creating the session.

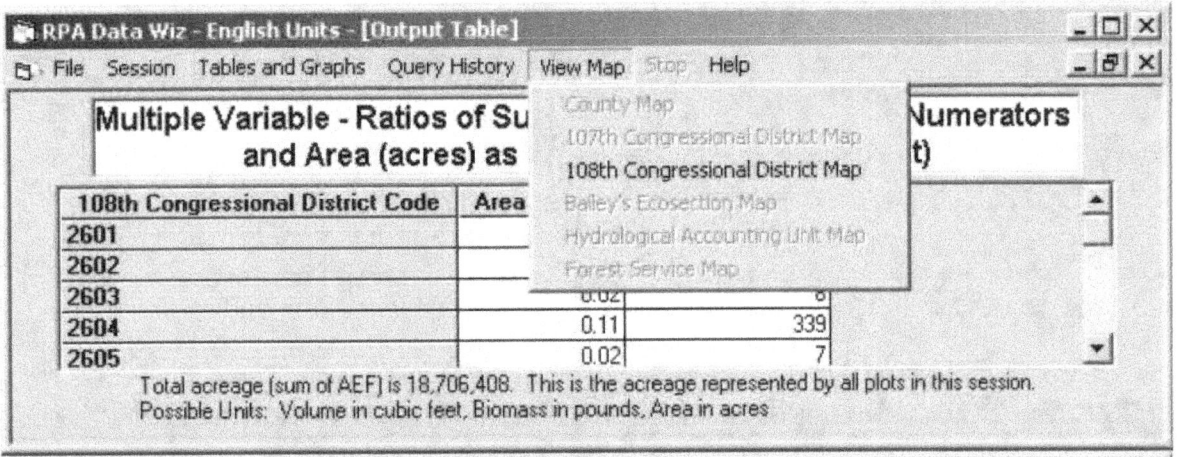

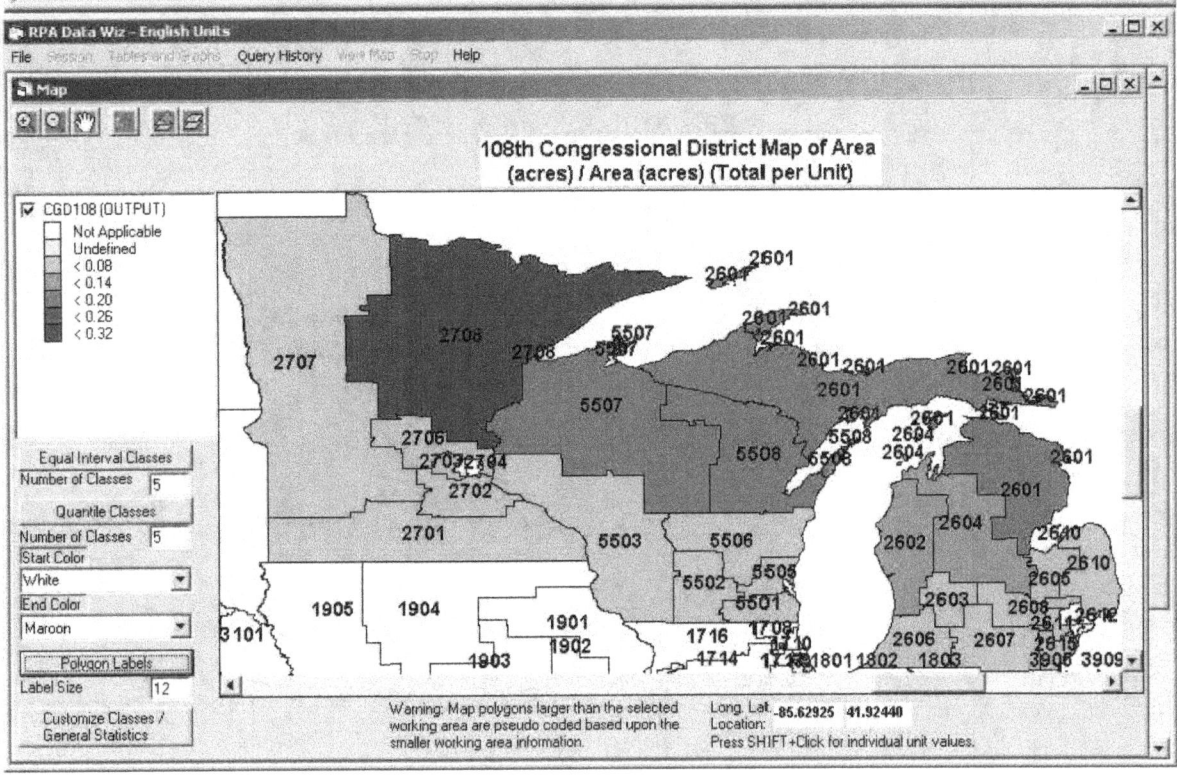

### Quantile Map

1. Choose *Quantile Classes* to display a map where the classes are divided such that an equal number of geographic units occur in each class.
2. Again, change the number of classes by typing in a different number for **Number of Classes**.
3. As previously mentioned, ramp the colors by selecting the **Start Color** and **End Color**.

Again, the example is the 108th Congressional District map of public timberland acreage to all land acreage. This time, five quantile classes are applied and the congressional district polygon labels are not displayed. Notice the contrast in the colors and class intervals between this example and the last example.

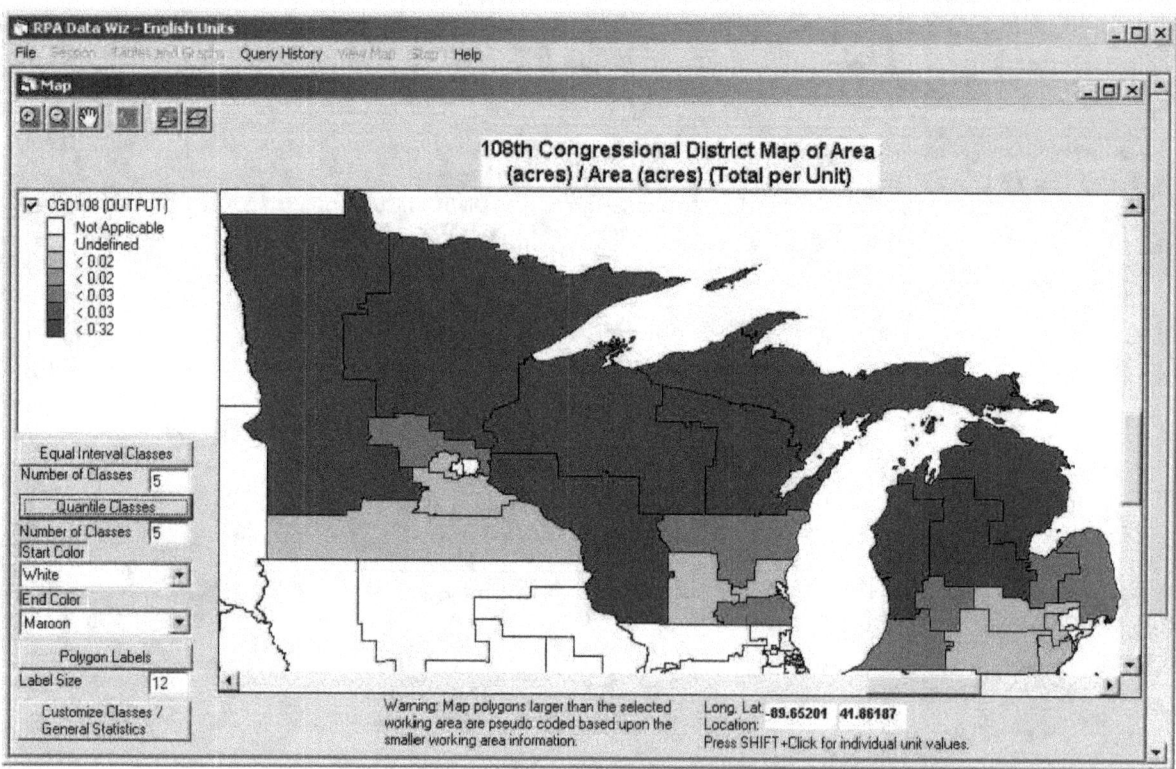

### Custom Map

1. Choose **Customize Classes / General Statistics** to display a map with user-defined ranges and colors for each class.
2. Define the class breaks and pick their associated colors. Two breaks are automatically assigned. You must define at least one more break.
3. There is an option to ramp colors in this dialog. Click the **Check to ramp colors from Class 1 to Last Class** box.

The Customize Classes dialog displays some basic statistics such as the mean, minimum, and maximum of the sum variable or ratio. It also shows the number of geographic units (not counting geographic units labeled as "Not Applicable" or "Undefined") involved in the map. These statistics can help determine the distribution of the data and how the classes should be defined. Like the two previous examples, the example below uses five classes, but the class breaks are defined differently. The same ramping color scheme is applied. Notice that this user-defined example represents the differences among the congressional districts better than the two previous examples.

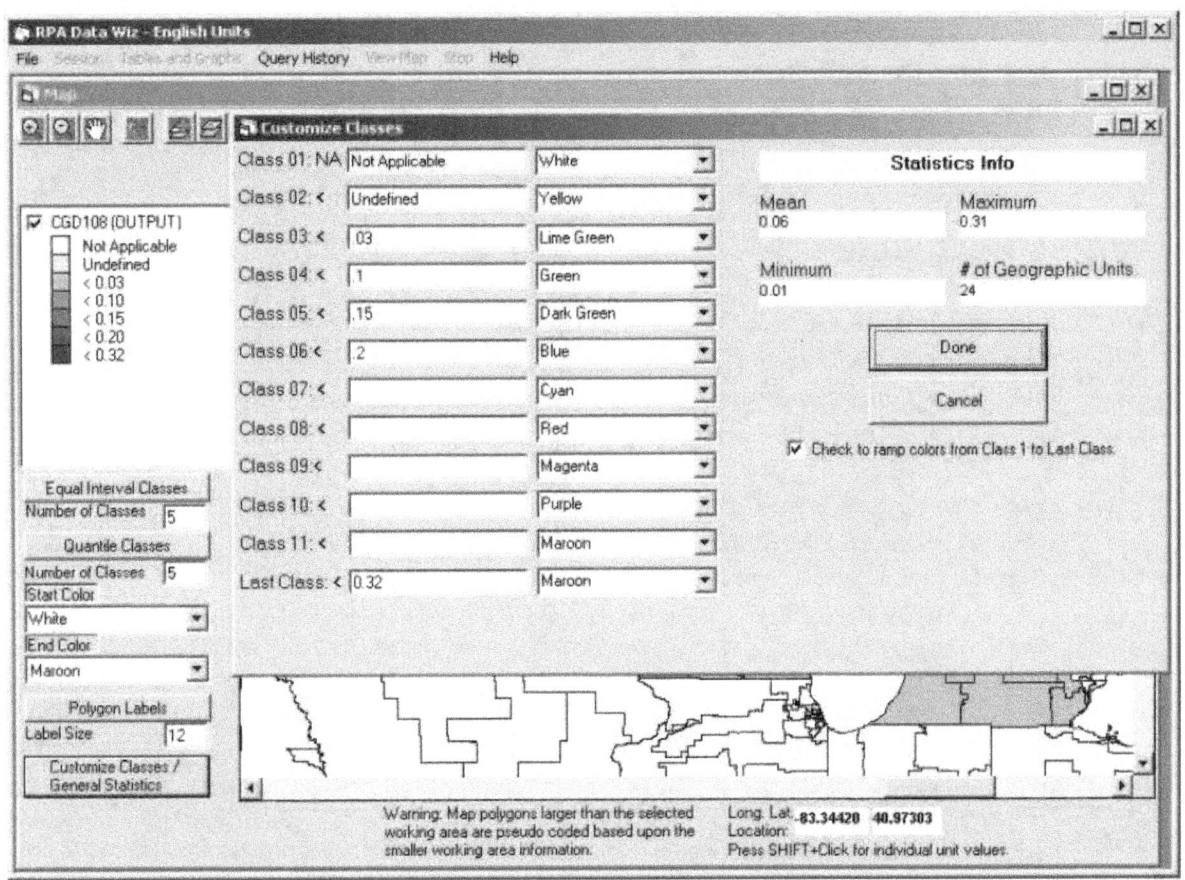

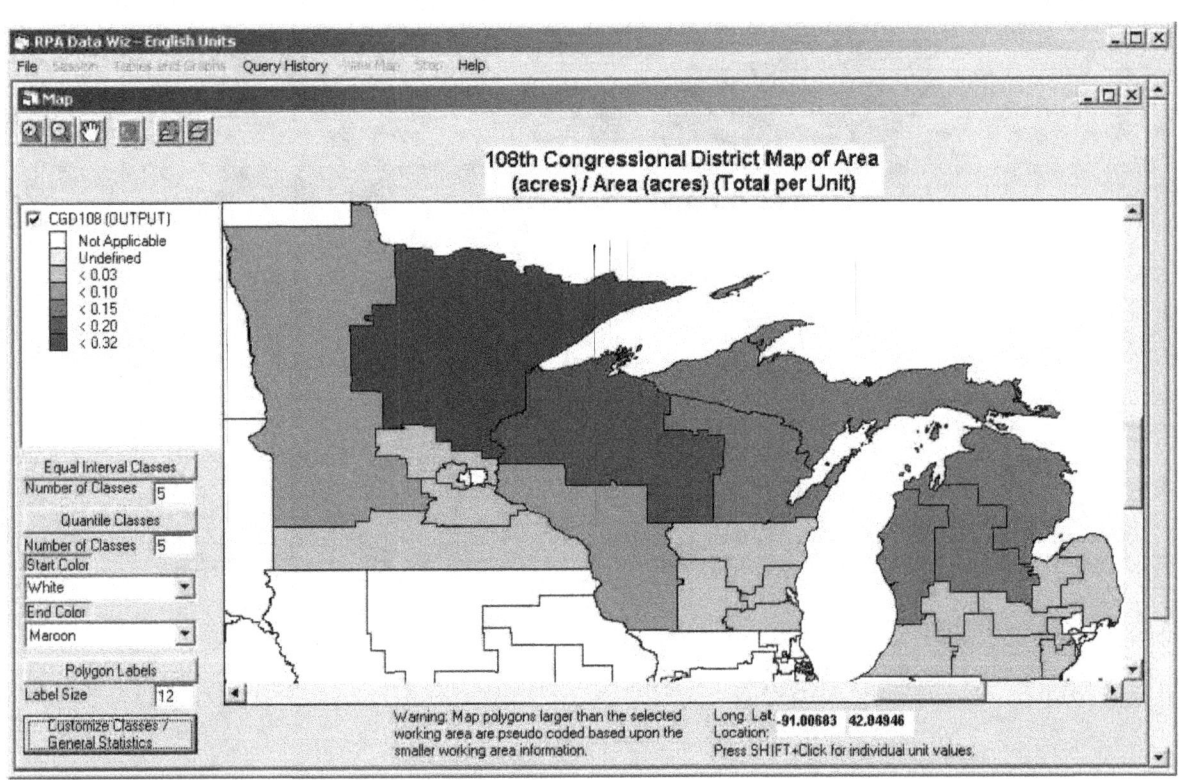

Keep in mind that you do not have to select every option before redisplaying a map. Change only the options you wish. The map will redisplay anytime one of the Equal Interval Classes, Quantile Classes, or Done (in Customize Classes dialog) buttons is clicked. In addition, the polygon labels are cleared anytime one of these buttons is clicked.

## Applying the GIS Tools

The Map form in RPA Data Wiz provides a number of *Geographic Information System (GIS)* capabilities. A short definition for GIS is a system where people apply computer technology to store and manipulate geographic information. Throughout this chapter, examples have been provided showing how you can manipulate the geographic information associated with the RPA database. This section describes the GIS tools available in RPA Data Wiz that are common in most GIS computer applications.

First, notice the **Long. Lat.** (longitude measuring east-west, latitude measuring north-south) coordinates in the lower right section of the Map form. Move the cursor throughout the map extent and notice the coordinates changing. The *latitude-longitude* coordinate system is a common geographic coordinate system used to identify locations on the earth (Aronoff 1995).

Next, use the cursor to display the exact value associated with a geographic unit. Place the cursor over a polygon of interest, hold **SHIFT**, and click the left button on the mouse. The value displays. Notice that the left-most shaded polygon in the example below is associated with 0.05.

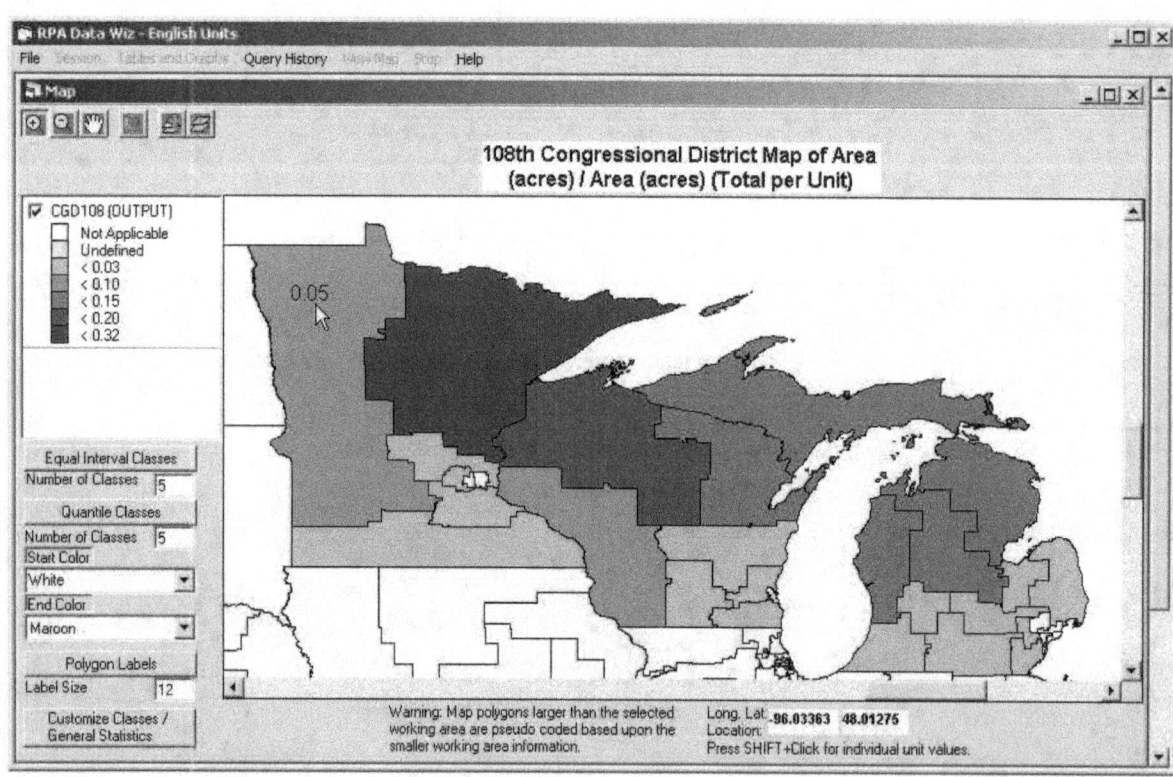

The following tools are displayed in the upper-left corner of the Map form. Placing the cursor over each tool displays a tool tip. Only one of the Zoom In, Zoom Out, or Pan tools can be active at a time. Click one of the tools and it will function with the cursor while in the map extent.

 Zoom In Tool. Activate the Zoom In Tool by clicking it. Hold the left button on the mouse and drag the cursor over the new map extent. Release the mouse button and the map display will reflect the new area in a larger map scale (smaller map area displayed in same computer screen area).

 Zoom Out Tool. Activate the Zoom Out Tool by clicking it. Unlike the Zoom In Tool, this tool does not allow you to delineate a box over the area of interest. Click the left button on the mouse over the point of interest to decrease the map scale by a factor of two.

 Pan Tool. Activate the Pan Tool by clicking it. Hold down the left button on the mouse and move the mouse from one point to another to change the map extent.

Click the next tool and it works immediately to increase the map extent.

 Zoom to Full Extent Tool. Activate the Zoom to Full Extent Tool by clicking it. The map extent changes to show all the geographic units of every map layer present.

Click the tools below to add and delete map layers to and from the map extent. The base map (map that displays initially in the Map form) cannot be removed. All of the map layers in RPA Data Wiz are located in the RPA Data Wiz application directory (usually C:\Program Files\RPA Data Wiz\). These map layers are ArcView shapefiles. You cannot and should not add the same theme that displays as the base map. Double-clicking on an added map layer name in the legend and then choosing a new color in the Color dialog changes the color of the map layer. Any polygon shapefiles or polygon, ArcInfo coverages (basically a different type of map layer) are displayed with no fill color so the base map is not covered. Note that adding any map layer that does not use the latitude-longitude coordinate system will have unpredictable consequences. The map layers will not overlay correctly upon each other.

 Add Map Layer Tool. Activate the Add Map Layer Tool by clicking it. The Add Map Layers dialog displays. Choose Shapefile, ArcInfo Polygon or Point Coverage, or ArcInfo Line Coverage. If Shapefile was chosen, then select Add Layer to use the Open dialog and locate the shapefile of interest. If an ArcInfo coverage option was chosen, a directory listing appears. ArcInfo coverage names will appear as directories. Select the one of interest and click Add Layer. Close the Add Map Layers dialog by clicking the upper-right 'X' button on the dialog.

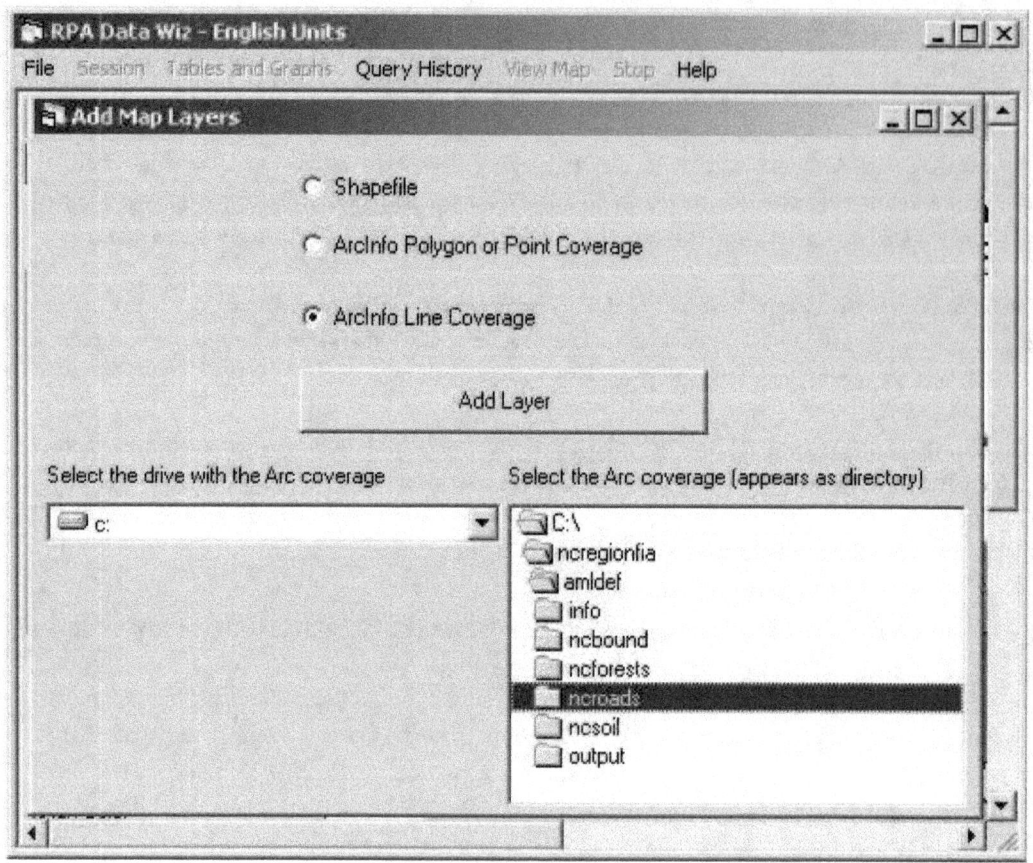

 Delete Map Layer Tool. Remove an ancillary map layer by first clicking on its name in the legend. Now click the Delete Map Layer Tool.

Extra map layers can provide a frame of reference. Depending on your audience and the point you are trying to make, extra map layers like roads and waterways help others relate to the maps you make in RPA Data Wiz. A number of Web sites offer free digital map layers that work in RPA Data Wiz (e.g., http://data.geocomm.com and http://nationalatlas.gov/atlasftp.html). Be sure to obtain map layers in the latitude-longitude coordinate system. A noteworthy extra map layer available with RPA Data Wiz is "statesp020." This is a State boundary map layer. The following example shows the congressional districts from previous examples with the previously mentioned state boundary map layer and a road map layer.

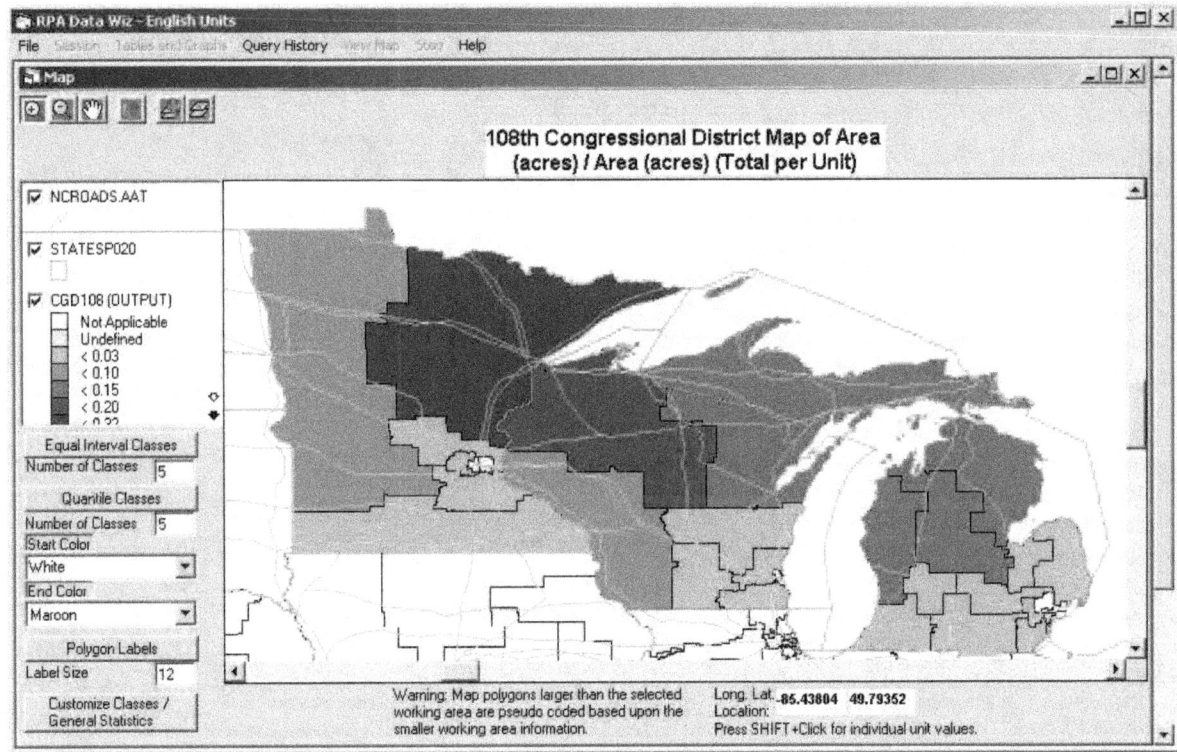

## Warnings

Some geographic units have multiple polygons. For example, a county could be composed of an island and mainland. The island would be coded the same as the mainland area. You can usually tell if a geographic unit has multiple polygons by selecting **Polygon Labels**. Multiple polygons that are part of the same geographic unit will be labeled the same.

In the bottom section of the Map form there is a warning indicating that polygons larger than the selected working area are pseudo coded based upon the smaller working area information. What does this mean? The previous examples showed congressional districts that follow State boundaries. It was mentioned earlier that the session leading up to the examples narrowed the working RPA plots or records down to public timberland in MI, MN, and WI. In this situation, the warning does not apply because the congressional districts do not move outside of the State boundaries chosen as the selected working area. Suppose the example is changed by one factor. Instead of creating a 108th Congressional District Map, a Baileys' Ecosection Map is created. Look at the example below and note where the State boundaries (statesp020) are in comparison to the ecosection boundaries (ecoregs). Now the warning applies. Some of the ecosection geographic units extend outside of the tri-state boundary area (the smaller working area). These ecosections are coded based only upon information occurring in the tri-state area. In other words, even though the map shows ecosections extending past State boundaries, the color codes of the ecosections only reflect plot information for the selected States.

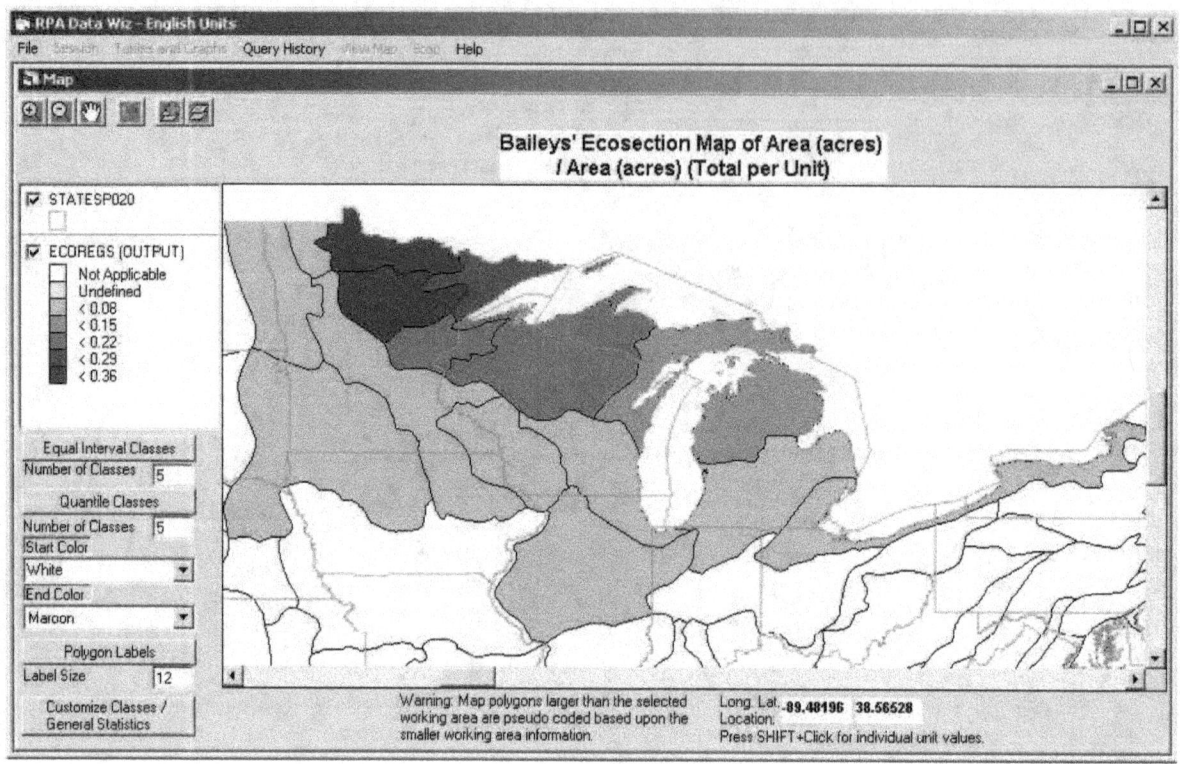

The 107th and 108th Congressional District Codes, Baileys' Ecosections, and Hydrological Accounting Units were assigned to plots using a GIS overlay analysis (appendix A). The analysis was applied using fuzzed plot locations. The fuzzed locations are usually within a mile of the true plot location. Consequently, there is some error introduced in the estimates when grouping by these variables. Furthermore, the maps associated with these variables will inherit this error. The StateCounty and Administrative Forest codes were directly assigned using the correct plot locations, so the estimates and maps associated with these grouping variables are not subject to this error.

## File Menu and Map Output Options

As with tables and graphs, a number of output options are available for maps in RPA Data Wiz. The legend and the map are output separately to allow more freedom when producing a final product in another software package like Microsoft PowerPoint or Adobe Photoshop. You can import or paste the legend and map into another software package and manipulate them to suit your needs. A map title does not come with the map image. This allows you the freedom to make your own title. The map can be output as a bitmap or a Windows enhanced metafile. Windows metafiles sometimes result in a sharper image, especially when the map has many line features like roads or waterways. However, the bitmap usually handles manipulation better than the metafile. Sometimes resizing the metafile adversely alters the image. Bitmap is the safest format to use.

### Exporting the Map and Legend

1.  Choose **File \ Export Map** to display the **Save – Copy** dialog.
2.  Select **Export to Bitmap** or **Export to Windows Enhanced Metafile**.
3.  Click **Export** to save the map portion of the Map form.
4.  Close the **Save - Copy** dialog by clicking the upper-right "X" button on the dialog. If you are working in PowerPoint, select **Insert \ Picture \ From File** and then choose the file.
5.  Choose **File \ Export Legend** to save the legend as a bitmap. The output files can be saved to any available directory, but the default directory is "temp" in the RPA Data Wiz application folder.

## Copying the Map and Legend to the Windows Clipboard

1. Select File \ Copy Map to Clipboard to display the Save – Copy dialog. The clipboard holds copied objects in memory and not as files. Consequently, you are not asked to save to a file.

2. Select Copy as Bitmap or Copy as Windows Enhanced Metafile.

3. Click Copy Map to Clipboard to copy the map portion of the Map form to the Windows clipboard.

4. Close the Save - Copy dialog by clicking the upper-right 'X' button on the dialog. Now you can paste the map into another software program. If you are working in PowerPoint and you chose bitmap, we recommend you choose Edit \ Paste Special... and select Device Independent Bitmap. If you are working in PowerPoint and you chose Windows enhanced metafile, we recommend you choose Edit \ Paste Special... and select Picture (Enhanced Metafile).

5. Choose File \ Copy Legend to Clipboard to automatically copy the legend to the clipboard. The legend only copies in the bitmap format. The legend is now ready to be pasted into another software program. In PowerPoint, choose Edit \ Paste Special... and select Device Independent Bitmap.

Whether you are opening the image from a saved file or you are pasting from the clipboard, you may need to resize the map to fit your area of interest. This is usually done by selecting the pasted image and then changing the size properties of the image or by clicking on a corner of the image and dragging it. In PowerPoint, select Format \ Picture \ Size and change the size making sure not to change the east-west and north-south dimensions disproportionately.

Select File \ Print Map to display the Print dialog and print the map portion of the Map form. The legend and title will not be printed. Landscape is the recommended and default orientation.

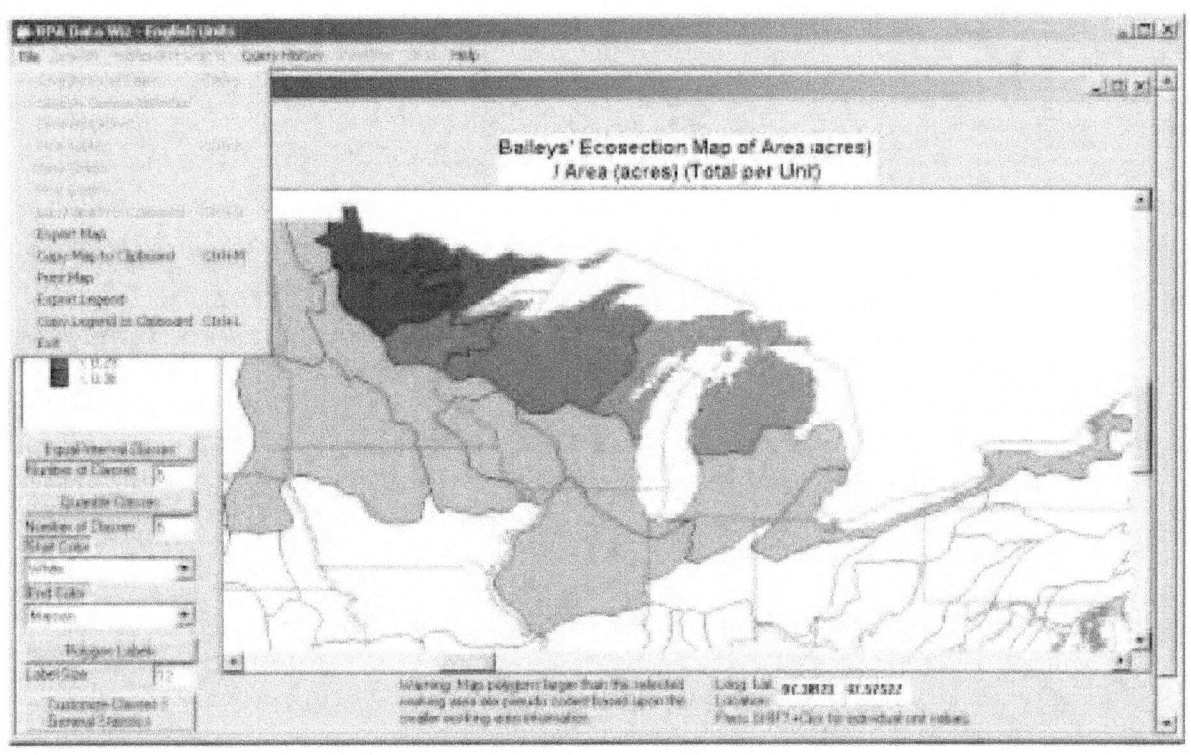

Figure 1 is an example of a final product produced in less than 15 minutes in PowerPoint. Notice that this is the example map presented in "View Map." The map layer, statesp020, that comes with RPA Data Wiz was added in the Map form and the class intervals were customized (used Customize Classes dialog) to bring out the contrast among the congressional districts. The map and legend were each copied to the clipboard and pasted into PowerPoint as bitmaps. A north arrow was added from the clip art in PowerPoint. Text was added to label the states. Finally a new title was created and the legend was labeled as "Legend."

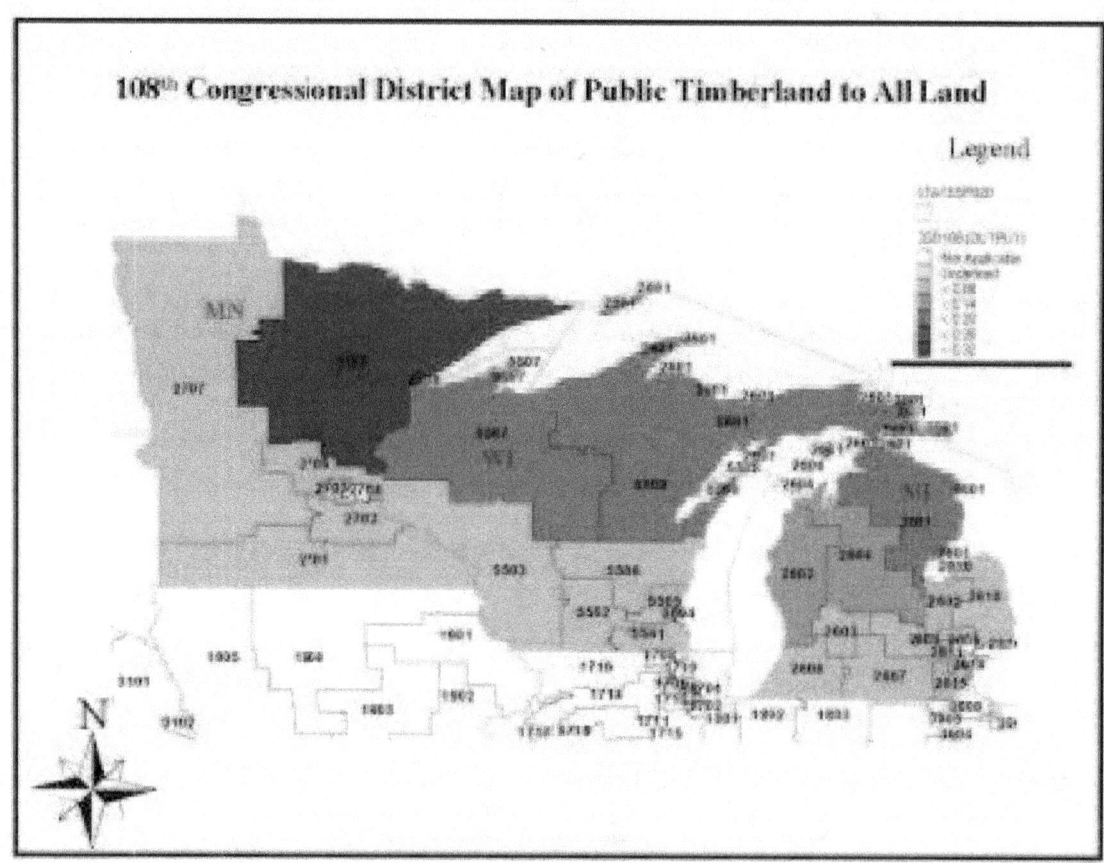

Figure 1.—Final map produced using RPA Data Wiz and Microsoft PowerPoint.

## Quantile and Equal Interval Mapping – Discussion and Notes

Theoretically, *quantile classes* have an equal number of geographic units. The total number of geographic units is divided by the total number of classes to come up with the number of units in each class. If you have 16 units and you want to group them into 4 quantile classes, then there should be 4 units in each class. The first class should have the first 25 percent of the units. The second class should have the next 25 percent of the units and so forth. The values of the variable in question (e.g., acreage) are sorted and each geographic unit is placed in a class based upon the relative magnitude of its value (fig. 2 and table 1). Practically there are some complications with the definition given and RPA Data Wiz compensates for these complications.

Theoretically, *equal interval classes* have an equal range of values. The range of data values (max - min) is divided by the total number of classes to determine the range of values in each class (fig. 2 and table 1). Again, there are some complications with this definition and RPA Data Wiz compensates for these.

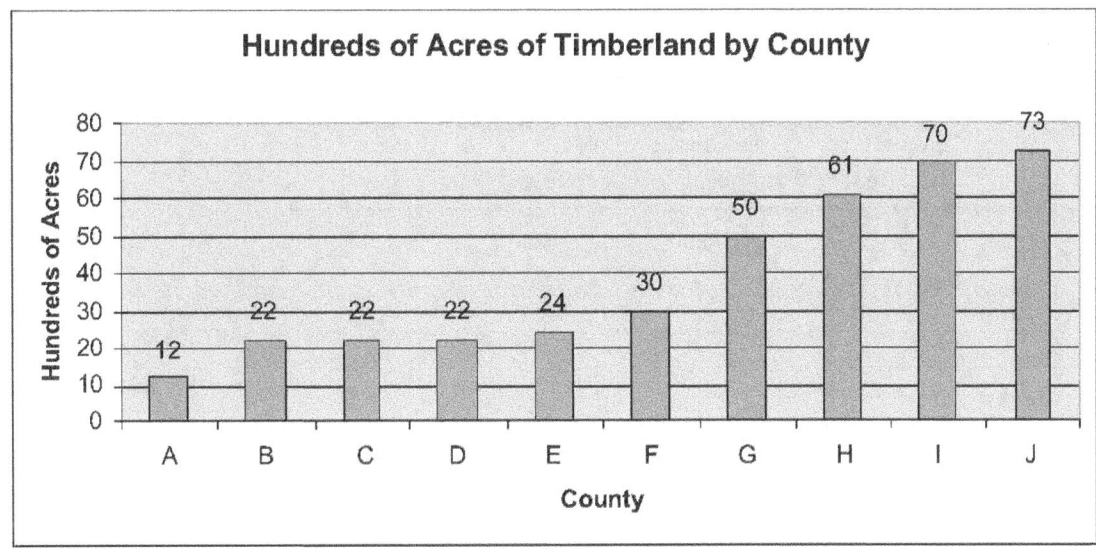

Figure 2.—Histogram of hundreds of acres of timberland by county.

Table 1.—Comparison of quantile and equal interval mapping techniques using figure 2.

| Classes | Quantiles | | | | Equal intervals | | | |
|---|---|---|---|---|---|---|---|---|
| | Theoretical counties | Theoretical ranges | Wiz counties | Wiz legend | Theoretical counties | Theoretical ranges | Wiz counties | Wiz legend |
| Class 1 | AB | 12 - 22 | ABCD | < 23 | ABCDE | 12 - 24 | ABCDE | < 25 |
| Class 2 | CD | 22 - 22 | | < 23 | F | 25 - 36 | F | < 37 |
| Class 3 | EF | 24 - 30 | EF | < 31 | | 37 - 48 | | < 49 |
| Class 4 | GH | 50 - 61 | GH | < 62 | G | 49 - 60 | G | < 61 |
| Class 5 | IJ | 70 - 73 | IJ | < 74 | HI | 61 - 72 | HIJ | < 74 |

## Quantile Class Exceptions

In RPA Data Wiz, there are some exceptions to the definition of quantile classes. First, if the resulting quotient is not an integer, then the quotient is truncated. Consequently, there may not be an equal number of geographic units per class. For example, if there are only 10 geographic units and 6 classes are requested, the result is 1 (10/6 = 1.66, truncated to 1) geographic unit per class (fig. 2 and table 2). With 6 classes and 1 geographic unit per class, only 6 of the 10 geographic units are recognized. In this situation, RPA Data Wiz puts 5 geographic units in the last class with the greatest upper limit. The last class will have a disproportionately greater number of geographic units. RPA Data Wiz does not round quotients up; the result would be a deficient number of classes (2 geographic units in the previous example results in only 5 classes). As the ratio of geographic units to classes increases, this exception has less of an effect. Most of the time, you will be working with enough geographic units to make the effects of this exception minimal.

Table 2.—*Quantile mapping using 6 classes and a truncated range of 1 with data from figure 2*

| Classes | Quantiles | | | |
|---------|-----------|--|--|--|
| | **Theoretical counties** | **Theoretical ranges** | **Wiz counties** | **Wiz legend** |
| **Class 1** | A | 12 - 12 | A | < 13 |
| **Class 2** | B | 22 - 22 | BCD | < 23 |
| **Class 3** | C | 22 - 22 | | < 23 |
| **Class 4** | D | 22 - 22 | | < 23 |
| **Class 5** | E | 24 - 24 | E | < 25 |
| **Class 6** | F | 30 - 30 | FGHIJ | < 74 |

The second exception occurs when more than 1 class has the same upper limit. Notice in table 1 that Class 1 and Class 2 each have 22 as the upper limit in the "Theoretical Ranges" column. The problem becomes worse when using more classes. Notice in table 2 that now there are 3 classes with 22 as the theoretical upper limit. Geographic units with the same value can belong to different classes using the quantile mapping technique. However, RPA Data Wiz keeps all the geographic units with the same values in the same class and displays them with the same color even though the legend indicates there are multiple classes for the same value. Figure 3 shows a quantile classification where 4 different classes have the same upper limit of 0.01, but all counties in the map with 0.01 are shaded with the same color (the topmost color for 0.01 in the legend).

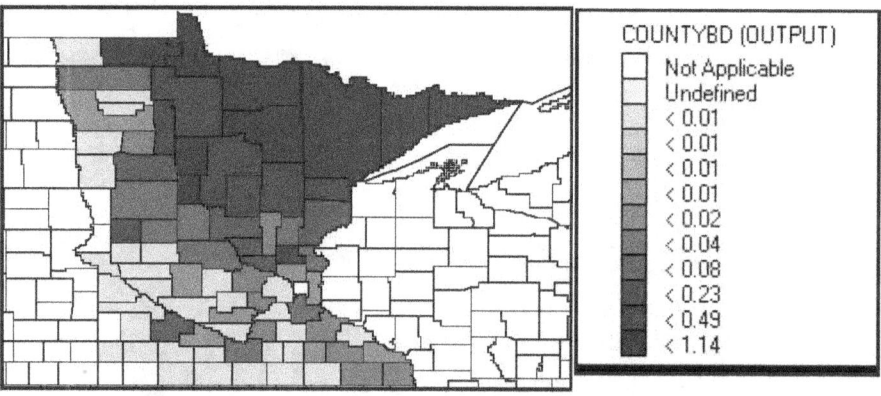

Figure 3 —*Quantile map of SW to HW cubic-foot volume on timberland in MN.*

## *Equal Interval Class Exceptions*

The equal interval mapping technique in RPA Data Wiz can result in exceptions to the definition (fig. 2 and table 1). As previously mentioned, the range is divided by the number of requested classes. If the quotient is not an integer, then the quotient is rounded to the nearest integer. In table 1 and figure 2, the range is 61 (73 – 12) and the quotient is 12.2 (61/5). Consequently, the quotient is rounded to provide a class interval of 12. When rounding down, some geographic units with high values may not be recognized in the last class. In table 1, County J does not make it into the "Theoretical Counties" column. When rounding up, the uppermost limit of the greatest class can result in a value greater than the maximum value of the geographic units. RPA Data Wiz violates the equal interval class definition and always uses the maximum value to define the uppermost limit of the greatest class. Consequently, the interval for the greatest class may not equal the interval used for all the other classes. This ensures that all geographic units are accounted for and the uppermost limit in the legend provides extra information (working with all values except ratios the uppermost limit is 1 more than the maximum value; the uppermost limit working with ratios is 0.01 more than the maximum value).

## Creating the Most Informative Map

When creating your map, you should usually focus on the following rules:

- Maximize the between-class differences
- Minimize the within-class differences

Quantile or equal interval maps can sometimes meet the previous criteria. However, problems do arise with these techniques. The quantile mapping technique can place geographic units with the same value in different classes and it can group geographic units with drastically different values in the same class (table 1). The equal interval mapping technique can create classes that contain no geographic units (Class 3 in table 1, Classes 3 and 4 in table 2). The Customize Classes dialog allows you to overcome these problems by entering your own class breaks derived by any means you choose. The easiest way to observe the previous rules is to study the data in the table and find the naturally occurring breaks. You may wish to export the data to a spreadsheet and then sort it to find the natural breaks. After identifying these breaks, you can enter them in the Customize Classes dialog.

There may be times when you are not concerned with maximizing the differences among groups that appear naturally in a map. For example, you may be only interested in highlighting geographic units that are above or below some threshold value. In this case, you may elect to group everything into two classes even though there may be a number of naturally occurring groups in each of these classes. Ultimately, your objectives will dictate the number and location of class breaks for your map.

# Chapter 6
# Tutorials

The tutorials are provided to give step-by-step examples of applying RPA Data Wiz. However, the tutorials are not meant to cover every aspect of RPA Data Wiz and they do not come with many detailed explanations of features and techniques. Refer to rest of this manual for this type of information.

## Exercise 1: Tables and Graphs

This exercise will help you become familiar with the tables and graphs in RPA Data Wiz. This will be an exploratory analysis of some of the information for the Southeast Assessment Subregion.

### Multiple Variable Sums Table

1. If RPA Data Wiz is not already running, then start it. Typical way is to select **Start \ Programs \ RPA Data Wiz**.
2. Click in the gray area of the initial screen to start.
3. If you have the English and metric versions, then pick one of them.
4. Choose **Session \ New Session**.
5. Select **Southeast Assessment Subregion** in Select RPA Subregion(s).
6. Click **Done Selecting RPA Subregion(s)**.
7. Choose **Land Cover Class** in RPA Variable Selection.
8. Select **Forest Land** in Select Field Value(s).
9. Click **Done Selecting Field Value(s)**.
10. Choose **Mean Stand Dia 2" Class or Larger** (5 cm class or larger for metric version) in RPA Variable Selection.
11. Select all values greater than or equal to 10 in Select Field Value(s). Hold **SHIFT** and click on **10** or the next highest number available. Keep holding **SHIFT** and scroll to the bottom of the list and click on the greatest value.
12. Click **Done Selecting Field Value(s)**.
13. Choose **Done Selecting** in RPA Variable Selection.
14. Create a multivariable sums table.
    A. Choose **Tables and Graphs \ Multiple Variable Tables and Graphs**. The Multiple Variable Sums Table and Graph Generator dialog appears.
    B. In order, select **Owner Group**, **Forest Type Group**, and **Site Productivity Class** for the grouping variable. Click each separately with the mouse without using any other keys. If you have accidentally chosen a variable, then deselect it by clicking on it a second time.
    C. Select all of the sum variables. Click on the first variable, **Area**. Scroll down to the bottom of the list. Hold SHIFT and click the last variable. All the sum variables are chosen.
    D. Select **Add number of samples as extra column**.
    E. Choose **Create Summary Table** (see example below). Make sure your form sizes are maximized to see the table well (click on box in upper right-hand corner of each form to maximize size). Scroll through the table and investigate the information. The last column contains the number of samples associated with the estimates in each row. This provides a measure of accuracy for the estimates. Notice that many rows have a low number of associated plots. The confidence in the corresponding estimates is low.
    F. Choose **File** in the main menu and notice the options for table output. Experiment with these options. Microsoft Excel tables can only be produced if you have Excel on your computer.

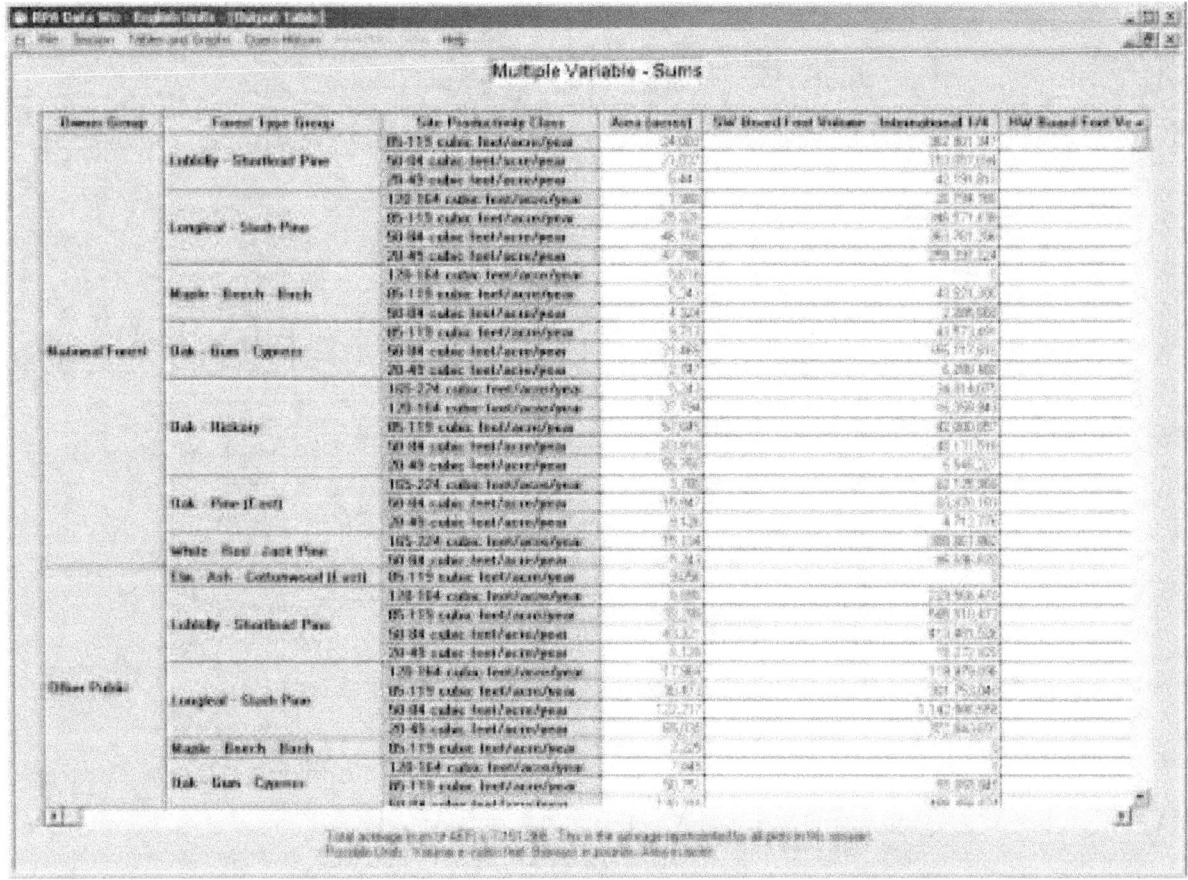

## Multiple Variable Sums Graph

1. Choose Tables and Graphs \ Multiple Variable Tables and Graphs. The Multiple Variable Sums Table and Graph Generator dialog appears.

2. Select Site Productivity Class for the grouping variable. Select only one grouping variable when producing graphs.

3. Select SW Gross Biomass 6' Class or Larger and HW Gross Biomass 6' Class or Larger for the sum variables. Scroll down to find the variables. Hold CTRL and click each variable.

4. Select Area as the optional ratio variable (under `Optional, only for Ratio of Sums:`).

5. Choose Create Graph (see example below). Make sure your form sizes are maximized to see the graph well (click on box in upper right-hand corner of each form to maximize size).

    A. Click on a series in the graph or in the legend to highlight the corresponding row in the table.

6. Select File in the main menu and notice there are options to output the table and the graph.

7. Output the graph to another software package.

    A. Choose Copy Graph to Clipboard or press CTRL + G to copy the graph as a Windows metafile to the Windows clipboard. The data in the graph are also pasted into memory. Depending upon where and how you perform a paste, the data or the image of the graph are pasted.

    B. Open another software package like Microsoft Excel

    C. If you are working in Excel, then select Edit \ Paste to paste the number data in the spread-sheet. Note that the row heading may not paste with the rest of the data. This appears to be a Microsoft bug in the software.

    D. Paste an image of the graph. In Excel, choose Edit \ Paste Special... and select the Bitmap type. In Microsoft PowerPoint, choose Edit \ Paste Special... and select Device Independent Bitmap.

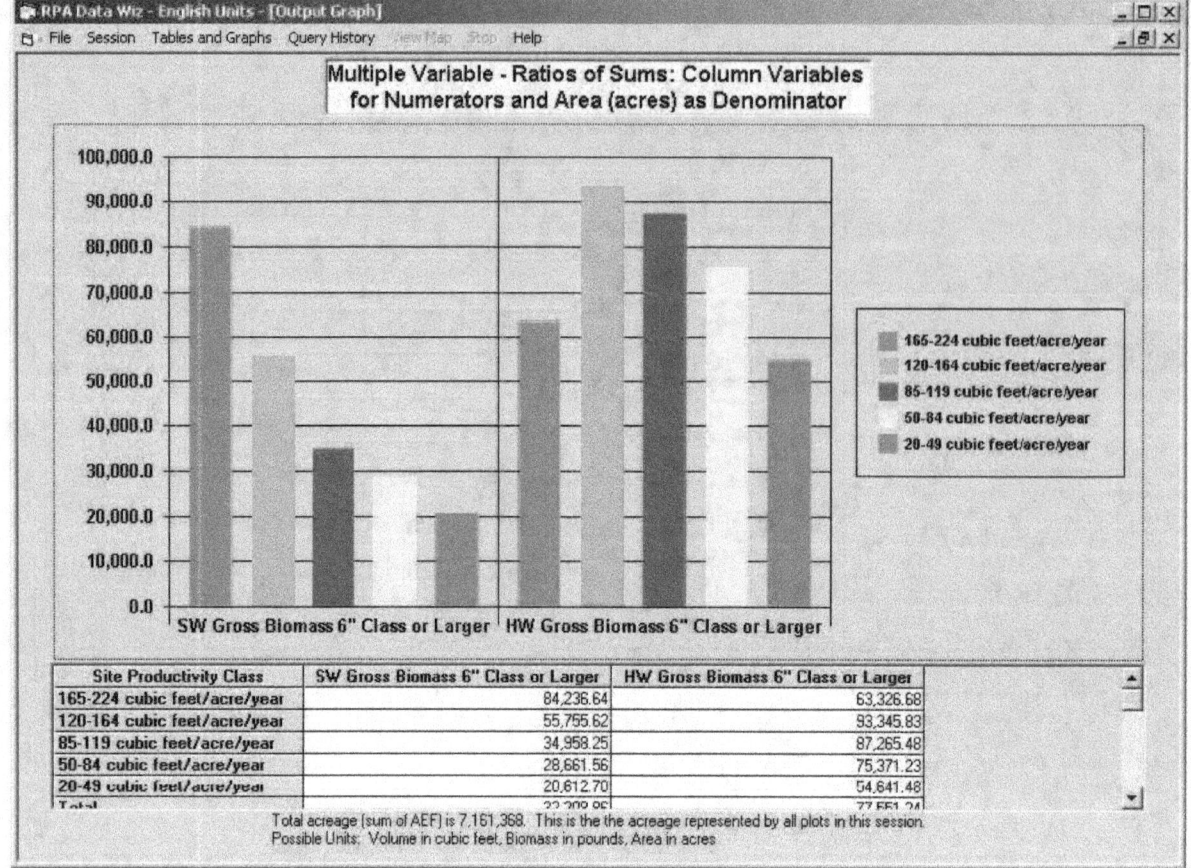

File   Session   Tables and Graphs   Query History   New Map   Stop   Help

**Multiple Variable - Ratios of Sums: Column Variables**
**for Numerators and Area (acres) as Denominator**

Legend:
- 165-224 cubic feet/acre/year
- 120-164 cubic feet/acre/year
- 85-119 cubic feet/acre/year
- 50-84 cubic feet/acre/year
- 20-49 cubic feet/acre/year

| Site Productivity Class | SW Gross Biomass 6" Class or Larger | HW Gross Biomass 6" Class or Larger |
|---|---|---|
| 165-224 cubic feet/acre/year | 84,236.64 | 63,326.68 |
| 120-164 cubic feet/acre/year | 55,755.62 | 93,345.83 |
| 85-119 cubic feet/acre/year | 34,958.25 | 87,265.48 |
| 50-84 cubic feet/acre/year | 28,661.56 | 75,371.23 |
| 20-49 cubic feet/acre/year | 20,612.70 | 54,641.48 |
| Total | 22,309.96 | 77,551.24 |

Total acreage (sum of AEF) is 7,161,368. This is the the acreage represented by all plots in this session.
Possible Units: Volume in cubic feet, Biomass in pounds, Area in acres

44

## Crosstab Graphs

1. Choose **Tables and Graphs \ Crosstab Tables and Graphs**.
2. Select **Forested Land Code** for the grouping variable.
3. Select **Forest Type Group** for the pivot variable.
4. Choose **Area** for the sum variable.
5. Choose **Create Graph** (see example below).
6. Select **Productive Reserved Forest Land** in the legend. The corresponding row is highlighted in the table. This series occupies much less area than the other series. As a result, this series is hard to distinguish on the graph. This problem is solved in the following step.

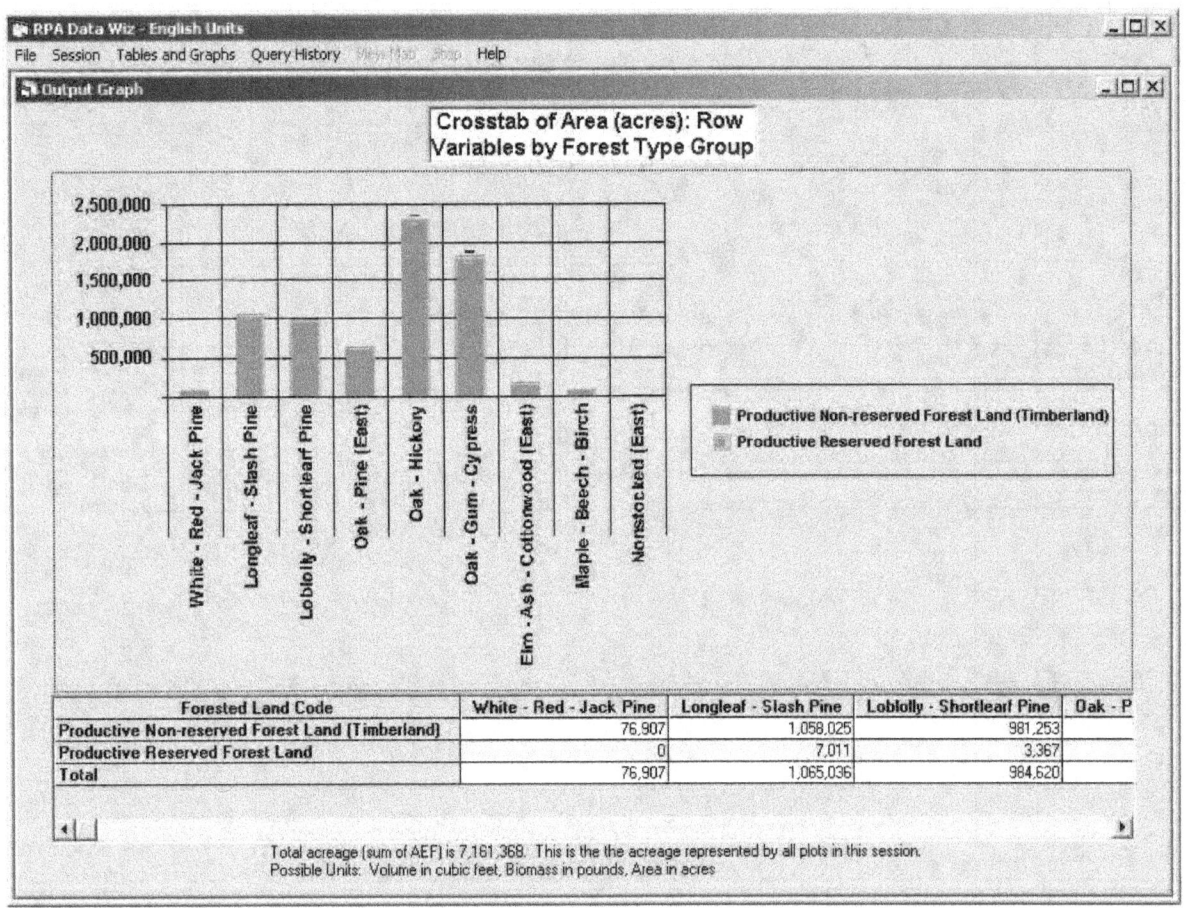

7. Hold **SHIFT** and click on the **Productive Reserved Forest Land** series again. The graph changes to only show the Productive Reserved Forest Land series (see example below). The scale bar changes to provide more detail.
8. Some annoying selection brackets are present on the graph. Click within the dotted line but off from the bars or legend to remove these selection brackets from the display.
9. Click outside the graph outline (outside the dotted line) to restore the display to the original graph.
10. Select **File** in the main menu to see the options for output.

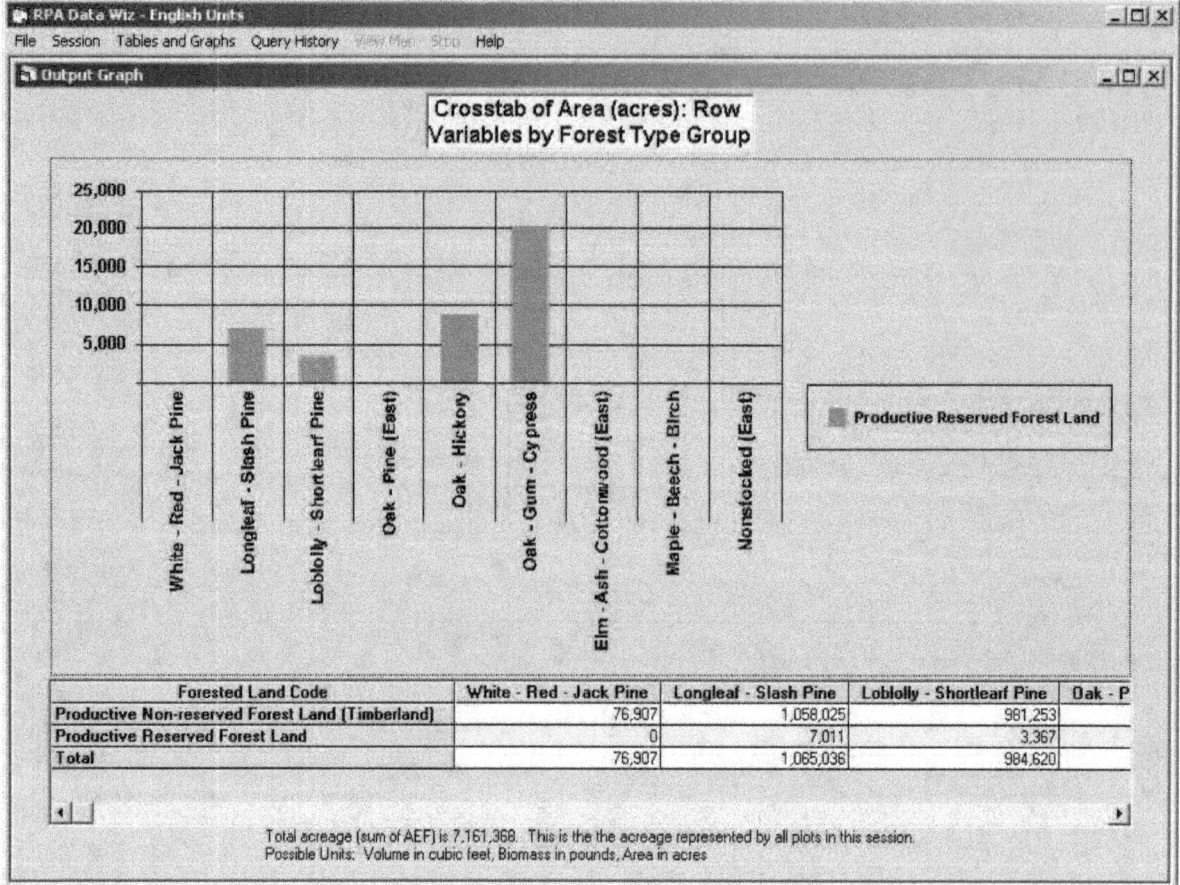

| Forested Land Code | White - Red - Jack Pine | Longleaf - Slash Pine | Loblolly - Shortlearf Pine | Oak - P |
|---|---|---|---|---|
| Productive Non-reserved Forest Land (Timberland) | 76,907 | 1,058,025 | 981,253 | |
| Productive Reserved Forest Land | 0 | 7,011 | 3,367 | |
| Total | 76,907 | 1,065,036 | 984,620 | |

Total acreage (sum of AEF) is 7,161,368. This is the the acreage represented by all plots in this session.
Possible Units: Volume in cubic feet, Biomass in pounds, Area in acres

## Exercise 2: Maps

This exercise will help you become familiar with the maps in RPA Data Wiz. You will create a map showing the amount of area of "old" (250 years and older) forest stands on lands administered by the USDA Forest Service in the Pacific Southwest Assessment Subregion. In RPA Data Wiz, most of the administrated lands throughout the United States are national forests. Other administered lands include areas like national grasslands.

1. If RPA Data Wiz is not already running, then start it. Typical way is to select **Start \ Programs \ RPA Data Wiz**.

2. Click in the gray area of the initial screen to start.

3. If you have the English and metric versions, then pick one of them.

4. Choose **Session \ New Session**.

5. Select **Pacific Southwest Assessment Subregion** in Select RPA Subregion(s).

6. Click **Done Selecting RPA Subregion(s)**.

7. Choose **Land Cover Class** in RPA Variable Selection.

8. Select **Forest Land** in Select Field Value(s).

9. Click **Done Selecting Field Value(s)**.

10. Choose **Ageclass** in RPA Variable Selection.

11. Select all values greater than or equal to 250 in Select Field Value(s). Hold **SHIFT** and click on **250** or the next highest number if 250 is unavailable. Keep holding **SHIFT** and scroll to the bottom of the list and click on the greatest value.

12. Click **Done Selecting Field Value(s)**.

13. Choose **Stand Size Class** in RPA Variable Selection.

14. Select **Large Diameter** in Select Field Value(s).

15. Click **Done Selecting Field Value(s)**.

16. Choose **Done Selecting** in RPA Variable Selection.

17. Create a multivariable sums table.

    A. Choose **Tables and Graphs \ Multiple Variable Tables and Graphs**. The Multiple Variable Sums Table and Graph Generator dialog appears.

    B. Select **Administrative Forest** for the grouping variable. Notice the note on the right side of the dialog that states which grouping variables have associated maps. It also points out that only one sum variable can be mapped. A ratio can also be mapped.

    C. Select **Area** for the sum variable.

    D. Select **Add number of samples as extra column**.

    E. Choose **Create Summary Table** (see example below). Compare the total area listed in the **Total** row to the total area listed in the bottom of the **Output Table** form. U.S. Administrative Forests represent most of the forest land in the subregion.

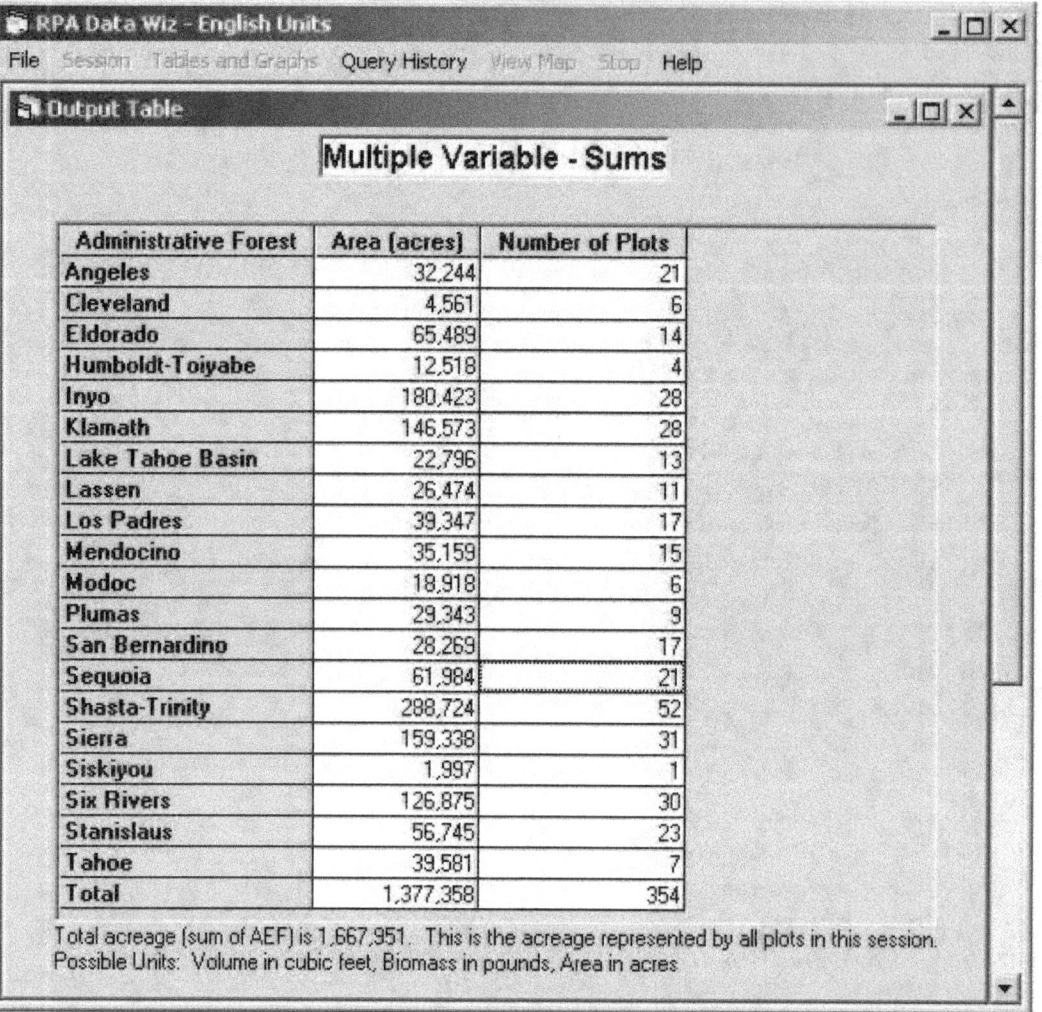

**Multiple Variable - Sums**

| Administrative Forest | Area (acres) | Number of Plots |
|---|---|---|
| Angeles | 32,244 | 21 |
| Cleveland | 4,561 | 6 |
| Eldorado | 65,489 | 14 |
| Humboldt-Toiyabe | 12,518 | 4 |
| Inyo | 180,423 | 28 |
| Klamath | 146,573 | 28 |
| Lake Tahoe Basin | 22,796 | 13 |
| Lassen | 26,474 | 11 |
| Los Padres | 39,347 | 17 |
| Mendocino | 35,159 | 15 |
| Modoc | 18,918 | 6 |
| Plumas | 29,343 | 9 |
| San Bernardino | 28,269 | 17 |
| Sequoia | 61,984 | 21 |
| Shasta-Trinity | 288,724 | 52 |
| Sierra | 159,338 | 31 |
| Siskiyou | 1,997 | 1 |
| Six Rivers | 126,875 | 30 |
| Stanislaus | 56,745 | 23 |
| Tahoe | 39,581 | 7 |
| Total | 1,377,358 | 354 |

Total acreage (sum of AEF) is 1,667,951. This is the acreage represented by all plots in this session.
Possible Units: Volume in cubic feet, Biomass in pounds, Area in acres

18. Select View Map \ Forest Service Map. A map with lands administered by the USDA Forest Service appears.

19. Select Equal Interval Classes with the default of 5 classes (see example below). Apply the tools in the map form.

   A. Click [icon] (Add Map Layer Tool). The Add Map Layers dialog displays. Choose Shapefile. Select Add Layer to use the Open dialog and locate statesp020 in the RPA Data Wiz application directory. Close the Add Map Layers dialog by clicking the upper-right "X" button on the dialog. The map display shows a state boundary layer.

   B. Change the color of the state boundary layer. Double-click on the name, statesp020, in the legend. A color dialog appears. Click on the desired color and select OK.

   C. Click [icon] (Zoom Out Tool). Click the left button on the mouse over the point of interest to decrease the map scale by a factor of two.

   D. Click [icon] (Zoom to Full Extent Tool). The map extent changes to show all the geographic units of every map layer present.

   E. Click [icon] (Zoom In Tool). Hold the left button on the mouse and drag the cursor over the California area. Release the mouse button and the map display reflects the new area in a larger map scale (smaller map area displayed in same computer screen area).

F. Click (Pan Tool). Hold down the left button on the mouse and move the mouse from one point to another to change the map extent.

G. Place the cursor over a polygon of interest, hold SHIFT and click the left button on the mouse. The value associated with the polygon displays. There may be more than one polygon associated with a U.S. National Forest (collectively they are called a geographic unit). If this is the case, then each polygon will have the same value. Notice the cursor and value displayed in the example below.

H. Click Polygon Labels to display the names of the geographic units.

I. Adjust the size (points) of the polygon labels by changing the number for Label Size and pressing Polygon Labels again.

J. Make the state boundary layer invisible by clicking the check box next to the associated name in the legend and clicking Equal Interval Classes.

K. Click the check box next to the name again. Click Equal Interval Classes again to redisplay the state boundary layer.

L. Change the order that the map layers are displayed in the map extent. Click and hold on statesp020 in the legend. Drag the layer name to the bottom of the legend area and release the mouse button. The state boundary layer will be displayed underneath USDA Forest Service layer.

M. Remove the state boundary layer. First, click on statesp020 in the legend. Next click (Delete Map Layer Tool) to remove the map layer from the map form.

N. Add the state boundary layer back in the map form for a frame of reference (see 'A' above).

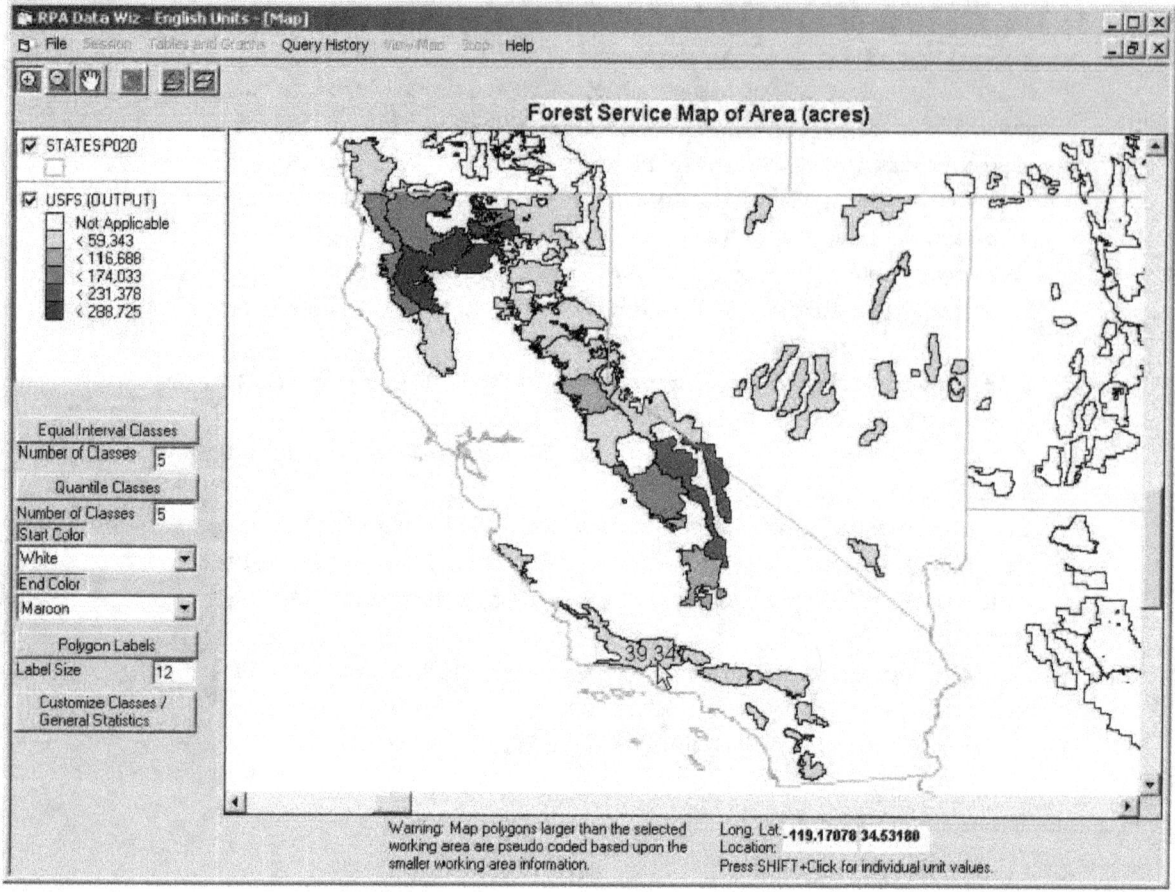

20. Select **Quantile Classes** with the default of 5 classes. Notice the difference. The map and legend indicate that most of the national forests have relatively low amounts of area in older, large-diameter forest stands. Looking back at the table also verifies this.

21. Choose **Customize Classes / General Statistics** (see examples below). Look at the Statistics Info section.

   A.   Type in numbers for class breaks that you would like to see.
   B.   Check **Check to ramp colors from Class 1 to Last Class**.
   C.   Click on the Last Class color box and change the color to Maroon.
   D.   Select **Done**. Move or close the Customize Classes dialog so you can see the map.

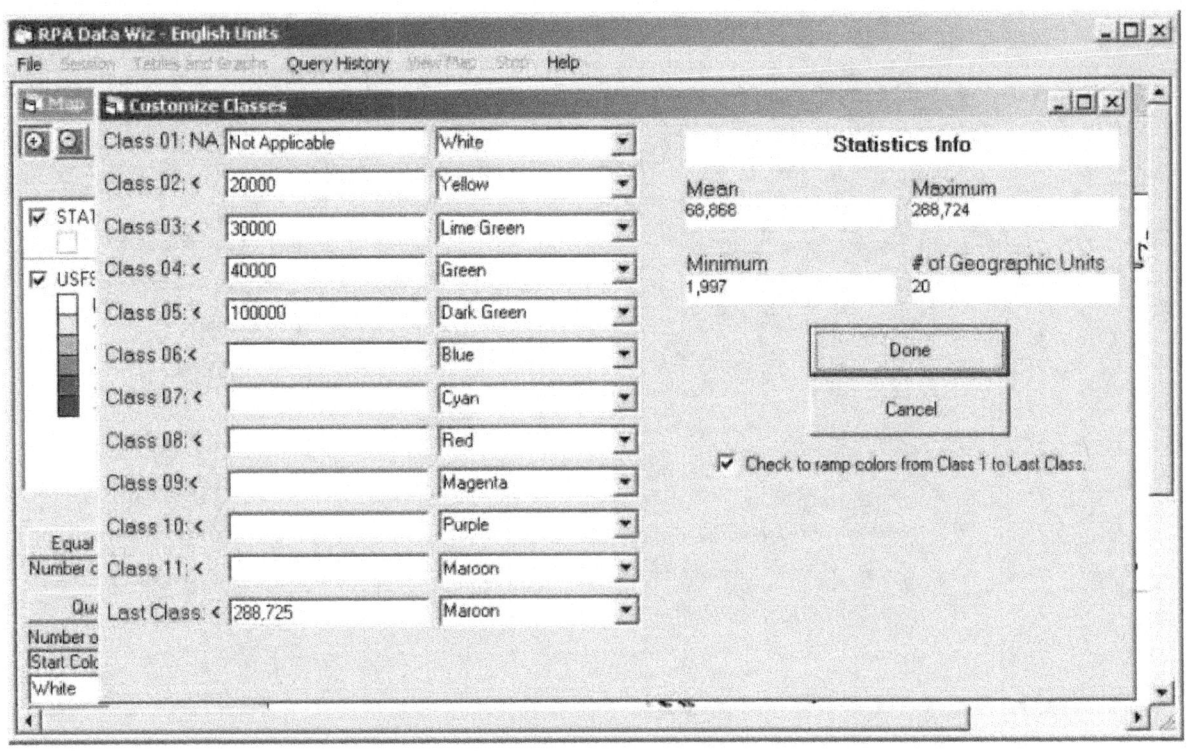

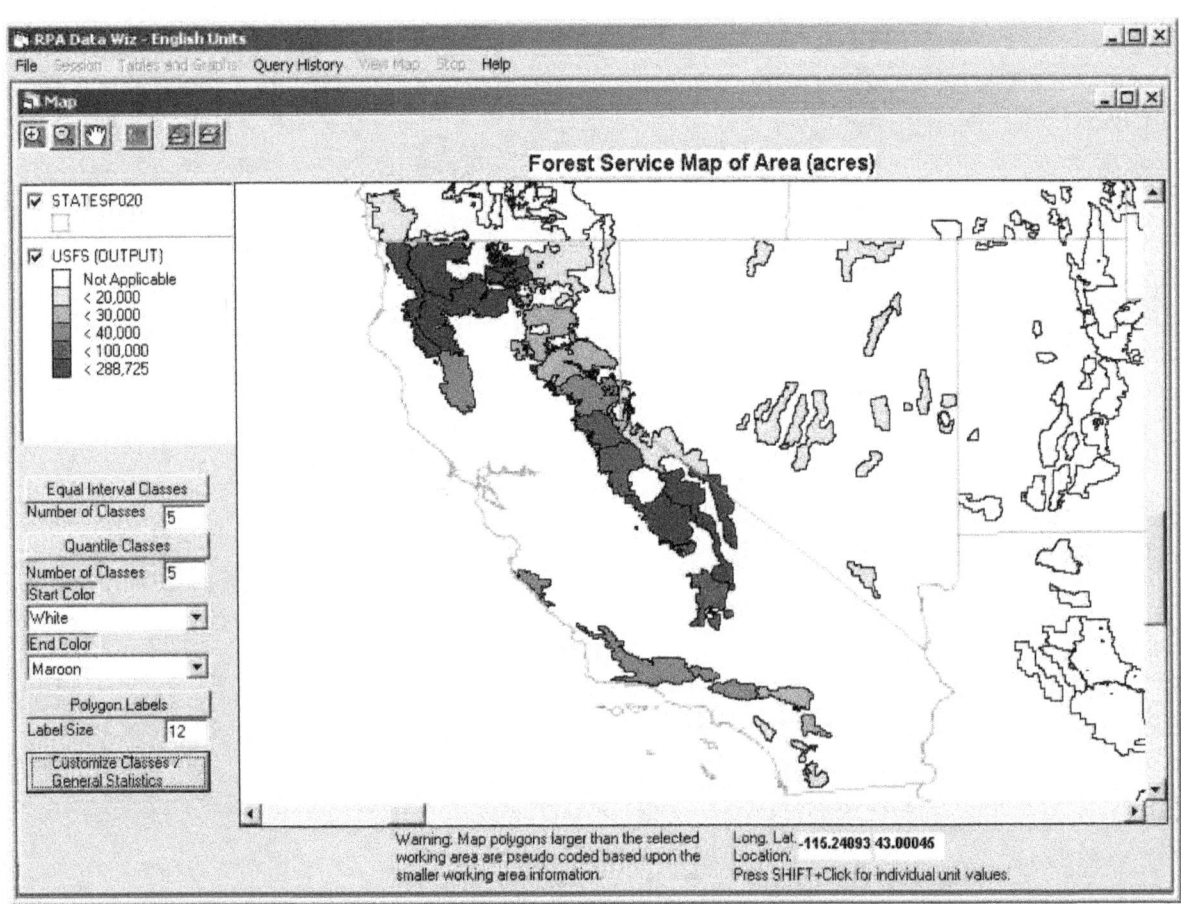

22. Choose **File** in the main RPA Data Wiz menu. Notice the options to output the map and the legend. The legend is output separately from the map. No title is output with the map.

   A. Select **File \ Copy Map to Clipboard** to display the **Save – Copy** dialog.

   B. Select **Copy as Bitmap**.

   C. Click **Copy Map to Clipboard** to copy the map portion of the Map form to the Windows clipboard.

   D. Close the **Save - Copy** dialog by clicking the upper-right "X" button on the dialog.

   E. Paste the map into another software program. In Microsoft PowerPoint, choose **Edit \ Paste Special…** and select **Device Independent Bitmap**. You may need to change the size of the image in your other software program. Remember to change the map equally in the east-west and north-south directions.

   F. Choose **File \ Copy Legend to Clipboard** to automatically copy the legend to the clipboard. The legend only copies in the bitmap format.

   G. Paste the legend into another software program. In PowerPoint, choose **Edit \ Paste Special…** and select **Device Independent Bitmap**.

23. Close the **Map** and **Output Table** forms.

## Exercise 3: Ratios

This exercise shows how RPA Data Wiz can be applied to answer several typical questions dealing with ratios. Even though the tables answer many questions directly, additional questions can be answered with a little manipulation.

### *Ratio of Mortality to Netgrowth on Forest Land in Baileys' Ecosections*

1. If RPA Data Wiz is not already running, then start it. Typical way is to select Start \ Programs \ RPA Data Wiz.
2. Click in the gray area of the initial screen to start.
3. If you have the English and metric versions, then pick one of them.
4. Choose Session \ New Session.
5. Select Pacific Northwest Assessment Subregion in Select RPA Subregion(s).
6. Click Done Selecting RPA Subregion(s).
7. Choose Land Cover Class in RPA Variable Selection.
8. Select Forest Land in Select Field Value(s).
9. Click Done Selecting Field Value(s).
10. Click Done Selecting in RPA Variable Selection.
11. Create a table of mortality to netgrowth volume for Baileys' Ecosections.
    A. Choose Tables and Graphs \ Multiple Variable Tables and Graphs. The Multiple Variable Sums Table and Graph Generator dialog appears.
    B. Select Baileys' Ecosection for the grouping variable.
    C. Select Mortality for the sum variable.
    D. Select Netgrowth as the optional ratio variable (under "Optional, only for Ratio of Sums").
    E. Check Add number of samples as extra column.
    F. Choose Create Summary Table (see example below).

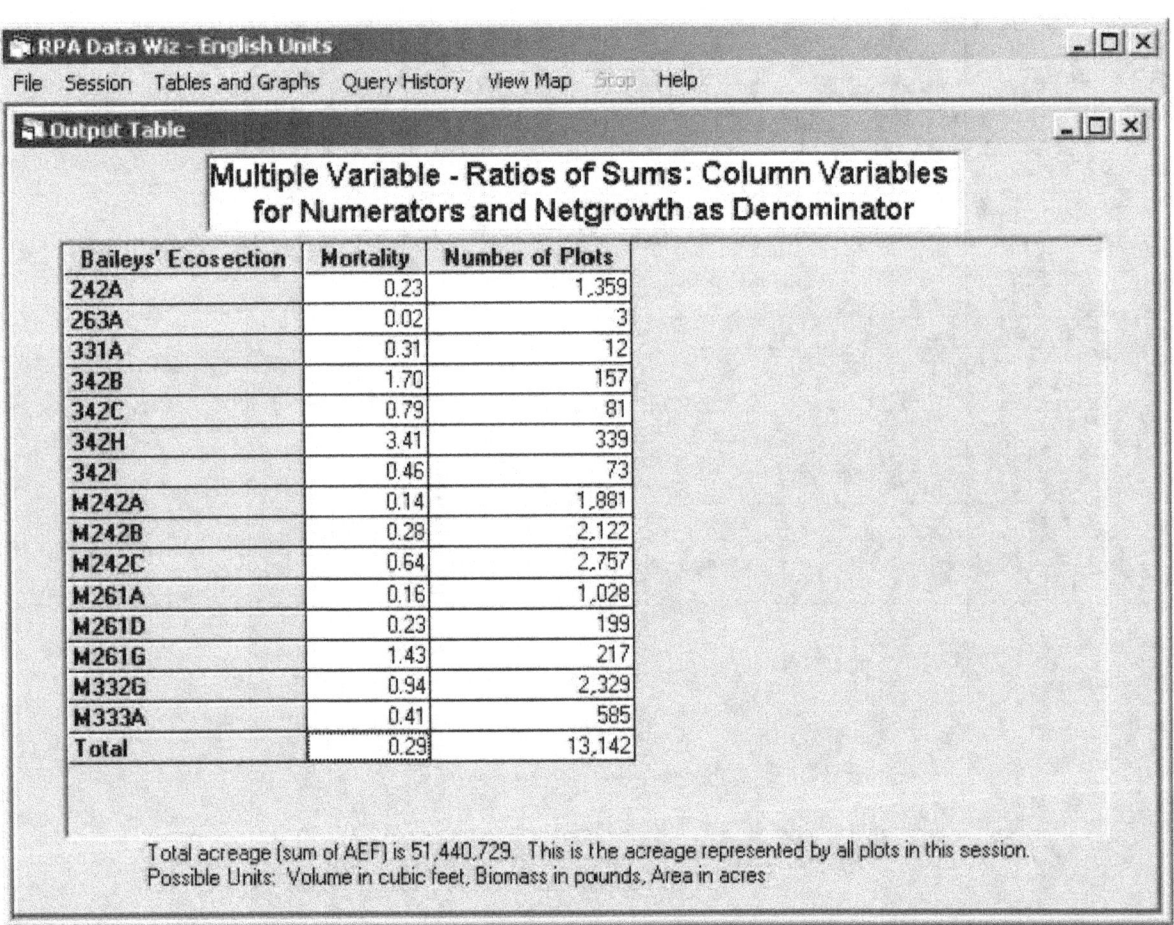

**RPA Data Wiz - English Units**

File   Session   Tables and Graphs   Query History   View Map   Stop   Help

**Output Table**

## Multiple Variable - Ratios of Sums: Column Variables for Numerators and Netgrowth as Denominator

| Baileys' Ecosection | Mortality | Number of Plots |
|---|---|---|
| 242A | 0.23 | 1,359 |
| 263A | 0.02 | 3 |
| 331A | 0.31 | 12 |
| 342B | 1.70 | 157 |
| 342C | 0.79 | 81 |
| 342H | 3.41 | 339 |
| 342I | 0.46 | 73 |
| M242A | 0.14 | 1,881 |
| M242B | 0.28 | 2,122 |
| M242C | 0.64 | 2,757 |
| M261A | 0.16 | 1,028 |
| M261D | 0.23 | 199 |
| M261G | 1.43 | 217 |
| M332G | 0.94 | 2,329 |
| M333A | 0.41 | 585 |
| Total | 0.29 | 13,142 |

Total acreage (sum of AEF) is 51,440,729. This is the acreage represented by all plots in this session.
Possible Units: Volume in cubic feet, Biomass in pounds, Area in acres

### *Ratio of Productive Reserved Forest Land to All Land by County*

1.  Choose Session \ Select from Existing Selection.
2.  Choose Forested Land Code in RPA Variable Selection.
3.  Select Productive Reserved Forest Land in Select Field Value(s).
4.  Click Done Selecting Field Value(s).
5.  Click Done Selecting in RPA Variable Selection.
6.  Create a table of productive reserved forest land to all land by county.

    A.  Choose Tables and Graphs \ Multiple Variable Tables and Graphs. The Multiple Variable Sums Table and Graph Generator dialog appears.
    B.  Select StateCounty for the grouping variable.
    C.  Select Area for the sum variable.
    D.  Select Area as the optional ratio variable.
    E.  Check Add number of samples as extra column.
    F.  Check Mapping Ratios: Divide by total sum associated with each geographic unit.

7.  Choose Create Summary Table (see example below). This may take a few minutes if you have a slower computer.

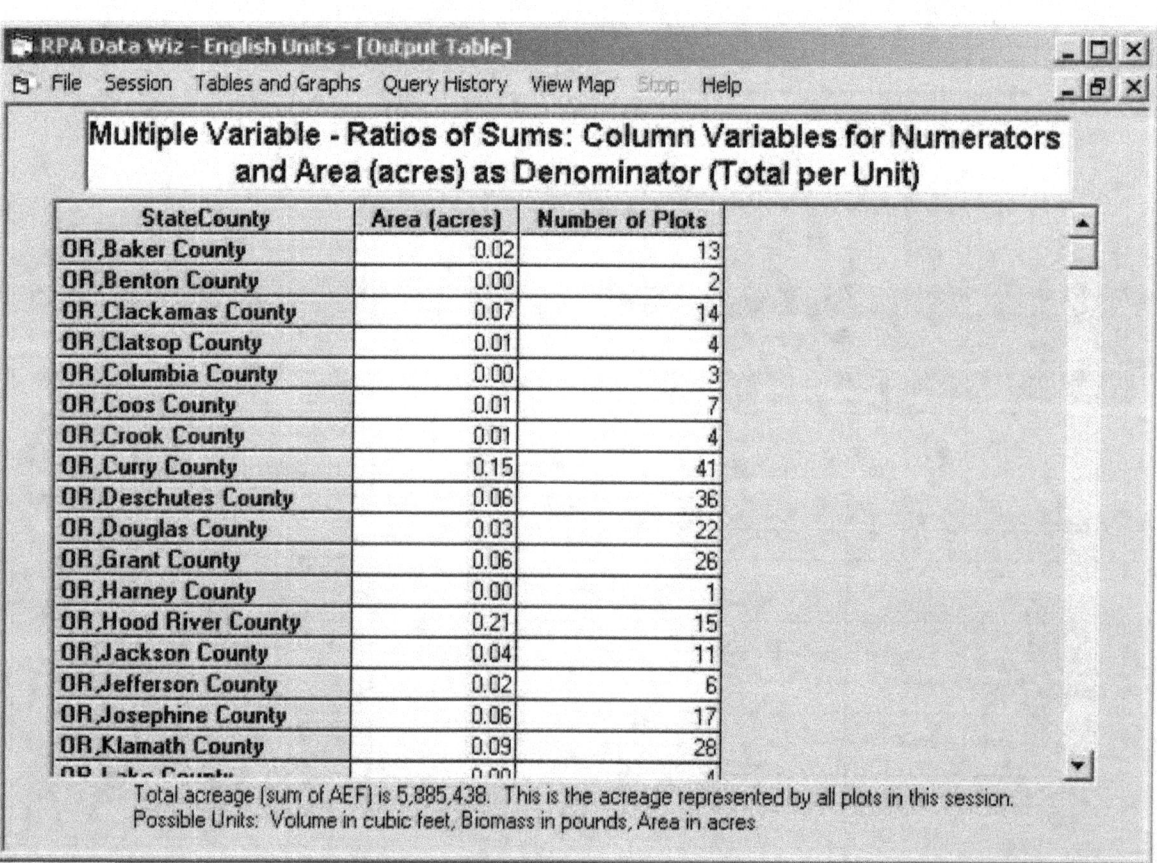

Multiple Variable - Ratios of Sums: Column Variables for Numerators and Area (acres) as Denominator (Total per Unit)

| StateCounty | Area (acres) | Number of Plots |
|---|---|---|
| OR,Baker County | 0.02 | 13 |
| OR,Benton County | 0.00 | 2 |
| OR,Clackamas County | 0.07 | 14 |
| OR,Clatsop County | 0.01 | 4 |
| OR,Columbia County | 0.00 | 3 |
| OR,Coos County | 0.01 | 7 |
| OR,Crook County | 0.01 | 4 |
| OR,Curry County | 0.15 | 41 |
| OR,Deschutes County | 0.06 | 36 |
| OR,Douglas County | 0.03 | 22 |
| OR,Grant County | 0.06 | 26 |
| OR,Harney County | 0.00 | 1 |
| OR,Hood River County | 0.21 | 15 |
| OR,Jackson County | 0.04 | 11 |
| OR,Jefferson County | 0.02 | 6 |
| OR,Josephine County | 0.06 | 17 |
| OR,Klamath County | 0.09 | 28 |
| OR,Lake County | 0.00 | 4 |

Total acreage (sum of AEF) is 5,885,438. This is the acreage represented by all plots in this session.
Possible Units: Volume in cubic feet, Biomass in pounds, Area in acres

## Ratio of National Forest Timberland to Private Timberland by 108ᵗʰ Congressional District

1. Choose Session \ New Session.
2. Select Pacific Northwest Assessment Subregion in Select RPA Subregion(s).
3. Click Done Selecting RPA Subregion(s).
4. Choose Forested Land Code in RPA Variable Selection.
5. Select timberland. In Select Field Value(s), choose Productive Non-reserved Forest Land (Timberland).
6. Click Done Selecting Field Value(s).
7. Click Done Selecting in RPA Variable Selection.
8. Create a crosstab table of 108ᵗʰ Congressional District by ownership group.
   A. Choose Tables and Graphs \ Crosstab Tables and Graphs.
   B. Select 108ᵗʰ Congressional District Code for the grouping variable.
   C. Select Owner Group for the pivot variable and Area for the sum variable.
9. Choose Create Summary Table (see example below). Note that this is not the final table with the ratios of national forest timberland to private timberland by 108ᵗʰ Congressional District. RPA Data Wiz cannot directly provide this information. With a few steps, you can derive the information by using this table in a spreadsheet like Microsoft Excel.

| RPA Data Wiz - English Units - [Output Table] | | | | |
|---|---|---|---|---|
| File   Session   Tables and Graphs   Query History   View Map   Stop   Help | | | | |

### Crosstab of Area (acres): Row Variables by Owner Group

| 108th Congressional District Code | National Forest | Other Public | Private | Total |
|---|---|---|---|---|
| 4101 | 27,301 | 249,044 | 869,769 | 1,146,114 |
| 4102 | 7,861,500 | 640,387 | 3,281,847 | 11,783,734 |
| 4103 | 158,419 | 14,232 | 197,240 | 369,891 |
| 4104 | 3,193,326 | 1,674,305 | 3,311,798 | 8,179,429 |
| 4105 | 737,364 | 569,307 | 1,045,405 | 2,352,076 |
| 5301 | 0 | 32,082 | 96,499 | 128,581 |
| 5302 | 830,803 | 365,929 | 879,385 | 2,076,117 |
| 5303 | 963,693 | 497,547 | 2,158,616 | 3,619,856 |
| 5304 | 1,253,773 | 261,135 | 1,011,725 | 2,526,633 |
| 5305 | 2,181,106 | 509,975 | 2,257,211 | 4,948,292 |
| 5306 | 520,942 | 548,509 | 1,755,091 | 2,824,542 |
| 5307 | 1,855 | 0 | 16,640 | 18,495 |
| 5308 | 180,880 | 169,334 | 690,499 | 1,040,713 |
| 5309 | 0 | 61,847 | 101,995 | 163,842 |
| Total | 17,910,962 | 5,593,633 | 17,673,720 | 41,178,315 |

Total acreage (sum of AEF) is 41,178,315. This is the acreage represented by all plots in this session.
Possible Units: Volume in cubic feet, Biomass in pounds, Area in acres

10. Work with the table in a spreadsheet to derive the ratio. If you have Excel, output the table in Excel format.
   A. Choose **File \ Save As Excel Table**. Save the file.
   B. Start Excel and choose **File \ Open**. Choose the file you just saved in RPA Data Wiz.
   C. Create a new column with the ratio of national forest timberland to private timberland.
      1. In a non-occupied column, select a cell in the second row (the first row under the column headings).
      2. In the cell, type the formula that will divide the column of national forest ownership by the column of private ownership (e.g., "= B2/D2").
      3. Press **ENTER**.
      4. Now select the cell again. Copy the cell (select **Edit \ Copy**).
      5. Select the rest of the cells in the current column that are associated with a congressional district (including the total) and paste the formula in these cells (select **Edit \ Paste**). The resulting numbers are the ratios of national forest timberland to private timberland by 108th Congressional District (see example below). You can express these numbers as percentages by adjusting the formula (e.g., "= (B2/D2) * 100").

| 108th Congressional District Code | National Forest | Other public | Private | Total | National Forest timberland to private timberland |
|---|---|---|---|---|---|
| 4101 | 27,301 | 249,044 | 869,769 | 1,146,114 | 0.031388794 |
| 4102 | 7,861,500 | 640,387 | 3,281,847 | 11,783,734 | 2.395449879 |
| 4103 | 158,419 | 14,232 | 197,240 | 369,891 | 0.803178868 |
| 4104 | 3,193,326 | 1,674,305 | 3,311,798 | 8,179,429 | 0.964227287 |
| 4105 | 737,364 | 569,307 | 1,045,405 | 2,352,076 | 0.705338123 |
| 5301 | 0 | 32,082 | 96,499 | 128,581 | 0 |
| 5302 | 830,803 | 365,929 | 879,385 | 2,076,117 | 0.944754573 |
| 5303 | 963,693 | 497,547 | 2,158,616 | 3,619,856 | 0.446440219 |
| 5304 | 1,253,773 | 261,135 | 1,011,725 | 2,526,633 | 1.239242877 |
| 5305 | 2,181,106 | 509,975 | 2,257,211 | 4,948,292 | 0.966283613 |
| 5306 | 520,942 | 548,509 | 1,755,091 | 2,824,542 | 0.296817658 |
| 5307 | 1,855 | 0 | 16,640 | 18,495 | 0.111478365 |
| 5308 | 180,880 | 169,334 | 690,499 | 1,040,713 | 0.261955484 |
| 5309 | 0 | 61,847 | 101,995 | 163,842 | 0 |
| Total | 17,910,962 | 5,593,633 | 17,673,720 | 41,178,315 | 1.013423433 |

# Exercise 4: Wildlife Habitat Identification

In this exercise you will identify counties that have critical habitat for animals. Birds and mammals use dead trees like snags for shelter. The pileated and red-headed woodpeckers favor larger snags (> 20-inch or > 50-cm size classes). Medium snags (10- to 20-inch or 25- to 50-cm size classes) are used by squirrels and the American kestrel. Birds like the eastern bluebird and black-capped chickadee prefer smaller snags (6- to 10-inch or 15- to 25-cm size classes). In addition, many animals opt to live in particular forest types at specific ages. For example, gray squirrels prefer hardwood stands like oak that are mature enough to provide shelter and food. This exercise will help identify some counties that may have higher preference for some species based upon the dead wood present. You will use Salvable Dead Biomass 6" Class or Larger (salvable dead biomass 15-cm class or larger in metric version) to indicate the amount of shelter available.

## *Tables and Graphs - Salvable Dead Biomass 6" Class or Larger*

1. If RPA Data Wiz is not already running, then start it. Typical way is to select **Start \ Programs \ RPA Data Wiz**.
2. Click in the gray area of the initial screen to start.
3. If you have the English and metric versions, then pick one of them.
4. Choose **Session \ New Session**.
5. Select **North Central Assessment Subregion** in Select RPA Subregion(s).
6. Click **Done Selecting RPA Subregion(s)**.
7. Select **State** in RPA Variable Selection.
8. Choose **WI** in Select Field Value(s).
9. Click **Done Selecting Field Value(s)**.
10. Choose **Land Cover Class** in RPA Variable Selection.
11. Select **Forest Land** in Select Field Value(s).
12. Click **Done Selecting Field Value(s)**.
13. Choose **Done Selecting** in RPA Variable Selection.
14. Create a table with biomass per area estimates for each county.
    A. Choose **Tables and Graphs \ Multiple Variable Tables and Graphs**. The Multiple Variable Sums Table and Graph Generator dialog appears.
    B. Select **StateCounty** for the grouping variable.
    C. Select **SW Salvable Dead Biomass 6" Class or Larger**, **HW Salvable Dead Biomass 6" Class or Larger**, and **Salvable Dead Biomass 6" Class or Larger** for the sum variables (15 cm class or larger for metric version). Use CTRL or SHIFT when selecting.
    D. Select **Area** as the optional ratio variable (under "Optional, only for Ratio of Sums:").
    E. Choose **Create Summary Table**. Notice that Iron, Menominee, and Rock Counties have the highest salvable dead biomass per area and that most of this is hardwood (HW).
15. Create a new session focusing on Iron, Menominee, and Rock Counties.
    A. Choose **Session \ Select from Existing Selection**.
    B. Choose **StateCounty** in RPA Variable Selection.
    C. Select **WI, Iron; WI, Menominee;** and **WI, Rock** from Select Field Value(s) using CTRL + Click.
    D. Click **Done Selecting Field Value(s)**.
    E. Select **Done Selecting** in RPA Variable Selection.
16. Choose **Query History** to see the queries you have performed so far.
17. Close the **Query History** form.
18. Create histograms comparing the amount of SW and HW salvable dead biomass in 6 inch or larger classes among the three counties.
    A. Choose **Tables and Graphs \ Multiple Variable Tables and Graphs**.
    B. Select **StateCounty** for the grouping variable.

C.  Select *SW Salvable Dead Biomass 6" Class or Larger*, *HW Salvable Dead Biomass 6" Class or Larger*, and *Salvable Dead Biomass 6" Class or Larger* (15 cm class or larger for metric version) for the sum variables.

D.  Select *Area* for the optional ratio variable.

E.  Choose *Create Graph* (see example below). Make sure your form sizes are maximized to see the graph well (click on box in upper right-hand corner of each form to maximize size). Look especially at the salvable dead biomass section of the graph (SW and HW combined). There is not much difference among the counties on a per area basis.

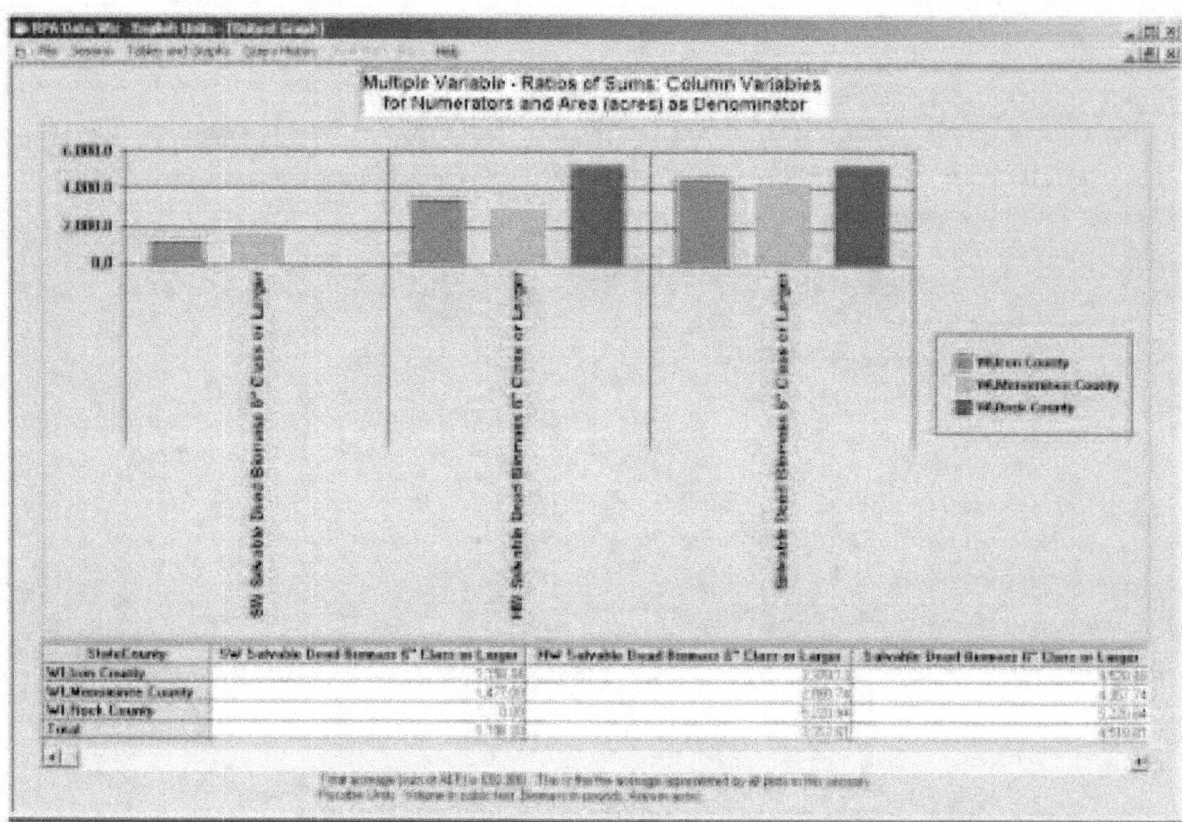

F.  Choose *Tables and Graphs \ Multiple Variable Tables and Graphs* again. Make the same histogram except do not choose an optional ratio variable. This shows the total dead biomass sums for each county. This is a cumulative histogram unlike the previous histogram. The graph and table show a great difference in totals among the counties with Iron County having more than the other two counties combined. Note that Iron County is much larger. Iron County definitely has the most salvable dead biomass in the 6-inch or larger class

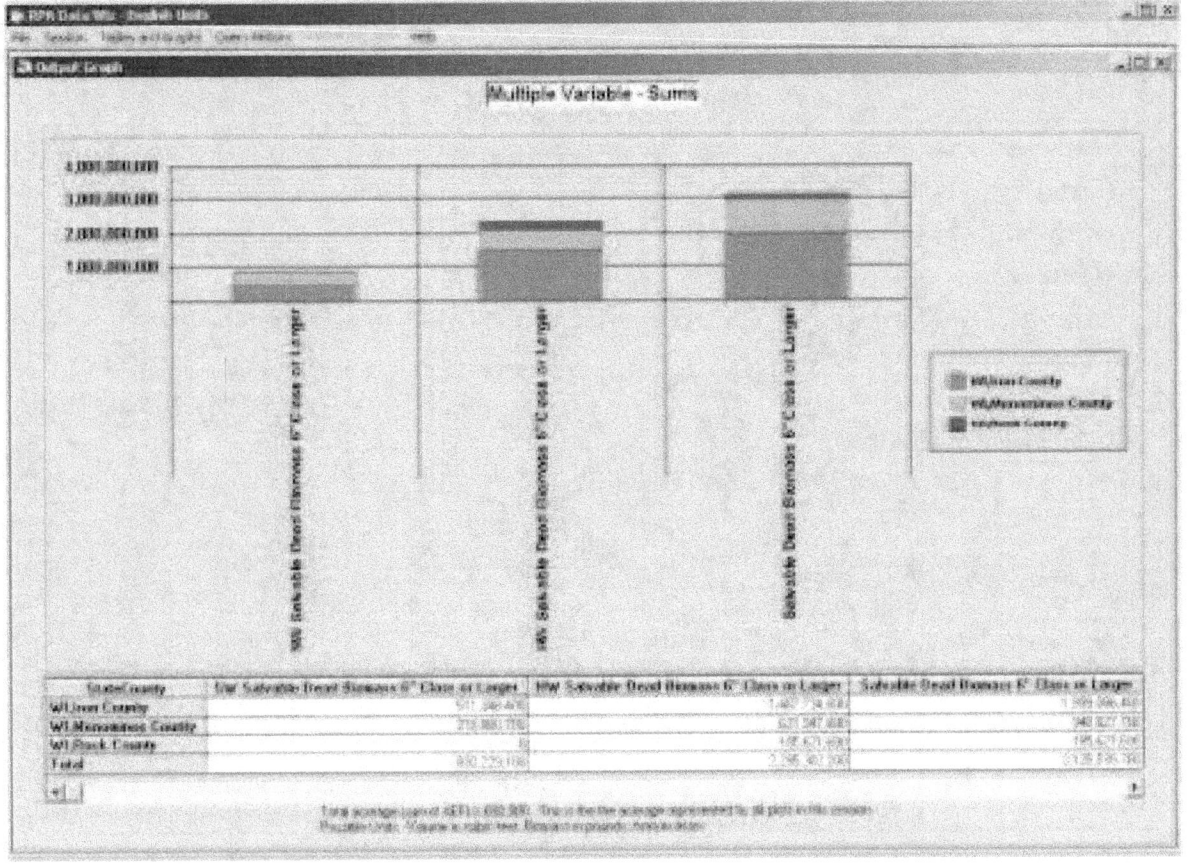

19. Look at the salvable dead biomass in the available forest types and age classes by stand diameter class for each of the three counties.
    A. Choose Tables and Graphs \ Crosstab Tables and Graphs.
    B. Select State County, Forest Type Group, and Ageclass for the grouping variables.
    C. Select Mean Stand DIA 2" Class or Larger (5-cm class or larger for metric version) for the pivot variable.
    D. Select Salvable Dead Biomass 6" Class or Larger (15-cm class or larger for metric version) for the sum variable.
    E. Click Create Summary Table. Look at the Total row on the bottom. Notice that most of the salvable dead biomass is present in the smaller stand-size classes (8-inch or 20-cm mean stand-size class and smaller). There is no salvable dead biomass listed for forest stands larger than the 14-inch mean stand-size class (35-cm mean stand-size class). Look at the Total column on the right. You can quickly scan the relative amounts of salvable dead biomass for each county-forest type-age class combination. Depending upon the animal species in question, one county can hold more promise than the others.

20. Compare the amount of salvable dead biomass among forest types.
    A. Choose Tables and Graphs \ Crosstab Tables and Graphs.
    B. Select Forest Type Group as the grouping variable.
    C. Select Mean Stand DIA 2" Class or Larger (5-cm class or larger for metric version) for the pivot variable.
    D. Select Salvable Dead Biomass 6" Class or Larger (15-cm class or larger for metric version) for the sum variable.
    E. Click Create Graph (see example next page). The histogram shows Maple-Beech-Birch with the most salvable dead biomass.

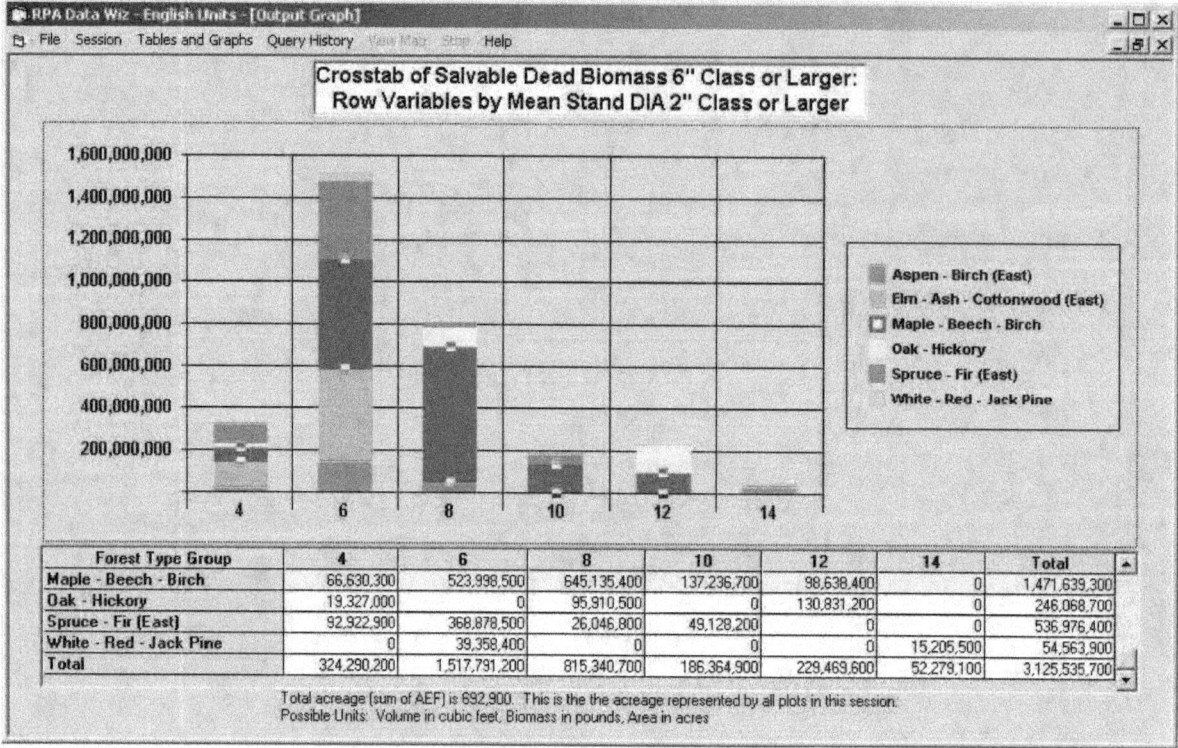

**Crosstab of Salvable Dead Biomass 6" Class or Larger: Row Variables by Mean Stand DIA 2" Class or Larger**

Legend:
- Aspen - Birch (East)
- Elm - Ash - Cottonwood (East)
- Maple - Beech - Birch
- Oak - Hickory
- Spruce - Fir (East)
- White - Red - Jack Pine

| Forest Type Group | 4 | 6 | 8 | 10 | 12 | 14 | Total |
|---|---|---|---|---|---|---|---|
| Maple - Beech - Birch | 66,630,300 | 523,998,500 | 645,135,400 | 137,236,700 | 98,638,400 | 0 | 1,471,639,300 |
| Oak - Hickory | 19,327,000 | 0 | 95,910,500 | 0 | 130,831,200 | 0 | 246,068,700 |
| Spruce - Fir (East) | 92,922,900 | 368,878,500 | 26,046,800 | 49,128,200 | 0 | 0 | 536,976,400 |
| White - Red - Jack Pine | 0 | 39,358,400 | 0 | 0 | 0 | 15,205,500 | 54,563,900 |
| Total | 324,290,200 | 1,517,791,200 | 815,340,700 | 186,364,900 | 229,469,600 | 52,279,100 | 3,125,535,700 |

Total acreage (sum of AEF) is 692,900. This is the the acreage represented by all plots in this session.
Possible Units: Volume in cubic feet, Biomass in pounds, Area in acres

F.  Use **SHIFT** + click to select the **Maple-Beech-Birch** series on the graph. A new histogram showing only the Maple-Beech-Birch series appears and the Maple-Beech-Birch series is highlighted in the table. This forest type comprises approximately half of the total salvable biomass for the three counties.

G.  Click outside the present histogram to return to the original graph. The graph clearly shows that most of the salvable dead biomass is in the 6-inch mean stand-size class (15-cm mean stand-size class).

21. Assuming salvable dead biomass in the 6-inch or larger classes signifies dead snags, this analysis highlights several counties in Wisconsin that may have favorable habitat for animal species preferring smaller forest stand sizes in the Maple-Beech-Birch forest type.

### Map - Salvable Dead Biomass 6" Class or Larger

1. Create a table of salvable dead biomass per area for each county.

    A.  Choose **Tables and Graphs \ Multiple Variable Tables and Graphs**

    B.  Select **StateCounty** for the grouping variable.

    C.  Select **Salvable Dead Biomass 6" Class or Larger** (15-cm class or larger for metric version) for the sum variable.

    D.  Select **Area** for the optional ratio variable.

    E.  Select **Create Summary Table**.

2. Identify the natural groupings or groupings of interest for the biomass per area estimates associated with the counties. Output the table to read into a spreadsheet and sort the biomass per area estimates. If you have Microsoft Excel, output the table in Excel format.

    A.  Choose **File \ Save As Excel Table** and save the file.

    B.  Open the file in Excel.

    C.  Delete the first (row headings) and last (totals) rows. Select the last row and choose **Edit \ Delete**. Select the first row and choose **Edit \ Delete**.

    D.  Select both columns of numbers and choose **Data \ Sort**. Sort by column B, the salvable dead biomass per area column. Look at the sorted biomass numbers. Look for natural or interesting groupings and breaks in the sorted numbers. Identify 5 or more breaks that you think delineate the groups. Remember these break numbers for later.

3. Select **View Map \ County Map**. A county map appears.
4. Select **Equal Interval Classes** with the default of 5 classes.
5. Select **Quantile Classes** with the default of 5 classes. Notice the difference. The map and legend indicate that most counties have relatively low amounts of salvable dead biomass per area in the 6-inch and larger classes.
6. Choose **Customize Classes / General Statistics**. Look at the **Statistics Info** section.
   A. Type in numbers for the class breaks you previously identified.
   B. Check **Check to ramp colors from Class 1 to Last Class**.
   C. Click on the **Last Class** color box and change the color to Maroon.
   D. Select **Done** but leave the Customize Classes dialog open. Move the dialog so you can see the map.
   E. Compare your custom map to the equal interval and quantile class maps by selecting the **Equal Interval Classes** and **Quantile Classes** buttons. Experiment with the number of classes designated with each type of map. Which is the best map? The answer to this can vary depending upon your objective. You may want a map that does the best job of identifying the differences in salvable dead biomass per area among all the counties. In this case, you will need a number of classes (e.g., 5 or more) preferably occurring close to any natural breaks. In contrast, you may only wish to highlight the few counties with the highest salvable dead biomass per area. With this objective in mind, a few classes would suffice. Below is an example where the class intervals were set manually using the Customize Classes dialog.
7. Close the Map and Output Table forms.
8. Choose **File \ Exit** to stop the program.

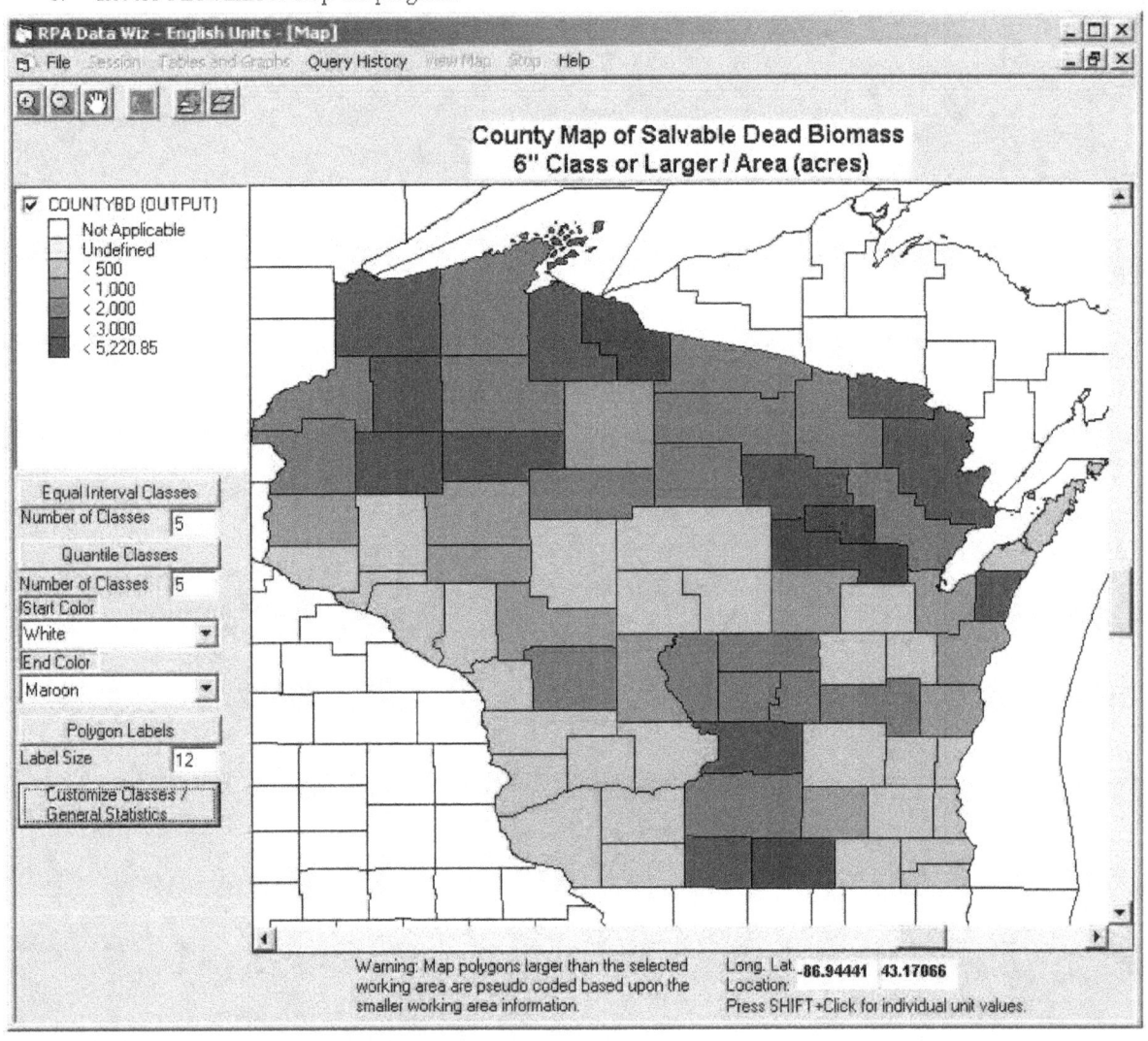

# Chapter 7
# Literature Cited

Aronoff, Stan. 1995. Geographic information systems: a management perspective. Ottawa, Canada: WDL Publications. 294 p.

ESRI. 1992 - 2000. Environmental Systems Research Institute, Inc., Redlands, CA.

Microsoft. 1987 – 2000. Microsoft Corporation.

Miles, Patrick D.; Brand, Gary J.; Alerich, Carol L.; Bednar, Larry F.; Woudenberg, Sharon W.; Glover, Joseph F.; Ezzell, Edward N. 2001. The forest inventory and analysis database: database description and users manual version 1.0. Gen Tech. Rep. NC-218. St. Paul, MN: U.S. Department of Agriculture, Forest Service, North Central Research Station. 130 p.

Miles, Patrick D.; Vissage, John S. In prep. The 2002 RPA plot summary database users manual version 1.0. St. Paul, MN: U.S. Department of Agriculture, Forest Service, North Central Research Station.

# Appendix A
## Selection Variables

These are the definitions for the selection variables in RPA Data Wiz. The corresponding field names in the RPA Data Wiz databases (English, rpadb2002.mdb; metric, rpadb2002met.mdb) are also provided. RPA Data Wiz uses Microsoft Access databases. Most of the data in RPA Data Wiz (rpadb2002.mdb and rpadb2002met.mdb, Access databases) originally came from the 2002 RPA Assessment database, an Oracle database. Most of the definitions presented here come directly from *The 2002 RPA Plot Summary Database Users Manual Version 1.0* (Miles and Vissage, In prep.) associated with the 2002 RPA Assessment database. Some fields have been added and some field definitions have been modified to work in RPA Data Wiz. The field definitions that may be unique to RPA Data Wiz or may have been changed to work in RPA Data Wiz are marked with an asterisk. The definitions follow the order presented in the RPA Variable Selection dialog of RPA Data Wiz. D.b.h. (diameter at breast height) is mentioned in this appendix. It is defined as the stem diameter, outside bark, at a point 4.5 feet (137.16 cm) above ground. Any other variables mentioned but not defined in this appendix are defined by Miles and Vissage (In prep.).

| RPA Data Wiz Name Access FIELD NAME | Definition |
|---|---|
| 1. Year YEAR | RPA year. This is set to 2002 for all records in the 2002 RPA plot summary database. |
| 2. Region or Station ID # RSID | Region or station identification number. This coded value uniquely identifies each of the 16 locations contributing data to the RPA Database. |

| Code | Region or Station |
|---|---|
| 1 | Region 1 |
| 2 | Region 2 |
| 3 | Region 3 |
| 4 | Region 4 |
| 5 | Region 5 |
| 6 | Region 6 |
| 7 | Bureau of Land Management (Oregon) |
| 8 | Region 8 |
| 9 | Region 9 |
| 10 | Region 10 |
| 22 | Rocky Mountain Research Station |
| 23 | North Central Research Station |
| 24 | Northeastern Research Station |
| 26 | Pacific Northwest Research Station |
| 27 | Alaska – PNW Research Station |
| 33 | Southern Research Station |

3.  Source of Inventory        Source of the inventory data. A coded value identifying the source of the data on the record. Sources include
    Data                       variations of original inventory data and inventory data updated by bookkeeping or projection. Code 1 is
    INVSOURCE                  used for all State inventories except for parts of Alaska and Hawaii.

    | Code | Source |
    |------|--------|
    | 1 | PLOT LEVEL - Original Eastwide/Westwide or FIADB format |
    | 2 | PLOT LEVEL - Updated Eastwide/Westwide standard format |
    | 3 | PLOT LEVEL - Original inventory data |
    | 4 | PLOT LEVEL - Updated inventory data |
    | 5 | STAND LEVEL - Original inventory data |
    | 6 | STAND LEVEL - Updated inventory data |
    | 7 | STRATUM LEVEL - Original inventory data |
    | 8 | STRATUM LEVEL - Updated inventory data |

4.  Source Date               Source date. The year of the field inventory for the plot.
    SRCDATE

5.  State                     State FIPS code. The State in which the plot is located.
    STATE

    | Code | Abbreviation | Name |
    |------|--------------|------|
    | 01 | AL | Alabama |
    | 02 | AK | Alaska |
    | 04 | AZ | Arizona |
    | 05 | AR | Arkansas |
    | 06 | CA | California |
    | 08 | CO | Colorado |
    | 09 | CT | Connecticut |
    | 10 | DE | Delaware |
    | 11 | DC | District of Columbia |
    | 12 | FL | Florida |
    | 13 | GA | Georgia |
    | 15 | HI | Hawaii |
    | 16 | ID | Idaho |
    | 17 | IL | Illinois |
    | 18 | IN | Indiana |
    | 19 | IA | Iowa |
    | 20 | KS | Kansas |
    | 21 | KY | Kentucky |
    | 22 | LA | Louisiana |
    | 23 | ME | Maine |
    | 24 | MD | Maryland |
    | 25 | MA | Massachusetts |
    | 26 | MI | Michigan |
    | 27 | MN | Minnesota |
    | 28 | MS | Mississippi |
    | 29 | MO | Missouri |
    | 30 | MT | Montana |
    | 31 | NE | Nebraska |
    | 32 | NV | Nevada |
    | 33 | NH | New Hampshire |

| | | |
|---|---|---|
| 34 | NJ | New Jersey |
| 35 | NM | New Mexico |
| 36 | NY | New York |
| 37 | NC | North Carolina |
| 38 | ND | North Dakota |
| 39 | OH | Ohio |
| 40 | OK | Oklahoma |
| 41 | OR | Oregon |
| 42 | PA | Pennsylvania |
| 44 | RI | Rhode Island |
| 45 | SC | South Carolina |
| 46 | SD | South Dakota |
| 47 | TN | Tennessee |
| 48 | TX | Texas |
| 49 | UT | Utah |
| 50 | VT | Vermont |
| 51 | VA | Virginia |
| 53 | WA | Washington |
| 54 | WV | West Virginia |
| 55 | WI | Wisconsin |
| 56 | WY | Wyoming |
| 72 | PR | Puerto Rico - Not in 2002 Database |

6. *StateCounty
   STATE and COUNTY

A combined State-county FIPS code ((STATE * 1000) + COUNTY). This field provides a unique identifier for each county in the country. FIPS codes for States are unique, but FIPS codes for counties are not unique among States. Consequently, StateCounty was created. Some special codes represent areas other than counties.

| Code | StateCounty | Code | StateCounty |
|---|---|---|---|
| 0 | Unknown | 29211 | MO,Sullivan County |
| 1001 | AL,Autauga County | 29213 | MO,Taney County |
| 1003 | AL,Baldwin County | 29215 | MO,Texas County |
| 1005 | AL,Barbour County | 29217 | MO,Vernon County |
| 1007 | AL,Bibb County | 29219 | MO,Warren County |
| 1009 | AL,Blount County | 29221 | MO,Washington County |
| 1011 | AL,Bullock County | 29223 | MO,Wayne County |
| 1013 | AL,Butler County | 29225 | MO,Webster County |
| 1015 | AL,Calhoun County | 29227 | MO,Worth County |
| 1017 | AL,Chambers County | 29229 | MO,Wright County |
| 1019 | AL,Cherokee County | 29510 | MO,St. Louis City |
| 1021 | AL,Chilton County | 30001 | MT,Beaverhead County |
| 1023 | AL,Choctaw County | 30003 | MT,Big Horn County |
| 1025 | AL,Clarke County | 30005 | MT,Blaine County |
| 1027 | AL,Clay County | 30007 | MT,Broadwater County |
| 1029 | AL,Cleburne County | 30009 | MT,Carbon County |
| 1031 | AL,Coffee County | 30011 | MT,Carter County |
| 1033 | AL,Colbert County | 30013 | MT,Cascade County |

| | | | |
|---|---|---|---|
| 1035 | AL,Conecuh County | 30015 | MT,Chouteau County |
| 1037 | AL,Coosa County | 30017 | MT,Custer County |
| 1039 | AL,Covington County | 30019 | MT,Daniels County |
| 1041 | AL,Crenshaw County | 30021 | MT,Dawson County |
| 1043 | AL,Cullman County | 30023 | MT,Deer Lodge County |
| 1045 | AL,Dale County | 30025 | MT,Fallon County |
| 1047 | AL,Dallas County | 30027 | MT,Fergus County |
| 1049 | AL,DeKalb County | 30029 | MT,Flathead County |
| 1051 | AL,Elmore County | 30031 | MT,Gallatin County |
| 1053 | AL,Escambia County | 30033 | MT,Garfield County |
| 1055 | AL,Etowah County | 30035 | MT,Glacier County |
| 1057 | AL,Fayette County | 30037 | MT,Golden Valley County |
| 1059 | AL,Franklin County | 30039 | MT,Granite County |
| 1061 | AL,Geneva County | 30041 | MT,Hill County |
| 1063 | AL,Greene County | 30043 | MT,Jefferson County |
| 1065 | AL,Hale County | 30045 | MT,Judith Basin County |
| 1067 | AL,Henry County | 30047 | MT,Lake County |
| 1069 | AL,Houston County | 30049 | MT,Lewis and Clark County |
| 1071 | AL,Jackson County | 30051 | MT,Liberty County |
| 1073 | AL,Jefferson County | 30053 | MT,Lincoln County |
| 1075 | AL,Lamar County | 30055 | MT,McCone County |
| 1077 | AL,Lauderdale County | 30057 | MT,Madison County |
| 1079 | AL,Lawrence County | 30059 | MT,Meagher County |
| 1081 | AL,Lee County | 30061 | MT,Mineral County |
| 1083 | AL,Limestone County | 30063 | MT,Missoula County |
| 1085 | AL,Lowndes County | 30065 | MT,Musselshell County |
| 1087 | AL,Macon County | 30067 | MT,Park County |
| 1089 | AL,Madison County | 30069 | MT,Petroleum County |
| 1091 | AL,Marengo County | 30071 | MT,Phillips County |
| 1093 | AL,Marion County | 30073 | MT,Pondera County |
| 1095 | AL,Marshall County | 30075 | MT,Powder River County |
| 1097 | AL,Mobile County | 30077 | MT,Powell County |
| 1099 | AL,Monroe County | 30079 | MT,Prairie County |
| 1101 | AL,Montgomery County | 30081 | MT,Ravalli County |
| 1103 | AL,Morgan County | 30083 | MT,Richland County |
| 1105 | AL,Perry County | 30085 | MT,Roosevelt County |
| 1107 | AL,Pickens County | 30087 | MT,Rosebud County |
| 1109 | AL,Pike County | 30089 | MT,Sanders County |
| 1111 | AL,Randolph County | 30091 | MT,Sheridan County |
| 1113 | AL,Russell County | 30093 | MT,Silver Bow County |
| 1115 | AL,St. Clair County | 30095 | MT,Stillwater County |
| 1117 | AL,Shelby County | 30097 | MT,Sweet Grass County |
| 1119 | AL,Sumter County | 30099 | MT,Teton County |
| 1121 | AL,Talladega County | 30101 | MT,Toole County |
| 1123 | AL,Tallapoosa County | 30103 | MT,Treasure County |
| 1125 | AL,Tuscaloosa County | 30105 | MT,Valley County |
| 1127 | AL,Walker County | 30107 | MT,Wheatland County |
| 1129 | AL,Washington County | 30109 | MT,Wibaux County |

| | | | |
|---|---|---|---|
| 1131 | AL,Wilcox County | 30111 | MT,Yellowstone County |
| 1133 | AL,Winston County | 30113 | MT,Yellowstone National Park |
| 2000 | AK,Undetermined | 30999 | MT,Undetermined County |
| 2100 | AK,Haines Borough | 31001 | NE,Adams County |
| 2110 | AK,Juneau Borough | 31003 | NE,Antelope County |
| 2130 | AK,Ketchikan Gateway Borough | 31005 | NE,Arthur County |
| 2201 | AK,Prince of Wales Outer | 31007 | NE,Banner County |
| | Ketchikan Census | 31009 | NE,Blaine County |
| 2220 | AK,Sitka Borough | 31011 | NE,Boone County |
| 2231 | AK,Skagway Yakutat | 31013 | NE,Box Butte County |
| | Angoon Census | 31015 | NE,Boyd County |
| 2280 | AK,Wrangell Petersburg Census | 31017 | NE,Brown County |
| 4001 | AZ,Apache County | 31019 | NE,Buffalo County |
| 4003 | AZ,Cochise County | 31021 | NE,Burt County |
| 4005 | AZ,Coconino County | 31023 | NE,Butler County |
| 4007 | AZ,Gila County | 31025 | NE,Cass County |
| 4009 | AZ,Graham County | 31027 | NE,Cedar County |
| 4011 | AZ,Greenlee County | 31029 | NE,Chase County |
| 4012 | AZ,La Paz County | 31031 | NE,Cherry County |
| 4013 | AZ,Maricopa County | 31033 | NE,Cheyenne County |
| 4015 | AZ,Mohave County | 31035 | NE,Clay County |
| 4017 | AZ,Navajo County | 31037 | NE,Colfax County |
| 4019 | AZ,Pima County | 31039 | NE,Cuming County |
| 4021 | AZ,Pinal County | 31041 | NE,Custer County |
| 4023 | AZ,Santa Cruz County | 31043 | NE,Dakota County |
| 4025 | AZ,Yavapai County | 31045 | NE,Dawes County |
| 4027 | AZ,Yuma County | 31047 | NE,Dawson County |
| 4999 | AZ,Undetermined County | 31049 | NE,Deuel County |
| 5001 | AR,Arkansas County | 31051 | NE,Dixon County |
| 5003 | AR,Ashley County | 31053 | NE,Dodge County |
| 5005 | AR,Baxter County | 31055 | NE,Douglas County |
| 5007 | AR,Benton County | 31057 | NE,Dundy County |
| 5009 | AR,Boone County | 31059 | NE,Fillmore County |
| 5011 | AR,Bradley County | 31061 | NE,Franklin County |
| 5013 | AR,Calhoun County | 31063 | NE,Frontier County |
| 5015 | AR,Carroll County | 31065 | NE,Furnas County |
| 5017 | AR,Chicot County | 31067 | NE,Gage County |
| 5019 | AR,Clark County | 31069 | NE,Garden County |
| 5021 | AR,Clay County | 31071 | NE,Garfield County |
| 5023 | AR,Cleburne County | 31073 | NE,Gosper County |
| 5025 | AR,Cleveland County | 31075 | NE,Grant County |
| 5027 | AR,Columbia County | 31077 | NE,Greeley County |
| 5029 | AR,Conway County | 31079 | NE,Hall County |
| 5031 | AR,Craighead County | 31081 | NE,Hamilton County |
| 5033 | AR,Crawford County | 31083 | NE,Harlan County |
| 5035 | AR,Crittenden County | 31085 | NE,Hayes County |
| 5037 | AR,Cross County | 31087 | NE,Hitchcock County |
| 5039 | AR,Dallas County | 31089 | NE,Holt County |

| | | | |
|---|---|---|---|
| 5041 | AR,Desha County | 31091 | NE,Hooker County |
| 5043 | AR,Drew County | 31093 | NE,Howard County |
| 5045 | AR,Faulkner County | 31095 | NE,Jefferson County |
| 5047 | AR,Franklin County | 31097 | NE,Johnson County |
| 5049 | AR,Fulton County | 31099 | NE,Kearney County |
| 5051 | AR,Garland County | 31101 | NE,Keith County |
| 5053 | AR,Grant County | 31103 | NE,Keya Paha County |
| 5055 | AR,Greene County | 31105 | NE,Kimball County |
| 5057 | AR,Hempstead County | 31107 | NE,Knox County |
| 5059 | AR,Hot Spring County | 31109 | NE,Lancaster County |
| 5061 | AR,Howard County | 31111 | NE,Lincoln County |
| 5063 | AR,Independence County | 31113 | NE,Logan County |
| 5065 | AR,Izard County | 31115 | NE,Loup County |
| 5067 | AR,Jackson County | 31117 | NE,McPherson County |
| 5069 | AR,Jefferson County | 31119 | NE,Madison County |
| 5071 | AR,Johnson County | 31121 | NE,Merrick County |
| 5073 | AR,Lafayette County | 31123 | NE,Morrill County |
| 5075 | AR,Lawrence County | 31125 | NE,Nance County |
| 5077 | AR,Lee County | 31127 | NE,Nemaha County |
| 5079 | AR,Lincoln County | 31129 | NE,Nuckolls County |
| 5081 | AR,Little River County | 31131 | NE,Otoe County |
| 5083 | AR,Logan County | 31133 | NE,Pawnee County |
| 5085 | AR,Lonoke County | 31135 | NE,Perkins County |
| 5087 | AR,Madison County | 31137 | NE,Phelps County |
| 5089 | AR,Marion County | 31139 | NE,Pierce County |
| 5091 | AR,Miller County | 31141 | NE,Platte County |
| 5093 | AR,Mississippi County | 31143 | NE,Polk County |
| 5095 | AR,Monroe County | 31145 | NE,Red Willow County |
| 5097 | AR,Montgomery County | 31147 | NE,Richardson County |
| 5099 | AR,Nevada County | 31149 | NE,Rock County |
| 5101 | AR,Newton County | 31151 | NE,Saline County |
| 5103 | AR,Ouachita County | 31153 | NE,Sarpy County |
| 5105 | AR,Perry County | 31155 | NE,Saunders County |
| 5107 | AR,Phillips County | 31157 | NE,Scotts Bluff County |
| 5109 | AR,Pike County | 31159 | NE,Seward County |
| 5111 | AR,Poinsett County | 31161 | NE,Sheridan County |
| 5113 | AR,Polk County | 31163 | NE,Sherman County |
| 5115 | AR,Pope County | 31165 | NE,Sioux County |
| 5117 | AR,Prairie County | 31167 | NE,Stanton County |
| 5119 | AR,Pulaski County | 31169 | NE,Thayer County |
| 5121 | AR,Randolph County | 31171 | NE,Thomas County |
| 5123 | AR,St. Francis County | 31173 | NE,Thurston County |
| 5125 | AR,Saline County | 31175 | NE,Valley County |
| 5127 | AR,Scott County | 31177 | NE,Washington County |
| 5129 | AR,Searcy County | 31179 | NE,Wayne County |
| 5131 | AR,Sebastian County | 31181 | NE,Webster County |
| 5133 | AR,Sevier County | 31183 | NE,Wheeler County |
| 5135 | AR,Sharp County | 31185 | NE,York County |

| | | | |
|---|---|---|---|
| 5137 | AR,Stone County | 32001 | NV,Churchill County |
| 5139 | AR,Union County | 32003 | NV,Clark County |
| 5141 | AR,Van Buren County | 32005 | NV,Douglas County |
| 5143 | AR,Washington County | 32007 | NV,Elko County |
| 5145 | AR,White County | 32009 | NV,Esmeralda County |
| 5147 | AR,Woodruff County | 32011 | NV,Eureka County |
| 5149 | AR,Yell County | 32013 | NV,Humboldt County |
| 6001 | CA,Alameda County | 32015 | NV,Lander County |
| 6003 | CA,Alpine County | 32017 | NV,Lincoln County |
| 6005 | CA,Amador County | 32019 | NV,Lyon County |
| 6007 | CA,Butte County | 32021 | NV,Mineral County |
| 6009 | CA,Calaveras County | 32023 | NV,Nye County |
| 6011 | CA,Colusa County | 32027 | NV,Pershing County |
| 6013 | CA,Contra Costa County | 32029 | NV,Storey County |
| 6015 | CA,Del Norte County | 32031 | NV,Washoe County |
| 6017 | CA,El Dorado County | 32033 | NV,White Pine County |
| 6019 | CA,Fresno County | 32510 | NV,Carson City |
| 6021 | CA,Glenn County | 32666 | NV,Toiybe National Forest |
| 6023 | CA,Humboldt County | 32999 | NV,Undetermined County |
| 6025 | CA,Imperial County | 33001 | NH,Belknap County |
| 6027 | CA,Inyo County | 33003 | NH,Carroll County |
| 6029 | CA,Kern County | 33005 | NH,Cheshire County |
| 6031 | CA,Kings County | 33007 | NH,Coos County |
| 6033 | CA,Lake County | 33009 | NH,Grafton County |
| 6035 | CA,Lassen County | 33011 | NH,Hillsborough County |
| 6037 | CA,Los Angeles County | 33013 | NH,Merrimack County |
| 6039 | CA,Madera County | 33015 | NH,Rockingham County |
| 6041 | CA,Marin County | 33017 | NH,Strafford County |
| 6043 | CA,Mariposa County | 33019 | NH,Sullivan County |
| 6045 | CA,Mendocino County | 34001 | NJ,Atlantic County |
| 6047 | CA,Merced County | 34003 | NJ,Bergen County |
| 6049 | CA,Modoc County | 34005 | NJ,Burlington County |
| 6051 | CA,Mono County | 34007 | NJ,Camden County |
| 6053 | CA,Monterey County | 34009 | NJ,Cape May County |
| 6055 | CA,Napa County | 34011 | NJ,Cumberland County |
| 6057 | CA,Nevada County | 34013 | NJ,Essex County |
| 6059 | CA,Orange County | 34015 | NJ,Gloucester County |
| 6061 | CA,Placer County | 34017 | NJ,Hudson County |
| 6063 | CA,Plumas County | 34019 | NJ,Hunterdon County |
| 6065 | CA,Riverside County | 34021 | NJ,Mercer County |
| 6067 | CA,Sacramento County | 34023 | NJ,Middlesex County |
| 6069 | CA,San Benito County | 34025 | NJ,Monmouth County |
| 6071 | CA,San Bernardino County | 34027 | NJ,Morris County |
| 6073 | CA,San Diego County | 34029 | NJ,Ocean County |
| 6075 | CA,San Francisco County | 34031 | NJ,Passaic County |
| 6077 | CA,San Joaquin County | 34033 | NJ,Salem County |
| 6079 | CA,San Luis Obispo County | 34035 | NJ,Somerset County |
| 6081 | CA,San Mateo County | 34037 | NJ,Sussex County |

| | | | |
|---|---|---|---|
| 6083 | CA,Santa Barbara County | 34039 | NJ,Union County |
| 6085 | CA,Santa Clara County | 34041 | NJ,Warren County |
| 6087 | CA,Santa Cruz County | 35001 | NM,Bernalillo County |
| 6089 | CA,Shasta County | 35003 | NM,Catron County |
| 6091 | CA,Sierra County | 35005 | NM,Chaves County |
| 6093 | CA,Siskiyou County | 35006 | NM,Cibola County |
| 6095 | CA,Solano County | 35007 | NM,Colfax County |
| 6097 | CA,Sonoma County | 35009 | NM,Curry County |
| 6099 | CA,Stanislaus County | 35011 | NM,DeBaca County |
| 6101 | CA,Sutter County | 35013 | NM,Dona Ana County |
| 6103 | CA,Tehama County | 35015 | NM,Eddy County |
| 6105 | CA,Trinity County | 35017 | NM,Grant County |
| 6107 | CA,Tulare County | 35019 | NM,Guadalupe County |
| 6109 | CA,Tuolumne County | 35021 | NM,Harding County |
| 6111 | CA,Ventura County | 35023 | NM,Hidalgo County |
| 6113 | CA,Yolo County | 35025 | NM,Lea County |
| 6115 | CA,Yuba County | 35027 | NM,Lincoln County |
| 6666 | CA,Toiyabe National Forest | 35028 | NM,Los Alamos |
| 8001 | CO,Adams County | 35029 | NM,Luna County |
| 8003 | CO,Alamosa County | 35031 | NM,McKinley County |
| 8005 | CO,Arapahoe County | 35033 | NM,Mora County |
| 8007 | CO,Archuleta County | 35035 | NM,Otero County |
| 8009 | CO,Baca County | 35037 | NM,Quay County |
| 8011 | CO,Bent County | 35039 | NM,Rio Arriba County |
| 8013 | CO,Boulder County | 35041 | NM,Roosevelt County |
| 8015 | CO,Chaffee County | 35043 | NM,Sandoval County |
| 8017 | CO,Cheyenne County | 35045 | NM,San Juan County |
| 8019 | CO,Clear Creek County | 35047 | NM,San Miguel County |
| 8021 | CO,Conejos County | 35049 | NM,Santa Fe County |
| 8023 | CO,Costilla County | 35051 | NM,Sierra County |
| 8025 | CO,Crowley County | 35053 | NM,Socorro County |
| 8027 | CO,Custer County | 35055 | NM,Taos County |
| 8029 | CO,Delta County | 35057 | NM,Torrance County |
| 8031 | CO,Denver County | 35059 | NM,Union County |
| 8033 | CO,Dolores County | 35061 | NM,Valencia County |
| 8035 | CO,Douglas County | 35999 | NM,Undetermined County |
| 8037 | CO,Eagle County | 36001 | NY,Albany County |
| 8039 | CO,Elbert County | 36003 | NY,Allegany County |
| 8041 | CO,El Paso County | 36005 | NY,Bronx County |
| 8043 | CO,Fremont County | 36007 | NY,Broome County |
| 8045 | CO,Garfield County | 36009 | NY,Cattaraugus County |
| 8047 | CO,Gilpin County | 36011 | NY,Cayuga County |
| 8049 | CO,Grand County | 36013 | NY,Chautauqua County |
| 8051 | CO,Gunnison County | 36015 | NY,Chemung County |
| 8053 | CO,Hinsdale County | 36017 | NY,Chenango County |
| 8055 | CO,Huerfano County | 36019 | NY,Clinton County |
| 8057 | CO,Jackson County | 36021 | NY,Columbia County |
| 8059 | CO,Jefferson County | 36023 | NY,Cortland County |

| | | | |
|---|---|---|---|
| 8061 | CO,Kiowa County | 36025 | NY,Delaware County |
| 8063 | CO,Kit Carson County | 36027 | NY,Dutchess County |
| 8065 | CO,Lake County | 36029 | NY,Erie County |
| 8067 | CO,La Plata County | 36031 | NY,Essex County |
| 8069 | CO,Larimer County | 36033 | NY,Franklin County |
| 8071 | CO,Las Animas County | 36035 | NY,Fulton County |
| 8073 | CO,Lincoln County | 36037 | NY,Genesee County |
| 8075 | CO,Logan County | 36039 | NY,Greene County |
| 8077 | CO,Mesa County | 36041 | NY,Hamilton County |
| 8079 | CO,Mineral County | 36043 | NY,Herkimer County |
| 8081 | CO,Moffat County | 36045 | NY,Jefferson County |
| 8083 | CO,Montezuma County | 36047 | NY,Kings County |
| 8085 | CO,Montrose County | 36049 | NY,Lewis County |
| 8087 | CO,Morgan County | 36051 | NY,Livingston County |
| 8089 | CO,Otero County | 36053 | NY,Madison County |
| 8091 | CO,Ouray County | 36055 | NY,Monroe County |
| 8093 | CO,Park County | 36057 | NY,Montgomery County |
| 8095 | CO,Phillips County | 36059 | NY,Nassau County |
| 8097 | CO,Pitkin County | 36061 | NY,New York County |
| 8099 | CO,Prowers County | 36063 | NY,Niagara County |
| 8101 | CO,Pueblo County | 36065 | NY,Oneida County |
| 8103 | CO,Rio Blanco County | 36067 | NY,Onondaga County |
| 8105 | CO,Rio Grande County | 36069 | NY,Ontario County |
| 8107 | CO,Routt County | 36071 | NY,Orange County |
| 8109 | CO,Saguache County | 36073 | NY,Orleans County |
| 8111 | CO,San Juan County | 36075 | NY,Oswego County |
| 8113 | CO,San Miguel County | 36077 | NY,Otsego County |
| 8115 | CO,Sedgwick County | 36079 | NY,Putnam County |
| 8117 | CO,Summit County | 36081 | NY,Queens County |
| 8119 | CO,Teller County | 36083 | NY,Rensselaer County |
| 8121 | CO,Washington County | 36085 | NY,Richmond County |
| 8123 | CO,Weld County | 36087 | NY,Rockland County |
| 8125 | CO,Yuma County | 36089 | NY,St. Lawrence County |
| 8660 | CO,GM-UNC-Gun National Forest | 36091 | NY,Saratoga County |
| | | 36093 | NY,Schenectady County |
| 8661 | CO,Rio Grande National Forest | 36095 | NY,Schoharie County |
| | | 36097 | NY,Schuyler County |
| 8662 | CO,Arapaho-Roosevelt National Forest | 36099 | NY,Seneca County |
| | | 36101 | NY,Steuben County |
| 8663 | CO,Routt National Forest | 36103 | NY,Suffolk County |
| 8664 | CO,Pike-San Isabel National Forest | 36105 | NY,Sullivan County |
| | | 36107 | NY,Tioga County |
| 8665 | CO,San Juan National Forest | 36109 | NY,Tompkins County |
| 8666 | CO,White River National Forest | 36111 | NY,Ulster County |
| 8999 | CO,Undetermined County | 36113 | NY,Warren County |
| 9001 | CT,Fairfield County | 36115 | NY,Washington County |
| 9003 | CT,Hartford County | 36117 | NY,Wayne County |
| 9005 | CT,Litchfield County | 36119 | NY,Westchester County |

| | | | |
|---|---|---|---|
| 9007 | CT,Middlesex County | 36121 | NY,Wyoming County |
| 9009 | CT,New Haven County | 36123 | NY,Yates County |
| 9011 | CT,New London County | 37001 | NC,Alamance County |
| 9013 | CT,Tolland County | 37003 | NC,Alexander County |
| 9015 | CT,Windham County | 37005 | NC,Alleghany County |
| 10001 | DE,Kent County | 37007 | NC,Anson County |
| 10003 | DE,New Castle County | 37009 | NC,Ashe County |
| 10005 | DE,Sussex County | 37011 | NC,Avery County |
| 11001 | District of Columbia | 37013 | NC,Beaufort County |
| 12001 | FL,Alachua County | 37015 | NC,Bertie County |
| 12003 | FL,Baker County | 37017 | NC,Bladen County |
| 12005 | FL,Bay County | 37019 | NC,Brunswick County |
| 12007 | FL,Bradford County | 37021 | NC,Buncombe County |
| 12009 | FL,Brevard County | 37023 | NC,Burke County |
| 12011 | FL,Broward County | 37025 | NC,Cabarrus County |
| 12013 | FL,Calhoun County | 37027 | NC,Caldwell County |
| 12015 | FL,Charlotte County | 37029 | NC,Camden County |
| 12017 | FL,Citrus County | 37031 | NC,Carteret County |
| 12019 | FL,Clay County | 37033 | NC,Caswell County |
| 12021 | FL,Collier County | 37035 | NC,Catawba County |
| 12023 | FL,Columbia County | 37037 | NC,Chatham County |
| 12025 | FL,Dade County | 37039 | NC,Cherokee County |
| 12027 | FL,DeSoto County | 37041 | NC,Chowan County |
| 12029 | FL,Dixie County | 37043 | NC,Clay County |
| 12031 | FL,Duval County | 37045 | NC,Cleveland County |
| 12033 | FL,Escambia County | 37047 | NC,Columbus County |
| 12035 | FL,Flagler County | 37049 | NC,Craven County |
| 12037 | FL,Franklin County | 37051 | NC,Cumberland County |
| 12039 | FL,Gadsden County | 37053 | NC,Currituck County |
| 12041 | FL,Gilchrist County | 37055 | NC,Dare County |
| 12043 | FL,Glades County | 37057 | NC,Davidson County |
| 12045 | FL,Gulf County | 37059 | NC,Davie County |
| 12047 | FL,Hamilton County | 37061 | NC,Duplin County |
| 12049 | FL,Hardee County | 37063 | NC,Durham County |
| 12051 | FL,Hendry County | 37065 | NC,Edgecombe County |
| 12053 | FL,Hernando County | 37067 | NC,Forsyth County |
| 12055 | FL,Highlands County | 37069 | NC,Franklin County |
| 12057 | FL,Hillsborough County | 37071 | NC,Gaston County |
| 12059 | FL,Holmes County | 37073 | NC,Gates County |
| 12061 | FL,Indian River County | 37075 | NC,Graham County |
| 12063 | FL,Jackson County | 37077 | NC,Granville County |
| 12065 | FL,Jefferson County | 37079 | NC,Greene County |
| 12067 | FL,Lafayette County | 37081 | NC,Guilford County |
| 12069 | FL,Lake County | 37083 | NC,Halifax County |
| 12071 | FL,Lee County | 37085 | NC,Harnett County |
| 12073 | FL,Leon County | 37087 | NC,Haywood County |
| 12075 | FL,Levy County | 37089 | NC,Henderson County |
| 12077 | FL,Liberty County | 37091 | NC,Hertford County |

| | | | |
|---|---|---|---|
| 12079 | FL,Madison County | 37093 | NC,Hoke County |
| 12081 | FL,Manatee County | 37095 | NC,Hyde County |
| 12083 | FL,Marion County | 37097 | NC,Iredell County |
| 12085 | FL,Martin County | 37099 | NC,Jackson County |
| 12087 | FL,Monroe County | 37101 | NC,Johnston County |
| 12089 | FL,Nassau County | 37103 | NC,Jones County |
| 12091 | FL,Okaloosa County | 37105 | NC,Lee County |
| 12093 | FL,Okeechobee County | 37107 | NC,Lenoir County |
| 12095 | FL,Orange County | 37109 | NC,Lincoln County |
| 12097 | FL,Osceola County | 37111 | NC,McDowell County |
| 12099 | FL,Palm Beach County | 37113 | NC,Macon County |
| 12101 | FL,Pasco County | 37115 | NC,Madison County |
| 12103 | FL,Pinellas County | 37117 | NC,Martin County |
| 12105 | FL,Polk County | 37119 | NC,Mecklenburg County |
| 12107 | FL,Putnam County | 37121 | NC,Mitchell County |
| 12109 | FL,St. Johns County | 37123 | NC,Montgomery County |
| 12111 | FL,St. Lucie County | 37125 | NC,Moore County |
| 12113 | FL,Santa Rosa County | 37127 | NC,Nash County |
| 12115 | FL,Sarasota County | 37129 | NC,New Hanover County |
| 12117 | FL,Seminole County | 37131 | NC,Northampton County |
| 12119 | FL,Sumter County | 37133 | NC,Onslow County |
| 12121 | FL,Suwannee County | 37135 | NC,Orange County |
| 12123 | FL,Taylor County | 37137 | NC,Pamlico County |
| 12125 | FL,Union County | 37139 | NC,Pasquotank County |
| 12127 | FL,Volusia County | 37141 | NC,Pender County |
| 12129 | FL,Wakulla County | 37143 | NC,Perquimans County |
| 12131 | FL,Walton County | 37145 | NC,Person County |
| 12133 | FL,Washington County | 37147 | NC,Pitt County |
| 13001 | GA,Appling County | 37149 | NC,Polk County |
| 13003 | GA,Atkinson County | 37151 | NC,Randolph County |
| 13005 | GA,Bacon County | 37153 | NC,Richmond County |
| 13007 | GA,Baker County | 37155 | NC,Robeson County |
| 13009 | GA,Baldwin County | 37157 | NC,Rockingham County |
| 13011 | GA,Banks County | 37159 | NC,Rowan County |
| 13013 | GA,Barrow County | 37161 | NC,Rutherford County |
| 13015 | GA,Bartow County | 37163 | NC,Sampson County |
| 13017 | GA,Ben Hill County | 37165 | NC,Scotland County |
| 13019 | GA,Berrien County | 37167 | NC,Stanly County |
| 13021 | GA,Bibb County | 37169 | NC,Stokes County |
| 13023 | GA,Bleckley County | 37171 | NC,Surry County |
| 13025 | GA,Brantley County | 37173 | NC,Swain County |
| 13027 | GA,Brooks County | 37175 | NC,Transylvania County |
| 13029 | GA,Bryan County | 37177 | NC,Tyrrell County |
| 13031 | GA,Bulloch County | 37179 | NC,Union County |
| 13033 | GA,Burke County | 37181 | NC,Vance County |
| 13035 | GA,Butts County | 37183 | NC,Wake County |
| 13037 | GA,Calhoun County | 37185 | NC,Warren County |
| 13039 | GA,Camden County | 37187 | NC,Washington County |

| | | | |
|---|---|---|---|
| 13043 | GA,Candler County | 37189 | NC,Watauga County |
| 13045 | GA,Carroll County | 37191 | NC,Wayne County |
| 13047 | GA,Catoosa County | 37193 | NC,Wilkes County |
| 13049 | GA,Charlton County | 37195 | NC,Wilson County |
| 13051 | GA,Chatham County | 37197 | NC,Yadkin County |
| 13053 | GA,Chattahoochee County | 37199 | NC,Yancey County |
| 13055 | GA,Chattooga County | 38001 | ND,Adams County |
| 13057 | GA,Cherokee County | 38003 | ND,Barnes County |
| 13059 | GA,Clarke County | 38005 | ND,Benson County |
| 13061 | GA,Clay County | 38007 | ND,Billings County |
| 13063 | GA,Clayton County | 38009 | ND,Bottineau County |
| 13065 | GA,Clinch County | 38011 | ND,Bowman County |
| 13067 | GA,Cobb County | 38013 | ND,Burke County |
| 13069 | GA,Coffee County | 38015 | ND,Burleigh County |
| 13071 | GA,Colquitt County | 38017 | ND,Cass County |
| 13073 | GA,Columbia County | 38019 | ND,Cavalier County |
| 13075 | GA,Cook County | 38021 | ND,Dickey County |
| 13077 | GA,Coweta County | 38023 | ND,Divide County |
| 13079 | GA,Crawford County | 38025 | ND,Dunn County |
| 13081 | GA,Crisp County | 38027 | ND,Eddy County |
| 13083 | GA,Dade County | 38029 | ND,Emmons County |
| 13085 | GA,Dawson County | 38031 | ND,Foster County |
| 13087 | GA,Decatur County | 38033 | ND,Golden Valley County |
| 13089 | GA,DeKalb County | 38035 | ND,Grand Forks County |
| 13091 | GA,Dodge County | 38037 | ND,Grant County |
| 13093 | GA,Dooly County | 38039 | ND,Griggs County |
| 13095 | GA,Dougherty County | 38041 | ND,Hettinger County |
| 13097 | GA,Douglas County | 38043 | ND,Kidder County |
| 13099 | GA,Early County | 38045 | ND,LaMoure County |
| 13101 | GA,Echols County | 38047 | ND,Logan County |
| 13103 | GA,Effingham County | 38049 | ND,McHenry County |
| 13105 | GA,Elbert County | 38051 | ND,McIntosh County |
| 13107 | GA,Emanuel County | 38053 | ND,McKenzie County |
| 13109 | GA,Evans County | 38055 | ND,McLean County |
| 13111 | GA,Fannin County | 38057 | ND,Mercer County |
| 13113 | GA,Fayette County | 38059 | ND,Morton County |
| 13115 | GA,Floyd County | 38061 | ND,Mountrail County |
| 13117 | GA,Forsyth County | 38063 | ND,Nelson County |
| 13119 | GA,Franklin County | 38065 | ND,Oliver County |
| 13121 | GA,Fulton County | 38067 | ND,Pembina County |
| 13123 | GA,Gilmer County | 38069 | ND,Pierce County |
| 13125 | GA,Glascock County | 38071 | ND,Ramsey County |
| 13127 | GA,Glynn County | 38073 | ND,Ransom County |
| 13129 | GA,Gordon County | 38075 | ND,Renville County |
| 13131 | GA,Grady County | 38077 | ND,Richland County |
| 13133 | GA,Greene County | 38079 | ND,Rolette County |
| 13135 | GA,Gwinnett County | 38081 | ND,Sargent County |
| 13137 | GA,Habersham County | 38083 | ND,Sheridan County |

| | | | |
|---|---|---|---|
| 13139 | GA,Hall County | 38085 | ND,Sioux County |
| 13141 | GA,Hancock County | 38087 | ND,Slope County |
| 13143 | GA,Haralson County | 38089 | ND,Stark County |
| 13145 | GA,Harris County | 38091 | ND,Steele County |
| 13147 | GA,Hart County | 38093 | ND,Stutsman County |
| 13149 | GA,Heard County | 38095 | ND,Towner County |
| 13151 | GA,Henry County | 38097 | ND,Traill County |
| 13153 | GA,Houston County | 38099 | ND,Walsh County |
| 13155 | GA,Irwin County | 38101 | ND,Ward County |
| 13157 | GA,Jackson County | 38103 | ND,Wells County |
| 13159 | GA,Jasper County | 38105 | ND,Williams County |
| 13161 | GA,Jeff Davis County | 39001 | OH,Adams County |
| 13163 | GA,Jefferson County | 39003 | OH,Allen County |
| 13165 | GA,Jenkins County | 39005 | OH,Ashland County |
| 13167 | GA,Johnson County | 39007 | OH,Ashtabula County |
| 13169 | GA,Jones County | 39009 | OH,Athens County |
| 13171 | GA,Lamar County | 39011 | OH,Auglaize County |
| 13173 | GA,Lanier County | 39013 | OH,Belmont County |
| 13175 | GA,Laurens County | 39015 | OH,Brown County |
| 13177 | GA,Lee County | 39017 | OH,Butler County |
| 13179 | GA,Liberty County | 39019 | OH,Carroll County |
| 13181 | GA,Lincoln County | 39021 | OH,Champaign County |
| 13183 | GA,Long County | 39023 | OH,Clark County |
| 13185 | GA,Lowndes County | 39025 | OH,Clermont County |
| 13187 | GA,Lumpkin County | 39027 | OH,Clinton County |
| 13189 | GA,McDuffie County | 39029 | OH,Columbiana County |
| 13191 | GA,McIntosh County | 39031 | OH,Coshocton County |
| 13193 | GA,Macon County | 39033 | OH,Crawford County |
| 13195 | GA,Madison County | 39035 | OH,Cuyahoga County |
| 13197 | GA,Marion County | 39037 | OH,Darke County |
| 13199 | GA,Meriwether County | 39039 | OH,Defiance County |
| 13201 | GA,Miller County | 39041 | OH,Delaware County |
| 13205 | GA,Mitchell County | 39043 | OH,Erie County |
| 13207 | GA,Monroe County | 39045 | OH,Fairfield County |
| 13209 | GA,Montgomery County | 39047 | OH,Fayette County |
| 13211 | GA,Morgan County | 39049 | OH,Franklin County |
| 13213 | GA,Murray County | 39051 | OH,Fulton County |
| 13215 | GA,Muscogee County | 39053 | OH,Gallia County |
| 13217 | GA,Newton County | 39055 | OH,Geauga County |
| 13219 | GA,Oconee County | 39057 | OH,Greene County |
| 13221 | GA,Oglethorpe County | 39059 | OH,Guernsey County |
| 13223 | GA,Paulding County | 39061 | OH,Hamilton County |
| 13225 | GA,Peach County | 39063 | OH,Hancock County |
| 13227 | GA,Pickens County | 39065 | OH,Hardin County |
| 13229 | GA,Pierce County | 39067 | OH,Harrison County |
| 13231 | GA,Pike County | 39069 | OH,Henry County |
| 13233 | GA,Polk County | 39071 | OH,Highland County |
| 13235 | GA,Pulaski County | 39073 | OH,Hocking County |

| | | | |
|---|---|---|---|
| 13237 | GA,Putnam County | 39075 | OH,Holmes County |
| 13239 | GA,Quitman County | 39077 | OH,Huron County |
| 13241 | GA,Rabun County | 39079 | OH,Jackson County |
| 13243 | GA,Randolph County | 39081 | OH,Jefferson County |
| 13245 | GA,Richmond County | 39083 | OH,Knox County |
| 13247 | GA,Rockdale County | 39085 | OH,Lake County |
| 13249 | GA,Schley County | 39087 | OH,Lawrence County |
| 13251 | GA,Screven County | 39089 | OH,Licking County |
| 13253 | GA,Seminole County | 39091 | OH,Logan County |
| 13255 | GA,Spalding County | 39093 | OH,Lorain County |
| 13257 | GA,Stephens County | 39095 | OH,Lucas County |
| 13259 | GA,Stewart County | 39097 | OH,Madison County |
| 13261 | GA,Sumter County | 39099 | OH,Mahoning County |
| 13263 | GA,Talbot County | 39101 | OH,Marion County |
| 13265 | GA,Taliaferro County | 39103 | OH,Medina County |
| 13267 | GA,Tattnall County | 39105 | OH,Meigs County |
| 13269 | GA,Taylor County | 39107 | OH,Mercer County |
| 13271 | GA,Telfair County | 39109 | OH,Miami County |
| 13273 | GA,Terrell County | 39111 | OH,Monroe County |
| 13275 | GA,Thomas County | 39113 | OH,Montgomery County |
| 13277 | GA,Tift County | 39115 | OH,Morgan County |
| 13279 | GA,Toombs County | 39117 | OH,Morrow County |
| 13281 | GA,Towns County | 39119 | OH,Muskingum County |
| 13283 | GA,Treutlen County | 39121 | OH,Noble County |
| 13285 | GA,Troup County | 39123 | OH,Ottawa County |
| 13287 | GA,Turner County | 39125 | OH,Paulding County |
| 13289 | GA,Twiggs County | 39127 | OH,Perry County |
| 13291 | GA,Union County | 39129 | OH,Pickaway County |
| 13293 | GA,Upson County | 39131 | OH,Pike County |
| 13295 | GA,Walker County | 39133 | OH,Portage County |
| 13297 | GA,Walton County | 39135 | OH,Preble County |
| 13299 | GA,Ware County | 39137 | OH,Putnam County |
| 13301 | GA,Warren County | 39139 | OH,Richland County |
| 13303 | GA,Washington County | 39141 | OH,Ross County |
| 13305 | GA,Wayne County | 39143 | OH,Sandusky County |
| 13307 | GA,Webster County | 39145 | OH,Scioto County |
| 13309 | GA,Wheeler County | 39147 | OH,Seneca County |
| 13311 | GA,White County | 39149 | OH,Shelby County |
| 13313 | GA,Whitfield County | 39151 | OH,Stark County |
| 13315 | GA,Wilcox County | 39153 | OH,Summit County |
| 13317 | GA,Wilkes County | 39155 | OH,Trumbull County |
| 13319 | GA,Wilkinson County | 39157 | OH,Tuscarawas County |
| 13321 | GA,Worth County | 39159 | OH,Union County |
| 15001 | HI,Hawaii County | 39161 | OH,Van Wert County |
| 16001 | ID,Ada County | 39163 | OH,Vinton County |
| 16003 | ID,Adams County | 39165 | OH,Warren County |
| 16005 | ID,Bannock County | 39167 | OH,Washington County |
| 16007 | ID,Bear Lake County | 39169 | OH,Wayne County |

| | | | |
|---|---|---|---|
| 16009 | ID,Benewah County | 39171 | OH,Williams County |
| 16011 | ID,Bingham County | 39173 | OH,Wood County |
| 16013 | ID,Blaine County | 39175 | OH,Wyandot County |
| 16015 | ID,Boise County | 40001 | OK,Adair County |
| 16017 | ID,Bonner County | 40003 | OK,Alfalfa County |
| 16019 | ID,Bonneville County | 40005 | OK,Atoka County |
| 16021 | ID,Boundary County | 40007 | OK,Beaver County |
| 16023 | ID,Butte County | 40009 | OK,Beckham County |
| 16025 | ID,Camas County | 40011 | OK,Blaine County |
| 16027 | ID,Canyon County | 40013 | OK,Bryan County |
| 16029 | ID,Caribou County | 40015 | OK,Caddo County |
| 16031 | ID,Cassia County | 40017 | OK,Canadian County |
| 16033 | ID,Clark County | 40019 | OK,Carter County |
| 16035 | ID,Clearwater County | 40021 | OK,Cherokee County |
| 16037 | ID,Custer County | 40023 | OK,Choctaw County |
| 16039 | ID,Elmore County | 40025 | OK,Cimarron County |
| 16041 | ID,Franklin County | 40027 | OK,Cleveland County |
| 16043 | ID,Fremont County | 40029 | OK,Coal County |
| 16045 | ID,Gem County | 40031 | OK,Comanche County |
| 16047 | ID,Gooding County | 40033 | OK,Cotton County |
| 16049 | ID,Idaho County | 40035 | OK,Craig County |
| 16051 | ID,Jefferson County | 40037 | OK,Creek County |
| 16053 | ID,Jerome County | 40039 | OK,Custer County |
| 16055 | ID,Kootenai County | 40041 | OK,Delaware County |
| 16057 | ID,Latah County | 40043 | OK,Dewey County |
| 16059 | ID,Lemhi County | 40045 | OK,Ellis County |
| 16061 | ID,Lewis County | 40047 | OK,Garfield County |
| 16063 | ID,Lincoln County | 40049 | OK,Garvin County |
| 16065 | ID,Madison County | 40051 | OK,Grady County |
| 16067 | ID,Minidoka County | 40053 | OK,Grant County |
| 16069 | ID,Nez Perce County | 40055 | OK,Greer County |
| 16071 | ID,Oneida County | 40057 | OK,Harmon County |
| 16073 | ID,Owyhee County | 40059 | OK,Harper County |
| 16075 | ID,Payette County | 40061 | OK,Haskell County |
| 16077 | ID,Power County | 40063 | OK,Hughes County |
| 16079 | ID,Shoshone County | 40065 | OK,Jackson County |
| 16081 | ID,Teton County | 40067 | OK,Jefferson County |
| 16083 | ID,Twin Falls County | 40069 | OK,Johnston County |
| 16085 | ID,Valley County | 40071 | OK,Kay County |
| 16087 | ID,Washington County | 40073 | OK,Kingfisher County |
| 16999 | ID,Undetermined County | 40075 | OK,Kiowa County |
| 17001 | IL,Adams County | 40077 | OK,Latimer County |
| 17003 | IL,Alexander County | 40079 | OK,Le Flore County |
| 17005 | IL,Bond County | 40081 | OK,Lincoln County |
| 17007 | IL,Boone County | 40083 | OK,Logan County |
| 17009 | IL,Brown County | 40085 | OK,Love County |
| 17011 | IL,Bureau County | 40087 | OK,McClain County |
| 17013 | IL,Calhoun County | 40089 | OK,McCurtain County |

| | | | |
|---|---|---|---|
| 17015 | IL,Carroll County | 40091 | OK,McIntosh County |
| 17017 | IL,Cass County | 40093 | OK,Major County |
| 17019 | IL,Champaign County | 40095 | OK,Marshall County |
| 17021 | IL,Christian County | 40097 | OK,Mayes County |
| 17023 | IL,Clark County | 40099 | OK,Murray County |
| 17025 | IL,Clay County | 40101 | OK,Muskogee County |
| 17027 | IL,Clinton County | 40103 | OK,Noble County |
| 17029 | IL,Coles County | 40105 | OK,Nowata County |
| 17031 | IL,Cook County | 40107 | OK,Okfuskee County |
| 17033 | IL,Crawford County | 40109 | OK,Oklahoma County |
| 17035 | IL,Cumberland County | 40111 | OK,Okmulgee County |
| 17037 | IL,DeKalb County | 40113 | OK,Osage County |
| 17039 | IL,De Witt County | 40115 | OK,Ottawa County |
| 17041 | IL,Douglas County | 40117 | OK,Pawnee County |
| 17043 | IL,DuPage County | 40119 | OK,Payne County |
| 17045 | IL,Edgar County | 40121 | OK,Pittsburg County |
| 17047 | IL,Edwards County | 40123 | OK,Pontotoc County |
| 17049 | IL,Effingham County | 40125 | OK,Pottawatomie County |
| 17051 | IL,Fayette County | 40127 | OK,Pushmataha County |
| 17053 | IL,Ford County | 40129 | OK,Roger Mills County |
| 17055 | IL,Franklin County | 40131 | OK,Rogers County |
| 17057 | IL,Fulton County | 40133 | OK,Seminole County |
| 17059 | IL,Gallatin County | 40135 | OK,Sequoyah County |
| 17061 | IL,Greene County | 40137 | OK,Stephens County |
| 17063 | IL,Grundy County | 40139 | OK,Texas County |
| 17065 | IL,Hamilton County | 40141 | OK,Tillman County |
| 17067 | IL,Hancock County | 40143 | OK,Tulsa County |
| 17069 | IL,Hardin County | 40145 | OK,Wagoner County |
| 17071 | IL,Henderson County | 40147 | OK,Washington County |
| 17073 | IL,Henry County | 40149 | OK,Washita County |
| 17075 | IL,Iroquois County | 40151 | OK,Woods County |
| 17077 | IL,Jackson County | 40153 | OK,Woodward County |
| 17079 | IL,Jasper County | 41001 | OR,Baker County |
| 17081 | IL,Jefferson County | 41003 | OR,Benton County |
| 17083 | IL,Jersey County | 41005 | OR,Clackamas County |
| 17085 | IL,Jo Daviess County | 41007 | OR,Clatsop County |
| 17087 | IL,Johnson County | 41009 | OR,Columbia County |
| 17089 | IL,Kane County | 41011 | OR,Coos County |
| 17091 | IL,Kankakee County | 41013 | OR,Crook County |
| 17093 | IL,Kendall County | 41015 | OR,Curry County |
| 17095 | IL,Knox County | 41017 | OR,Deschutes County |
| 17097 | IL,Lake County | 41019 | OR,Douglas County |
| 17099 | IL,La Salle County | 41021 | OR,Gilliam County |
| 17101 | IL,Lawrence County | 41023 | OR,Grant County |
| 17103 | IL,Lee County | 41025 | OR,Harney County |
| 17105 | IL,Livingston County | 41027 | OR,Hood River County |
| 17107 | IL,Logan County | 41029 | OR,Jackson County |
| 17109 | IL,McDonough County | 41031 | OR,Jefferson County |

| | | | |
|---|---|---|---|
| 17111 | IL,McHenry County | 41033 | OR,Josephine County |
| 17113 | IL,McLean County | 41035 | OR,Klamath County |
| 17115 | IL,Macon County | 41037 | OR,Lake County |
| 17117 | IL,Macoupin County | 41039 | OR,Lane County |
| 17119 | IL,Madison County | 41041 | OR,Lincoln County |
| 17121 | IL,Marion County | 41043 | OR,Linn County |
| 17123 | IL,Marshall County | 41045 | OR,Malheur County |
| 17125 | IL,Mason County | 41047 | OR,Marion County |
| 17127 | IL,Massac County | 41049 | OR,Morrow County |
| 17129 | IL,Menard County | 41051 | OR,Multnomah County |
| 17131 | IL,Mercer County | 41053 | OR,Polk County |
| 17133 | IL,Monroe County | 41055 | OR,Sherman County |
| 17135 | IL,Montgomery County | 41057 | OR,Tillamook County |
| 17137 | IL,Morgan County | 41059 | OR,Umatilla County |
| 17139 | IL,Moultrie County | 41061 | OR,Union County |
| 17141 | IL,Ogle County | 41063 | OR,Wallowa County |
| 17143 | IL,Peoria County | 41065 | OR,Wasco County |
| 17145 | IL,Perry County | 41067 | OR,Washington County |
| 17147 | IL,Piatt County | 41069 | OR,Wheeler County |
| 17149 | IL,Pike County | 41071 | OR,Yamhill County |
| 17151 | IL,Pope County | 42001 | PA,Adams County |
| 17153 | IL,Pulaski County | 42003 | PA,Allegheny County |
| 17155 | IL,Putnam County | 42005 | PA,Armstrong County |
| 17157 | IL,Randolph County | 42007 | PA,Beaver County |
| 17159 | IL,Richland County | 42009 | PA,Bedford County |
| 17161 | IL,Rock Island County | 42011 | PA,Berks County |
| 17163 | IL,St. Clair County | 42013 | PA,Blair County |
| 17165 | IL,Saline County | 42015 | PA,Bradford County |
| 17167 | IL,Sangamon County | 42017 | PA,Bucks County |
| 17169 | IL,Schuyler County | 42019 | PA,Butler County |
| 17171 | IL,Scott County | 42021 | PA,Cambria County |
| 17173 | IL,Shelby County | 42023 | PA,Cameron County |
| 17175 | IL,Stark County | 42025 | PA,Carbon County |
| 17177 | IL,Stephenson County | 42027 | PA,Centre County |
| 17179 | IL,Tazewell County | 42029 | PA,Chester County |
| 17181 | IL,Union County | 42031 | PA,Clarion County |
| 17183 | IL,Vermilion County | 42033 | PA,Clearfield County |
| 17185 | IL,Wabash County | 42035 | PA,Clinton County |
| 17187 | IL,Warren County | 42037 | PA,Columbia County |
| 17189 | IL,Washington County | 42039 | PA,Crawford County |
| 17191 | IL,Wayne County | 42041 | PA,Cumberland County |
| 17193 | IL,White County | 42043 | PA,Dauphin County |
| 17195 | IL,Whiteside County | 42045 | PA,Delaware County |
| 17197 | IL,Will County | 42047 | PA,Elk County |
| 17199 | IL,Williamson County | 42049 | PA,Erie County |
| 17201 | IL,Winnebago County | 42051 | PA,Fayette County |
| 17203 | IL,Woodford County | 42053 | PA,Forest County |
| 18001 | IN,Adams County | 42055 | PA,Franklin County |

| | | | |
|---|---|---|---|
| 18003 | IN,Allen County | 42057 | PA,Fulton County |
| 18005 | IN,Bartholomew County | 42059 | PA,Greene County |
| 18007 | IN,Benton County | 42061 | PA,Huntingdon County |
| 18009 | IN,Blackford County | 42063 | PA,Indiana County |
| 18011 | IN,Boone County | 42065 | PA,Jefferson County |
| 18013 | IN,Brown County | 42067 | PA,Juniata County |
| 18015 | IN,Carroll County | 42069 | PA,Lackawanna County |
| 18017 | IN,Cass County | 42071 | PA,Lancaster County |
| 18019 | IN,Clark County | 42073 | PA,Lawrence County |
| 18021 | IN,Clay County | 42075 | PA,Lebanon County |
| 18023 | IN,Clinton County | 42077 | PA,Lehigh County |
| 18025 | IN,Crawford County | 42079 | PA,Luzerne County |
| 18027 | IN,Daviess County | 42081 | PA,Lycoming County |
| 18029 | IN,Dearborn County | 42083 | PA,Mc Kean County |
| 18031 | IN,Decatur County | 42085 | PA,Mercer County |
| 18033 | IN,De Kalb County | 42087 | PA,Mifflin County |
| 18035 | IN,Delaware County | 42089 | PA,Monroe County |
| 18037 | IN,Dubois County | 42091 | PA,Montgomery County |
| 18039 | IN,Elkhart County | 42093 | PA,Montour County |
| 18041 | IN,Fayette County | 42095 | PA,Northampton County |
| 18043 | IN,Floyd County | 42097 | PA,Northumberland County |
| 18045 | IN,Fountain County | 42099 | PA,Perry County |
| 18047 | IN,Franklin County | 42101 | PA,Philadelphia County |
| 18049 | IN,Fulton County | 42103 | PA,Pike County |
| 18051 | IN,Gibson County | 42105 | PA,Potter County |
| 18053 | IN,Grant County | 42107 | PA,Schuylkill County |
| 18055 | IN,Greene County | 42109 | PA,Snyder County |
| 18057 | IN,Hamilton County | 42111 | PA,Somerset County |
| 18059 | IN,Hancock County | 42113 | PA,Sullivan County |
| 18061 | IN,Harrison County | 42115 | PA,Susquehanna County |
| 18063 | IN,Hendricks County | 42117 | PA,Tioga County |
| 18065 | IN,Henry County | 42119 | PA,Union County |
| 18067 | IN,Howard County | 42121 | PA,Venango County |
| 18069 | IN,Huntington County | 42123 | PA,Warren County |
| 18071 | IN,Jackson County | 42125 | PA,Washington County |
| 18073 | IN,Jasper County | 42127 | PA,Wayne County |
| 18075 | IN,Jay County | 42129 | PA,Westmoreland County |
| 18077 | IN,Jefferson County | 42131 | PA,Wyoming County |
| 18079 | IN,Jennings County | 42133 | PA,York County |
| 18081 | IN,Johnson County | 44001 | RI,Bristol County |
| 18083 | IN,Knox County | 44003 | RI,Kent County |
| 18085 | IN,Kosciusko County | 44005 | RI,Newport County |
| 18087 | IN,Lagrange County | 44007 | RI,Providence County |
| 18089 | IN,Lake County | 44009 | RI,Washington County |
| 18091 | IN,La Porte County | 45001 | SC,Abbeville County |
| 18093 | IN,Lawrence County | 45003 | SC,Aiken County |
| 18095 | IN,Madison County | 45005 | SC,Allendale County |
| 18097 | IN,Marion County | 45007 | SC,Anderson County |

| | | | |
|---|---|---|---|
| 18099 | IN,Marshall County | 45009 | SC,Bamberg County |
| 18101 | IN,Martin County | 45011 | SC,Barnwell County |
| 18103 | IN,Miami County | 45013 | SC,Beaufort County |
| 18105 | IN,Monroe County | 45015 | SC,Berkeley County |
| 18107 | IN,Montgomery County | 45017 | SC,Calhoun County |
| 18109 | IN,Morgan County | 45019 | SC,Charleston County |
| 18111 | IN,Newton County | 45021 | SC,Cherokee County |
| 18113 | IN,Noble County | 45023 | SC,Chester County |
| 18115 | IN,Ohio County | 45025 | SC,Chesterfield County |
| 18117 | IN,Orange County | 45027 | SC,Clarendon County |
| 18119 | IN,Owen County | 45029 | SC,Colleton County |
| 18121 | IN,Parke County | 45031 | SC,Darlington County |
| 18123 | IN,Perry County | 45033 | SC,Dillon County |
| 18125 | IN,Pike County | 45035 | SC,Dorchester County |
| 18127 | IN,Porter County | 45037 | SC,Edgefield County |
| 18129 | IN,Posey County | 45039 | SC,Fairfield County |
| 18131 | IN,Pulaski County | 45041 | SC,Florence County |
| 18133 | IN,Putnam County | 45043 | SC,Georgetown County |
| 18135 | IN,Randolph County | 45045 | SC,Greenville County |
| 18137 | IN,Ripley County | 45047 | SC,Greenwood County |
| 18139 | IN,Rush County | 45049 | SC,Hampton County |
| 18141 | IN,St. Joseph County | 45051 | SC,Horry County |
| 18143 | IN,Scott County | 45053 | SC,Jasper County |
| 18145 | IN,Shelby County | 45055 | SC,Kershaw County |
| 18147 | IN,Spencer County | 45057 | SC,Lancaster County |
| 18149 | IN,Starke County | 45059 | SC,Laurens County |
| 18151 | IN,Steuben County | 45061 | SC,Lee County |
| 18153 | IN,Sullivan County | 45063 | SC,Lexington County |
| 18155 | IN,Switzerland County | 45065 | SC,McCormick County |
| 18157 | IN,Tippecanoe County | 45067 | SC,Marion County |
| 18159 | IN,Tipton County | 45069 | SC,Marlboro County |
| 18161 | IN,Union County | 45071 | SC,Newberry County |
| 18163 | IN,Vanderburgh County | 45073 | SC,Oconee County |
| 18165 | IN,Vermillion County | 45075 | SC,Orangeburg County |
| 18167 | IN,Vigo County | 45077 | SC,Pickens County |
| 18169 | IN,Wabash County | 45079 | SC,Richland County |
| 18171 | IN,Warren County | 45081 | SC,Saluda County |
| 18173 | IN,Warrick County | 45083 | SC,Spartanburg County |
| 18175 | IN,Washington County | 45085 | SC,Sumter County |
| 18177 | IN,Wayne County | 45087 | SC,Union County |
| 18179 | IN,Wells County | 45089 | SC,Williamsburg County |
| 18181 | IN,White County | 45091 | SC,York County |
| 18183 | IN,Whitley County | 46003 | SD,Aurora County |
| 19001 | IA,Adair County | 46005 | SD,Beadle County |
| 19003 | IA,Adams County | 46007 | SD,Bennett County |
| 19005 | IA,Allamakee County | 46009 | SD,Bon Homme County |
| 19007 | IA,Appanoose County | 46011 | SD,Brookings County |
| 19009 | IA,Audubon County | 46013 | SD,Brown County |

| | | | |
|---|---|---|---|
| 19011 | IA,Benton County | 46015 | SD,Brule County |
| 19013 | IA,Black Hawk County | 46017 | SD,Buffalo County |
| 19015 | IA,Boone County | 46019 | SD,Butte County |
| 19017 | IA,Bremer County | 46021 | SD,Campbell County |
| 19019 | IA,Buchanan County | 46023 | SD,Charles Mix County |
| 19021 | IA,Buena Vista County | 46025 | SD,Clark County |
| 19023 | IA,Butler County | 46027 | SD,Clay County |
| 19025 | IA,Calhoun County | 46029 | SD,Codington County |
| 19027 | IA,Carroll County | 46031 | SD,Corson County |
| 19029 | IA,Cass County | 46033 | SD,Custer County |
| 19031 | IA,Cedar County | 46035 | SD,Davison County |
| 19033 | IA,Cerro Gordo County | 46037 | SD,Day County |
| 19035 | IA,Cherokee County | 46039 | SD,Deuel County |
| 19037 | IA,Chickasaw County | 46041 | SD,Dewey County |
| 19039 | IA,Clarke County | 46043 | SD,Douglas County |
| 19041 | IA,Clay County | 46045 | SD,Edmunds County |
| 19043 | IA,Clayton County | 46047 | SD,Fall River County |
| 19045 | IA,Clinton County | 46049 | SD,Faulk County |
| 19047 | IA,Crawford County | 46051 | SD,Grant County |
| 19049 | IA,Dallas County | 46053 | SD,Gregory County |
| 19051 | IA,Davis County | 46055 | SD,Haakon County |
| 19053 | IA,Decatur County | 46057 | SD,Hamlin County |
| 19055 | IA,Delaware County | 46059 | SD,Hand County |
| 19057 | IA,Des Moines County | 46061 | SD,Hanson County |
| 19059 | IA,Dickinson County | 46063 | SD,Harding County |
| 19061 | IA,Dubuque County | 46065 | SD,Hughes County |
| 19063 | IA,Emmet County | 46067 | SD,Hutchinson County |
| 19065 | IA,Fayette County | 46069 | SD,Hyde County |
| 19067 | IA,Floyd County | 46071 | SD,Jackson County |
| 19069 | IA,Franklin County | 46073 | SD,Jerauld County |
| 19071 | IA,Fremont County | 46075 | SD,Jones County |
| 19073 | IA,Greene County | 46077 | SD,Kingsbury County |
| 19075 | IA,Grundy County | 46079 | SD,Lake County |
| 19077 | IA,Guthrie County | 46081 | SD,Lawrence County |
| 19079 | IA,Hamilton County | 46083 | SD,Lincoln County |
| 19081 | IA,Hancock County | 46085 | SD,Lyman County |
| 19083 | IA,Hardin County | 46087 | SD,McCook County |
| 19085 | IA,Harrison County | 46089 | SD,McPherson County |
| 19087 | IA,Henry County | 46091 | SD,Marshall County |
| 19089 | IA,Howard County | 46093 | SD,Meade County |
| 19091 | IA,Humboldt County | 46095 | SD,Mellette County |
| 19093 | IA,Ida County | 46097 | SD,Miner County |
| 19095 | IA,Iowa County | 46099 | SD,Minnehaha County |
| 19097 | IA,Jackson County | 46101 | SD,Moody County |
| 19099 | IA,Jasper County | 46103 | SD,Pennington County |
| 19101 | IA,Jefferson County | 46105 | SD,Perkins County |
| 19103 | IA,Johnson County | 46107 | SD,Potter County |
| 19105 | IA,Jones County | 46109 | SD,Roberts County |

| | | | |
|---|---|---|---|
| 19107 | IA,Keokuk County | 46111 | SD,Sanborn County |
| 19109 | IA,Kossuth County | 46113 | SD,Shannon County |
| 19111 | IA,Lee County | 46115 | SD,Spink County |
| 19113 | IA,Linn County | 46117 | SD,Stanley County |
| 19115 | IA,Louisa County | 46119 | SD,Sully County |
| 19117 | IA,Lucas County | 46121 | SD,Todd County |
| 19119 | IA,Lyon County | 46123 | SD,Tripp County |
| 19121 | IA,Madison County | 46125 | SD,Turner County |
| 19123 | IA,Mahaska County | 46127 | SD,Union County |
| 19125 | IA,Marion County | 46129 | SD,Walworth County |
| 19127 | IA,Marshall County | 46135 | SD,Yankton County |
| 19129 | IA,Mills County | 46137 | SD,Ziebach County |
| 19131 | IA,Mitchell County | 46666 | SD,Black Hills National Forest |
| 19133 | IA,Monona County | 47001 | TN,Anderson County |
| 19135 | IA,Monroe County | 47003 | TN,Bedford County |
| 19137 | IA,Montgomery County | 47005 | TN,Benton County |
| 19139 | IA,Muscatine County | 47007 | TN,Bledsoe County |
| 19141 | IA,O'Brien County | 47009 | TN,Blount County |
| 19143 | IA,Osceola County | 47011 | TN,Bradley County |
| 19145 | IA,Page County | 47013 | TN,Campbell County |
| 19147 | IA,Palo Alto County | 47015 | TN,Cannon County |
| 19149 | IA,Plymouth County | 47017 | TN,Carroll County |
| 19151 | IA,Pocahontas County | 47019 | TN,Carter County |
| 19153 | IA,Polk County | 47021 | TN,Cheatham County |
| 19155 | IA,Pottawattamie County | 47023 | TN,Chester County |
| 19157 | IA,Poweshiek County | 47025 | TN,Claiborne County |
| 19159 | IA,Ringgold County | 47027 | TN,Clay County |
| 19161 | IA,Sac County | 47029 | TN,Cocke County |
| 19163 | IA,Scott County | 47031 | TN,Coffee County |
| 19165 | IA,Shelby County | 47033 | TN,Crockett County |
| 19167 | IA,Sioux County | 47035 | TN,Cumberland County |
| 19169 | IA,Story County | 47037 | TN,Davidson County |
| 19171 | IA,Tama County | 47039 | TN,Decatur County |
| 19173 | IA,Taylor County | 47041 | TN,DeKalb County |
| 19175 | IA,Union County | 47043 | TN,Dickson County |
| 19177 | IA,Van Buren County | 47045 | TN,Dyer County |
| 19179 | IA,Wapello County | 47047 | TN,Fayette County |
| 19181 | IA,Warren County | 47049 | TN,Fentress County |
| 19183 | IA,Washington County | 47051 | TN,Franklin County |
| 19185 | IA,Wayne County | 47053 | TN,Gibson County |
| 19187 | IA,Webster County | 47055 | TN,Giles County |
| 19189 | IA,Winnebago County | 47057 | TN,Grainger County |
| 19191 | IA,Winneshiek County | 47059 | TN,Greene County |
| 19193 | IA,Woodbury County | 47061 | TN,Grundy County |
| 19195 | IA,Worth County | 47063 | TN,Hamblen County |
| 19197 | IA,Wright County | 47065 | TN,Hamilton County |
| 20001 | KS,Allen County | 47067 | TN,Hancock County |
| 20003 | KS,Anderson County | 47069 | TN,Hardeman County |

| | | | |
|---|---|---|---|
| 20005 | KS,Atchison County | 47071 | TN,Hardin County |
| 20007 | KS,Barber County | 47073 | TN,Hawkins County |
| 20009 | KS,Barton County | 47075 | TN,Haywood County |
| 20011 | KS,Bourbon County | 47077 | TN,Henderson County |
| 20013 | KS,Brown County | 47079 | TN,Henry County |
| 20015 | KS,Butler County | 47081 | TN,Hickman County |
| 20017 | KS,Chase County | 47083 | TN,Houston County |
| 20019 | KS,Chautauqua County | 47085 | TN,Humphreys County |
| 20021 | KS,Cherokee County | 47087 | TN,Jackson County |
| 20023 | KS,Cheyenne County | 47089 | TN,Jefferson County |
| 20025 | KS,Clark County | 47091 | TN,Johnson County |
| 20027 | KS,Clay County | 47093 | TN,Knox County |
| 20029 | KS,Cloud County | 47095 | TN,Lake County |
| 20031 | KS,Coffey County | 47097 | TN,Lauderdale County |
| 20033 | KS,Comanche County | 47099 | TN,Lawrence County |
| 20035 | KS,Cowley County | 47101 | TN,Lewis County |
| 20037 | KS,Crawford County | 47103 | TN,Lincoln County |
| 20039 | KS,Decatur County | 47105 | TN,Loudon County |
| 20041 | KS,Dickinson County | 47107 | TN,McMinn County |
| 20043 | KS,Doniphan County | 47109 | TN,McNairy County |
| 20045 | KS,Douglas County | 47111 | TN,Macon County |
| 20047 | KS,Edwards County | 47113 | TN,Madison County |
| 20049 | KS,Elk County | 47115 | TN,Marion County |
| 20051 | KS,Ellis County | 47117 | TN,Marshall County |
| 20053 | KS,Ellsworth County | 47119 | TN,Maury County |
| 20055 | KS,Finney County | 47121 | TN,Meigs County |
| 20057 | KS,Ford County | 47123 | TN,Monroe County |
| 20059 | KS,Franklin County | 47125 | TN,Montgomery County |
| 20061 | KS,Geary County | 47127 | TN,Moore County |
| 20063 | KS,Gove County | 47129 | TN,Morgan County |
| 20065 | KS,Graham County | 47131 | TN,Obion County |
| 20067 | KS,Grant County | 47133 | TN,Overton County |
| 20069 | KS,Gray County | 47135 | TN,Perry County |
| 20071 | KS,Greeley County | 47137 | TN,Pickett County |
| 20073 | KS,Greenwood County | 47139 | TN,Polk County |
| 20075 | KS,Hamilton County | 47141 | TN,Putnam County |
| 20077 | KS,Harper County | 47143 | TN,Rhea County |
| 20079 | KS,Harvey County | 47145 | TN,Roane County |
| 20081 | KS,Haskell County | 47147 | TN,Robertson County |
| 20083 | KS,Hodgeman County | 47149 | TN,Rutherford County |
| 20085 | KS,Jackson County | 47151 | TN,Scott County |
| 20087 | KS,Jefferson County | 47153 | TN,Sequatchie County |
| 20089 | KS,Jewell County | 47155 | TN,Sevier County |
| 20091 | KS,Johnson County | 47157 | TN,Shelby County |
| 20093 | KS,Kearny County | 47159 | TN,Smith County |
| 20095 | KS,Kingman County | 47161 | TN,Stewart County |
| 20097 | KS,Kiowa County | 47163 | TN,Sullivan County |
| 20099 | KS,Labette County | 47165 | TN,Sumner County |

| | | | |
|---|---|---|---|
| 20101 | KS,Lane County | 47167 | TN,Tipton County |
| 20103 | KS,Leavenworth County | 47169 | TN,Trousdale County |
| 20105 | KS,Lincoln County | 47171 | TN,Unicoi County |
| 20107 | KS,Linn County | 47173 | TN,Union County |
| 20109 | KS,Logan County | 47175 | TN,Van Buren County |
| 20111 | KS,Lyon County | 47177 | TN,Warren County |
| 20113 | KS,McPherson County | 47179 | TN,Washington County |
| 20115 | KS,Marion County | 47181 | TN,Wayne County |
| 20117 | KS,Marshall County | 47183 | TN,Weakley County |
| 20119 | KS,Meade County | 47185 | TN,White County |
| 20121 | KS,Miami County | 47187 | TN,Williamson County |
| 20123 | KS,Mitchell County | 47189 | TN,Wilson County |
| 20125 | KS,Montgomery County | 48001 | TX,Anderson County |
| 20127 | KS,Morris County | 48003 | TX,Andrews County |
| 20129 | KS,Morton County | 48005 | TX,Angelina County |
| 20131 | KS,Nemaha County | 48007 | TX,Aransas County |
| 20133 | KS,Neosho County | 48009 | TX,Archer County |
| 20135 | KS,Ness County | 48011 | TX,Armstrong County |
| 20137 | KS,Norton County | 48013 | TX,Atascosa County |
| 20139 | KS,Osage County | 48015 | TX,Austin County |
| 20141 | KS,Osborne County | 48017 | TX,Bailey County |
| 20143 | KS,Ottawa County | 48019 | TX,Bandera County |
| 20145 | KS,Pawnee County | 48021 | TX,Bastrop County |
| 20147 | KS,Phillips County | 48023 | TX,Baylor County |
| 20149 | KS,Pottawatomie County | 48025 | TX,Bee County |
| 20151 | KS,Pratt County | 48027 | TX,Bell County |
| 20153 | KS,Rawlins County | 48029 | TX,Bexar County |
| 20155 | KS,Reno County | 48031 | TX,Blanco County |
| 20157 | KS,Republic County | 48033 | TX,Borden County |
| 20159 | KS,Rice County | 48035 | TX,Bosque County |
| 20161 | KS,Riley County | 48037 | TX,Bowie County |
| 20163 | KS,Rooks County | 48039 | TX,Brazoria County |
| 20165 | KS,Rush County | 48041 | TX,Brazos County |
| 20167 | KS,Russell County | 48043 | TX,Brewster County |
| 20169 | KS,Saline County | 48045 | TX,Briscoe County |
| 20171 | KS,Scott County | 48047 | TX,Brooks County |
| 20173 | KS,Sedgwick County | 48049 | TX,Brown County |
| 20175 | KS,Seward County | 48051 | TX,Burleson County |
| 20177 | KS,Shawnee County | 48053 | TX,Burnet County |
| 20179 | KS,Sheridan County | 48055 | TX,Caldwell County |
| 20181 | KS,Sherman County | 48057 | TX,Calhoun County |
| 20183 | KS,Smith County | 48059 | TX,Callahan County |
| 20185 | KS,Stafford County | 48061 | TX,Cameron County |
| 20187 | KS,Stanton County | 48063 | TX,Camp County |
| 20189 | KS,Stevens County | 48065 | TX,Carson County |
| 20191 | KS,Sumner County | 48067 | TX,Cass County |
| 20193 | KS,Thomas County | 48069 | TX,Castro County |
| 20195 | KS,Trego County | 48071 | TX,Chambers County |

| | | | |
|---|---|---|---|
| 20197 | KS,Wabaunsee County | 48073 | TX,Cherokee County |
| 20199 | KS,Wallace County | 48075 | TX,Childress County |
| 20201 | KS,Washington County | 48077 | TX,Clay County |
| 20203 | KS,Wichita County | 48079 | TX,Cochran County |
| 20205 | KS,Wilson County | 48081 | TX,Coke County |
| 20207 | KS,Woodson County | 48083 | TX,Coleman County |
| 20209 | KS,Wyandotte County | 48085 | TX,Collin County |
| 21001 | KY,Adair County | 48087 | TX,Collingsworth County |
| 21003 | KY,Allen County | 48089 | TX,Colorado County |
| 21005 | KY,Anderson County | 48091 | TX,Comal County |
| 21007 | KY,Ballard County | 48093 | TX,Comanche County |
| 21009 | KY,Barren County | 48095 | TX,Concho County |
| 21011 | KY,Bath County | 48097 | TX,Cooke County |
| 21013 | KY,Bell County | 48099 | TX,Coryell County |
| 21015 | KY,Boone County | 48101 | TX,Cottle County |
| 21017 | KY,Bourbon County | 48103 | TX,Crane County |
| 21019 | KY,Boyd County | 48105 | TX,Crockett County |
| 21021 | KY,Boyle County | 48107 | TX,Crosby County |
| 21023 | KY,Bracken County | 48109 | TX,Culberson County |
| 21025 | KY,Breathitt County | 48111 | TX,Dallam County |
| 21027 | KY,Breckinridge County | 48113 | TX,Dallas County |
| 21029 | KY,Bullitt County | 48115 | TX,Dawson County |
| 21031 | KY,Butler County | 48117 | TX,Deaf Smith County |
| 21033 | KY,Caldwell County | 48119 | TX,Delta County |
| 21035 | KY,Calloway County | 48121 | TX,Denton County |
| 21037 | KY,Campbell County | 48123 | TX,DeWitt County |
| 21039 | KY,Carlisle County | 48125 | TX,Dickens County |
| 21041 | KY,Carroll County | 48127 | TX,Dimmit County |
| 21043 | KY,Carter County | 48129 | TX,Donley County |
| 21045 | KY,Casey County | 48131 | TX,Duval County |
| 21047 | KY,Christian County | 48133 | TX,Eastland County |
| 21049 | KY,Clark County | 48135 | TX,Ector County |
| 21051 | KY,Clay County | 48137 | TX,Edwards County |
| 21053 | KY,Clinton County | 48139 | TX,Ellis County |
| 21055 | KY,Crittenden County | 48141 | TX,El Paso County |
| 21057 | KY,Cumberland County | 48143 | TX,Erath County |
| 21059 | KY,Daviess County | 48145 | TX,Falls County |
| 21061 | KY,Edmonson County | 48147 | TX,Fannin County |
| 21063 | KY,Elliott County | 48149 | TX,Fayette County |
| 21065 | KY,Estill County | 48151 | TX,Fisher County |
| 21067 | KY,Fayette County | 48153 | TX,Floyd County |
| 21069 | KY,Fleming County | 48155 | TX,Foard County |
| 21071 | KY,Floyd County | 48157 | TX,Fort Bend County |
| 21073 | KY,Franklin County | 48159 | TX,Franklin County |
| 21075 | KY,Fulton County | 48161 | TX,Freestone County |
| 21077 | KY,Gallatin County | 48163 | TX,Frio County |
| 21079 | KY,Garrard County | 48165 | TX,Gaines County |
| 21081 | KY,Grant County | 48167 | TX,Galveston County |

| | | | |
|---|---|---|---|
| 21083 | KY,Graves County | 48169 | TX,Garza County |
| 21085 | KY,Grayson County | 48171 | TX,Gillespie County |
| 21087 | KY,Green County | 48173 | TX,Glasscock County |
| 21089 | KY,Greenup County | 48175 | TX,Goliad County |
| 21091 | KY,Hancock County | 48177 | TX,Gonzales County |
| 21093 | KY,Hardin County | 48179 | TX,Gray County |
| 21095 | KY,Harlan County | 48181 | TX,Grayson County |
| 21097 | KY,Harrison County | 48183 | TX,Gregg County |
| 21099 | KY,Hart County | 48185 | TX,Grimes County |
| 21101 | KY,Henderson County | 48187 | TX,Guadalupe County |
| 21103 | KY,Henry County | 48189 | TX,Hale County |
| 21105 | KY,Hickman County | 48191 | TX,Hall County |
| 21107 | KY,Hopkins County | 48193 | TX,Hamilton County |
| 21109 | KY,Jackson County | 48195 | TX,Hansford County |
| 21111 | KY,Jefferson County | 48197 | TX,Hardeman County |
| 21113 | KY,Jessamine County | 48199 | TX,Hardin County |
| 21115 | KY,Johnson County | 48201 | TX,Harris County |
| 21117 | KY,Kenton County | 48203 | TX,Harrison County |
| 21119 | KY,Knott County | 48205 | TX,Hartley County |
| 21121 | KY,Knox County | 48207 | TX,Haskell County |
| 21123 | KY,Larue County | 48209 | TX,Hays County |
| 21125 | KY,Laurel County | 48211 | TX,Hemphill County |
| 21127 | KY,Lawrence County | 48213 | TX,Henderson County |
| 21129 | KY,Lee County | 48215 | TX,Hidalgo County |
| 21131 | KY,Leslie County | 48217 | TX,Hill County |
| 21133 | KY,Letcher County | 48219 | TX,Hockley County |
| 21135 | KY,Lewis County | 48221 | TX,Hood County |
| 21137 | KY,Lincoln County | 48223 | TX,Hopkins County |
| 21139 | KY,Livingston County | 48225 | TX,Houston County |
| 21141 | KY,Logan County | 48227 | TX,Howard County |
| 21143 | KY,Lyon County | 48229 | TX,Hudspeth County |
| 21145 | KY,McCracken County | 48231 | TX,Hunt County |
| 21147 | KY,McCreary County | 48233 | TX,Hutchinson County |
| 21149 | KY,McLean County | 48235 | TX,Irion County |
| 21151 | KY,Madison County | 48237 | TX,Jack County |
| 21153 | KY,Magoffin County | 48239 | TX,Jackson County |
| 21155 | KY,Marion County | 48241 | TX,Jasper County |
| 21157 | KY,Marshall County | 48243 | TX,Jeff Davis County |
| 21159 | KY,Martin County | 48245 | TX,Jefferson County |
| 21161 | KY,Mason County | 48247 | TX,Jim Hogg County |
| 21163 | KY,Meade County | 48249 | TX,Jim Wells County |
| 21165 | KY,Menifee County | 48251 | TX,Johnson County |
| 21167 | KY,Mercer County | 48253 | TX,Jones County |
| 21169 | KY,Metcalfe County | 48255 | TX,Karnes County |
| 21171 | KY,Monroe County | 48257 | TX,Kaufman County |
| 21173 | KY,Montgomery County | 48259 | TX,Kendall County |
| 21175 | KY,Morgan County | 48261 | TX,Kenedy County |
| 21177 | KY,Muhlenberg County | 48263 | TX,Kent County |

| | | | |
|---|---|---|---|
| 21179 | KY,Nelson County | 48265 | TX,Kerr County |
| 21181 | KY,Nicholas County | 48267 | TX,Kimble County |
| 21183 | KY,Ohio County | 48269 | TX,King County |
| 21185 | KY,Oldham County | 48271 | TX,Kinney County |
| 21187 | KY,Owen County | 48273 | TX,Kleberg County |
| 21189 | KY,Owsley County | 48275 | TX,Knox County |
| 21191 | KY,Pendleton County | 48277 | TX,Lamar County |
| 21193 | KY,Perry County | 48279 | TX,Lamb County |
| 21195 | KY,Pike County | 48281 | TX,Lampasas County |
| 21197 | KY,Powell County | 48283 | TX,La Salle County |
| 21199 | KY,Pulaski County | 48285 | TX,Lavaca County |
| 21201 | KY,Robertson County | 48287 | TX,Lee County |
| 21203 | KY,Rockcastle County | 48289 | TX,Leon County |
| 21205 | KY,Rowan County | 48291 | TX,Liberty County |
| 21207 | KY,Russell County | 48293 | TX,Limestone County |
| 21209 | KY,Scott County | 48295 | TX,Lipscomb County |
| 21211 | KY,Shelby County | 48297 | TX,Live Oak County |
| 21213 | KY,Simpson County | 48299 | TX,Llano County |
| 21215 | KY,Spencer County | 48301 | TX,Loving County |
| 21217 | KY,Taylor County | 48303 | TX,Lubbock County |
| 21219 | KY,Todd County | 48305 | TX,Lynn County |
| 21221 | KY,Trigg County | 48307 | TX,McCulloch County |
| 21223 | KY,Trimble County | 48309 | TX,McLennan County |
| 21225 | KY,Union County | 48311 | TX,McMullen County |
| 21227 | KY,Warren County | 48313 | TX,Madison County |
| 21229 | KY,Washington County | 48315 | TX,Marion County |
| 21231 | KY,Wayne County | 48317 | TX,Martin County |
| 21233 | KY,Webster County | 48319 | TX,Mason County |
| 21235 | KY,Whitley County | 48321 | TX,Matagorda County |
| 21237 | KY,Wolfe County | 48323 | TX,Maverick County |
| 21239 | KY,Woodford County | 48325 | TX,Medina County |
| 22001 | LA,Acadia Parish | 48327 | TX,Menard County |
| 22003 | LA,Allen Parish | 48329 | TX,Midland County |
| 22005 | LA,Ascension Parish | 48331 | TX,Milam County |
| 22007 | LA,Assumption Parish | 48333 | TX,Mills County |
| 22009 | LA,Avoyelles Parish | 48335 | TX,Mitchell County |
| 22011 | LA,Beauregard Parish | 48337 | TX,Montague County |
| 22013 | LA,Bienville Parish | 48339 | TX,Montgomery County |
| 22015 | LA,Bossier Parish | 48341 | TX,Moore County |
| 22017 | LA,Caddo Parish | 48343 | TX,Morris County |
| 22019 | LA,Calcasieu Parish | 48345 | TX,Motley County |
| 22021 | LA,Caldwell Parish | 48347 | TX,Nacogdoches County |
| 22023 | LA,Cameron Parish | 48349 | TX,Navarro County |
| 22025 | LA,Catahoula Parish | 48351 | TX,Newton County |
| 22027 | LA,Claiborne Parish | 48353 | TX,Nolan County |
| 22029 | LA,Concordia Parish | 48355 | TX,Nueces County |
| 22031 | LA,De Soto Parish | 48357 | TX,Ochiltree County |
| 22033 | LA,East Baton Rouge Parish | 48359 | TX,Oldham County |

| | | | |
|---|---|---|---|
| 22035 | LA,East Carroll Parish | 48361 | TX,Orange County |
| 22037 | LA,East Feliciana Parish | 48363 | TX,Palo Pinto County |
| 22039 | LA,Evangeline Parish | 48365 | TX,Panola County |
| 22041 | LA,Franklin Parish | 48367 | TX,Parker County |
| 22043 | LA,Grant Parish | 48369 | TX,Parmer County |
| 22045 | LA,Iberia Parish | 48371 | TX,Pecos County |
| 22047 | LA,Iberville Parish | 48373 | TX,Polk County |
| 22049 | LA,Jackson Parish | 48375 | TX,Potter County |
| 22051 | LA,Jefferson Parish | 48377 | TX,Presidio County |
| 22053 | LA,Jefferson Davis Parish | 48379 | TX,Rains County |
| 22055 | LA,Lafayette Parish | 48381 | TX,Randall County |
| 22057 | LA,Lafourche Parish | 48383 | TX,Reagan County |
| 22059 | LA,La Salle Parish | 48385 | TX,Real County |
| 22061 | LA,Lincoln Parish | 48387 | TX,Red River County |
| 22063 | LA,Livingston Parish | 48389 | TX,Reeves County |
| 22065 | LA,Madison Parish | 48391 | TX,Refugio County |
| 22067 | LA,Morehouse Parish | 48393 | TX,Roberts County |
| 22069 | LA,Natchitoches Parish | 48395 | TX,Robertson County |
| 22071 | LA,Orleans Parish | 48397 | TX,Rockwall County |
| 22073 | LA,Ouachita Parish | 48399 | TX,Runnels County |
| 22075 | LA,Plaquemines Parish | 48401 | TX,Rusk County |
| 22077 | LA,Pointe Coupee Parish | 48403 | TX,Sabine County |
| 22079 | LA,Rapides Parish | 48405 | TX,San Augustine County |
| 22081 | LA,Red River Parish | 48407 | TX,San Jacinto County |
| 22083 | LA,Richland Parish | 48409 | TX,San Patricio County |
| 22085 | LA,Sabine Parish | 48411 | TX,San Saba County |
| 22087 | LA,St. Bernard Parish | 48413 | TX,Schleicher County |
| 22089 | LA,St. Charles Parish | 48415 | TX,Scurry County |
| 22091 | LA,St. Helena Parish | 48417 | TX,Shackelford County |
| 22093 | LA,St. James Parish | 48419 | TX,Shelby County |
| 22095 | LA,St. John the Baptist Parish | 48421 | TX,Sherman County |
| 22097 | LA,St. Landry Parish | 48423 | TX,Smith County |
| 22099 | LA,St. Martin Parish | 48425 | TX,Somervell County |
| 22101 | LA,St. Mary Parish | 48427 | TX,Starr County |
| 22103 | LA,St. Tammany Parish | 48429 | TX,Stephens County |
| 22105 | LA,Tangipahoa Parish | 48431 | TX,Sterling County |
| 22107 | LA,Tensas Parish | 48433 | TX,Stonewall County |
| 22109 | LA,Terrebonne Parish | 48435 | TX,Sutton County |
| 22111 | LA,Union Parish | 48437 | TX,Swisher County |
| 22113 | LA,Vermilion Parish | 48439 | TX,Tarrant County |
| 22115 | LA,Vernon Parish | 48441 | TX,Taylor County |
| 22117 | LA,Washington Parish | 48443 | TX,Terrell County |
| 22119 | LA,Webster Parish | 48445 | TX,Terry County |
| 22121 | LA,West Baton Rouge Parish | 48447 | TX,Throckmorton County |
| 22123 | LA,West Carroll Parish | 48449 | TX,Titus County |
| 22125 | LA,West Feliciana Parish | 48451 | TX,Tom Green County |
| 22127 | LA,Winn Parish | 48453 | TX,Travis County |
| 23001 | ME,Androscoggin County | 48455 | TX,Trinity County |

| | | | |
|---|---|---|---|
| 23003 | ME,Aroostook County | 48457 | TX,Tyler County |
| 23005 | ME,Cumberland County | 48459 | TX,Upshur County |
| 23007 | ME,Franklin County | 48461 | TX,Upton County |
| 23009 | ME,Hancock County | 48463 | TX,Uvalde County |
| 23011 | ME,Kennebec County | 48465 | TX,Val Verde County |
| 23013 | ME,Knox County | 48467 | TX,Van Zandt County |
| 23015 | ME,Lincoln County | 48469 | TX,Victoria County |
| 23017 | ME,Oxford County | 48471 | TX,Walker County |
| 23019 | ME,Penobscot County | 48473 | TX,Waller County |
| 23021 | ME,Piscataquis County | 48475 | TX,Ward County |
| 23023 | ME,Sagadahoc County | 48477 | TX,Washington County |
| 23025 | ME,Somerset County | 48479 | TX,Webb County |
| 23027 | ME,Waldo County | 48481 | TX,Wharton County |
| 23029 | ME,Washington County | 48483 | TX,Wheeler County |
| 23031 | ME,York County | 48485 | TX,Wichita County |
| 24001 | MD,Allegany County | 48487 | TX,Wilbarger County |
| 24003 | MD,Anne Arundel County | 48489 | TX,Willacy County |
| 24005 | MD,Baltimore County | 48491 | TX,Williamson County |
| 24009 | MD,Calvert County | 48493 | TX,Wilson County |
| 24011 | MD,Caroline County | 48495 | TX,Winkler County |
| 24013 | MD,Carroll County | 48497 | TX,Wise County |
| 24015 | MD,Cecil County | 48499 | TX,Wood County |
| 24017 | MD,Charles County | 48501 | TX,Yoakum County |
| 24019 | MD,Dorchester County | 48503 | TX,Young County |
| 24021 | MD,Frederick County | 48505 | TX,Zapata County |
| 24023 | MD,Garrett County | 48507 | TX,Zavala County |
| 24025 | MD,Harford County | 49001 | UT,Beaver County |
| 24027 | MD,Howard County | 49003 | UT,Box Elder County |
| 24029 | MD,Kent County | 49005 | UT,Cache County |
| 24031 | MD,Montgomery County | 49007 | UT,Carbon County |
| 24033 | MD,Prince George's County | 49009 | UT,Daggett County |
| 24035 | MD,Queen Anne's County | 49011 | UT,Davis County |
| 24037 | MD,St. Mary's County | 49013 | UT,Duchesne County |
| 24039 | MD,Somerset County | 49015 | UT,Emery County |
| 24041 | MD,Talbot County | 49017 | UT,Garfield County |
| 24043 | MD,Washington County | 49019 | UT,Grand County |
| 24045 | MD,Wicomico County | 49021 | UT,Iron County |
| 24047 | MD,Worcester County | 49023 | UT,Juab County |
| 24510 | MD,Baltimore City | 49025 | UT,Kane County |
| 25001 | MA,Barnstable County | 49027 | UT,Millard County |
| 25003 | MA,Berkshire County | 49029 | UT,Morgan County |
| 25005 | MA,Bristol County | 49031 | UT,Piute County |
| 25007 | MA,Dukes County | 49033 | UT,Rich County |
| 25009 | MA,Essex County | 49035 | UT,Salt Lake County |
| 25011 | MA,Franklin County | 49037 | UT,San Juan County |
| 25013 | MA,Hampden County | 49039 | UT,Sanpete County |
| 25015 | MA,Hampshire County | 49041 | UT,Sevier County |
| 25017 | MA,Middlesex County | 49043 | UT,Summit County |

| | | | |
|---|---|---|---|
| 25019 | MA,Nantucket County | 49045 | UT,Tooele County |
| 25021 | MA,Norfolk County | 49047 | UT,Uintah County |
| 25023 | MA,Plymouth County | 49049 | UT,Utah County |
| 25025 | MA,Suffolk County | 49051 | UT,Wasatch County |
| 25027 | MA,Worcester County | 49053 | UT,Washington County |
| 26001 | MI,Alcona County | 49055 | UT,Wayne County |
| 26003 | MI,Alger County | 49057 | UT,Weber County |
| 26005 | MI,Allegan County | 50001 | VT,Addison County |
| 26007 | MI,Alpena County | 50003 | VT,Bennington County |
| 26009 | MI,Antrim County | 50005 | VT,Caledonia County |
| 26011 | MI,Arenac County | 50007 | VT,Chittenden County |
| 26013 | MI,Baraga County | 50009 | VT,Essex County |
| 26015 | MI,Barry County | 50011 | VT,Franklin County |
| 26017 | MI,Bay County | 50013 | VT,Grand Isle County |
| 26019 | MI,Benzie County | 50015 | VT,Lamoille County |
| 26021 | MI,Berrien County | 50017 | VT,Orange County |
| 26023 | MI,Branch County | 50019 | VT,Orleans County |
| 26025 | MI,Calhoun County | 50021 | VT,Rutland County |
| 26027 | MI,Cass County | 50023 | VT,Washington County |
| 26029 | MI,Charlevoix County | 50025 | VT,Windham County |
| 26031 | MI,Cheboygan County | 50027 | VT,Windsor County |
| 26033 | MI,Chippewa County | 51001 | VA,Accomack County |
| 26035 | MI,Clare County | 51003 | VA,Albemarle County |
| 26037 | MI,Clinton County | 51005 | VA,Alleghany County |
| 26039 | MI,Crawford County | 51007 | VA,Amelia County |
| 26041 | MI,Delta County | 51009 | VA,Amherst County |
| 26043 | MI,Dickinson County | 51011 | VA,Appomattox County |
| 26045 | MI,Eaton County | 51013 | VA,Arlington County |
| 26047 | MI,Emmet County | 51015 | VA,Augusta County |
| 26049 | MI,Genesee County | 51017 | VA,Bath County |
| 26051 | MI,Gladwin County | 51019 | VA,Bedford County |
| 26053 | MI,Gogebic County | 51021 | VA,Bland County |
| 26055 | MI,Grand Traverse County | 51023 | VA,Botetourt County |
| 26057 | MI,Gratiot County | 51025 | VA,Brunswick County |
| 26059 | MI,Hillsdale County | 51027 | VA,Buchanan County |
| 26061 | MI,Houghton County | 51029 | VA,Buckingham County |
| 26063 | MI,Huron County | 51031 | VA,Campbell County |
| 26065 | MI,Ingham County | 51033 | VA,Caroline County |
| 26067 | MI,Ionia County | 51035 | VA,Carroll County |
| 26069 | MI,Iosco County | 51036 | VA,Charles City County |
| 26071 | MI,Iron County | 51037 | VA,Charlotte County |
| 26073 | MI,Isabella County | 51041 | VA,Chesterfield County |
| 26075 | MI,Jackson County | 51043 | VA,Clarke County |
| 26077 | MI,Kalamazoo County | 51045 | VA,Craig County |
| 26079 | MI,Kalkaska County | 51047 | VA,Culpeper County |
| 26081 | MI,Kent County | 51049 | VA,Cumberland County |
| 26083 | MI,Keweenaw County | 51051 | VA,Dickenson County |
| 26085 | MI,Lake County | 51053 | VA,Dinwiddie County |

| | | | |
|---|---|---|---|
| 26087 | MI,Lapeer County | 51057 | VA,Essex County |
| 26089 | MI,Leelanau County | 51059 | VA,Fairfax County |
| 26091 | MI,Lenawee County | 51061 | VA,Fauquier County |
| 26093 | MI,Livingston County | 51063 | VA,Floyd County |
| 26095 | MI,Luce County | 51065 | VA,Fluvanna County |
| 26097 | MI,Mackinac County | 51067 | VA,Franklin County |
| 26099 | MI,Macomb County | 51069 | VA,Frederick County |
| 26101 | MI,Manistee County | 51071 | VA,Giles County |
| 26103 | MI,Marquette County | 51073 | VA,Gloucester County |
| 26105 | MI,Mason County | 51075 | VA,Goochland County |
| 26107 | MI,Mecosta County | 51077 | VA,Grayson County |
| 26109 | MI,Menominee County | 51079 | VA,Greene County |
| 26111 | MI,Midland County | 51081 | VA,Greensville County |
| 26113 | MI,Missaukee County | 51083 | VA,Halifax County |
| 26115 | MI,Monroe County | 51085 | VA,Hanover County |
| 26117 | MI,Montcalm County | 51087 | VA,Henrico County |
| 26119 | MI,Montmorency County | 51089 | VA,Henry County |
| 26121 | MI,Muskegon County | 51091 | VA,Highland County |
| 26123 | MI,Newaygo County | 51093 | VA,Isle of Wight County |
| 26125 | MI,Oakland County | 51095 | VA,James City County |
| 26127 | MI,Oceana County | 51097 | VA,King and Queen County |
| 26129 | MI,Ogemaw County | 51099 | VA,King George County |
| 26131 | MI,Ontonagon County | 51101 | VA,King William County |
| 26133 | MI,Osceola County | 51103 | VA,Lancaster County |
| 26135 | MI,Oscoda County | 51105 | VA,Lee County |
| 26137 | MI,Otsego County | 51107 | VA,Loudoun County |
| 26139 | MI,Ottawa County | 51109 | VA,Louisa County |
| 26141 | MI,Presque Isle County | 51111 | VA,Lunenburg County |
| 26143 | MI,Roscommon County | 51113 | VA,Madison County |
| 26145 | MI,Saginaw County | 51115 | VA,Mathews County |
| 26147 | MI,St. Clair County | 51117 | VA,Mecklenburg County |
| 26149 | MI,St. Joseph County | 51119 | VA,Middlesex County |
| 26151 | MI,Sanilac County | 51121 | VA,Montgomery County |
| 26153 | MI,Schoolcraft County | 51125 | VA,Nelson County |
| 26155 | MI,Shiawassee County | 51127 | VA,New Kent County |
| 26157 | MI,Tuscola County | 51131 | VA,Northampton County |
| 26159 | MI,Van Buren County | 51133 | VA,Northumberland County |
| 26161 | MI,Washtenaw County | 51135 | VA,Nottoway County |
| 26163 | MI,Wayne County | 51137 | VA,Orange County |
| 26165 | MI,Wexford County | 51139 | VA,Page County |
| 27001 | MN,Aitkin County | 51141 | VA,Patrick County |
| 27003 | MN,Anoka County | 51143 | VA,Pittsylvania County |
| 27005 | MN,Becker County | 51145 | VA,Powhatan County |
| 27007 | MN,Beltrami County | 51147 | VA,Prince Edward County |
| 27009 | MN,Benton County | 51149 | VA,Prince George County |
| 27011 | MN,Big Stone County | 51153 | VA,Prince William County |
| 27013 | MN,Blue Earth County | 51155 | VA,Pulaski County |
| 27015 | MN,Brown County | 51157 | VA,Rappahannock County |

| | | | |
|---|---|---|---|
| 27017 | MN,Carlton County | 51159 | VA,Richmond County |
| 27019 | MN,Carver County | 51161 | VA,Roanoke County |
| 27021 | MN,Cass County | 51163 | VA,Rockbridge County |
| 27023 | MN,Chippewa County | 51165 | VA,Rockingham County |
| 27025 | MN,Chisago County | 51167 | VA,Russell County |
| 27027 | MN,Clay County | 51169 | VA,Scott County |
| 27029 | MN,Clearwater County | 51171 | VA,Shenandoah County |
| 27031 | MN,Cook County | 51173 | VA,Smyth County |
| 27033 | MN,Cottonwood County | 51175 | VA,Southampton County |
| 27035 | MN,Crow Wing County | 51177 | VA,Spotsylvania County |
| 27037 | MN,Dakota County | 51179 | VA,Stafford County |
| 27039 | MN,Dodge County | 51181 | VA,Surry County |
| 27041 | MN,Douglas County | 51183 | VA,Sussex County |
| 27043 | MN,Faribault County | 51185 | VA,Tazewell County |
| 27045 | MN,Fillmore County | 51187 | VA,Warren County |
| 27047 | MN,Freeborn County | 51191 | VA,Washington County |
| 27049 | MN,Goodhue County | 51193 | VA,Westmoreland County |
| 27051 | MN,Grant County | 51195 | VA,Wise County |
| 27053 | MN,Hennepin County | 51197 | VA,Wythe County |
| 27055 | MN,Houston County | 51199 | VA,York County |
| 27057 | MN,Hubbard County | 51510 | VA,Alexandria City |
| 27059 | MN,Isanti County | 51515 | VA,Bedford City |
| 27061 | MN,Itasca County | 51520 | VA,Bristol City |
| 27063 | MN,Jackson County | 51530 | VA,Buena Vista City |
| 27065 | MN,Kanabec County | 51540 | VA,Charlottesville City |
| 27067 | MN,Kandiyohi County | 51550 | VA,Chesapeake City |
| 27069 | MN,Kittson County | 51560 | VA,Clifton Forge City |
| 27071 | MN,Koochiching County | 51570 | VA,Colonial Heights City |
| 27073 | MN,Lac qui Parle County | 51580 | VA,Covington City |
| 27075 | MN,Lake County | 51590 | VA,Danville City |
| 27077 | MN,Lake of the Woods County | 51595 | VA,Emporia City |
| 27079 | MN,Le Sueur County | 51600 | VA,Fairfax City |
| 27081 | MN,Lincoln County | 51610 | VA,Falls Church City |
| 27083 | MN,Lyon County | 51620 | VA,Franklin City |
| 27085 | MN,McLeod County | 51630 | VA,Fredericksburg City |
| 27087 | MN,Mahnomen County | 51640 | VA,Galax City |
| 27089 | MN,Marshall County | 51650 | VA,Hampton City |
| 27091 | MN,Martin County | 51660 | VA,Harrisonburg City |
| 27093 | MN,Meeker County | 51670 | VA,Hopewell City |
| 27095 | MN,Mille Lacs County | 51678 | VA,Lexington City |
| 27097 | MN,Morrison County | 51680 | VA,Lynchburg City |
| 27099 | MN,Mower County | 51683 | VA,Manassas City |
| 27101 | MN,Murray County | 51685 | VA,Manassas Park City |
| 27103 | MN,Nicollet County | 51690 | VA,Martinsville City |
| 27105 | MN,Nobles County | 51700 | VA,Newport News City |
| 27107 | MN,Norman County | 51710 | VA,Norfolk City |
| 27109 | MN,Olmsted County | 51720 | VA,Norton City |
| 27111 | MN,Otter Tail County | 51730 | VA,Petersburg City |

| | | | |
|---|---|---|---|
| 27113 | MN,Pennington County | 51735 | VA,Poquoson City |
| 27115 | MN,Pine County | 51740 | VA,Portsmouth City |
| 27117 | MN,Pipestone County | 51750 | VA,Radford City |
| 27119 | MN,Polk County | 51760 | VA,Richmond City |
| 27121 | MN,Pope County | 51770 | VA,Roanoke City |
| 27123 | MN,Ramsey County | 51775 | VA,Salem City |
| 27125 | MN,Red Lake County | 51780 | VA,South Boston City |
| 27127 | MN,Redwood County | 51790 | VA,Staunton City |
| 27129 | MN,Renville County | 51800 | VA,Suffolk City |
| 27131 | MN,Rice County | 51810 | VA,Virginia Beach City |
| 27133 | MN,Rock County | 51820 | VA,Waynesboro City |
| 27135 | MN,Roseau County | 51830 | VA,Williamsburg City |
| 27137 | MN,St. Louis County | 51840 | VA,Winchester City |
| 27139 | MN,Scott County | 53001 | WA,Adams County |
| 27141 | MN,Sherburne County | 53003 | WA,Asotin County |
| 27143 | MN,Sibley County | 53005 | WA,Benton County |
| 27145 | MN,Stearns County | 53007 | WA,Chelan County |
| 27147 | MN,Steele County | 53009 | WA,Clallam County |
| 27149 | MN,Stevens County | 53011 | WA,Clark County |
| 27151 | MN,Swift County | 53013 | WA,Columbia County |
| 27153 | MN,Todd County | 53015 | WA,Cowlitz County |
| 27155 | MN,Traverse County | 53017 | WA,Douglas County |
| 27157 | MN,Wabasha County | 53019 | WA,Ferry County |
| 27159 | MN,Wadena County | 53021 | WA,Franklin County |
| 27161 | MN,Waseca County | 53023 | WA,Garfield County |
| 27163 | MN,Washington County | 53025 | WA,Grant County |
| 27165 | MN,Watonwan County | 53027 | WA,Grays Harbor County |
| 27167 | MN,Wilkin County | 53029 | WA,Island County |
| 27169 | MN,Winona County | 53031 | WA,Jefferson County |
| 27171 | MN,Wright County | 53033 | WA,King County |
| 27173 | MN,Yellow Medicine County | 53035 | WA,Kitsap County |
| 28001 | MS,Adams County | 53037 | WA,Kittitas County |
| 28003 | MS,Alcorn County | 53039 | WA,Klickitat County |
| 28005 | MS,Amite County | 53041 | WA,Lewis County |
| 28007 | MS,Attala County | 53043 | WA,Lincoln County |
| 28009 | MS,Benton County | 53045 | WA,Mason County |
| 28011 | MS,Bolivar County | 53047 | WA,Okanogan County |
| 28013 | MS,Calhoun County | 53049 | WA,Pacific County |
| 28015 | MS,Carroll County | 53051 | WA,Pend Oreille County |
| 28017 | MS,Chickasaw County | 53053 | WA,Pierce County |
| 28019 | MS,Choctaw County | 53055 | WA,San Juan County |
| 28021 | MS,Claiborne County | 53057 | WA,Skagit County |
| 28023 | MS,Clarke County | 53059 | WA,Skamania County |
| 28025 | MS,Clay County | 53061 | WA,Snohomish County |
| 28027 | MS,Coahoma County | 53063 | WA,Spokane County |
| 28029 | MS,Copiah County | 53065 | WA,Stevens County |
| 28031 | MS,Covington County | 53067 | WA,Thurston County |
| 28033 | MS,DeSoto County | 53069 | WA,Wahkiakum County |

| | | | |
|---|---|---|---|
| 28035 | MS,Forrest County | 53071 | WA,Walla Walla County |
| 28037 | MS,Franklin County | 53073 | WA,Whatcom County |
| 28039 | MS,George County | 53075 | WA,Whitman County |
| 28041 | MS,Greene County | 53077 | WA,Yakima County |
| 28043 | MS,Grenada County | 53999 | WA,Undetermined County |
| 28045 | MS,Hancock County | 54001 | WV,Barbour County |
| 28047 | MS,Harrison County | 54003 | WV,Berkeley County |
| 28049 | MS,Hinds County | 54005 | WV,Boone County |
| 28051 | MS,Holmes County | 54007 | WV,Braxton County |
| 28053 | MS,Humphreys County | 54009 | WV,Brooke County |
| 28055 | MS,Issaquena County | 54011 | WV,Cabell County |
| 28057 | MS,Itawamba County | 54013 | WV,Calhoun County |
| 28059 | MS,Jackson County | 54015 | WV,Clay County |
| 28061 | MS,Jasper County | 54017 | WV,Doddridge County |
| 28063 | MS,Jefferson County | 54019 | WV,Fayette County |
| 28065 | MS,Jefferson Davis County | 54021 | WV,Gilmer County |
| 28067 | MS,Jones County | 54023 | WV,Grant County |
| 28069 | MS,Kemper County | 54025 | WV,Greenbrier County |
| 28071 | MS,Lafayette County | 54027 | WV,Hampshire County |
| 28073 | MS,Lamar County | 54029 | WV,Hancock County |
| 28075 | MS,Lauderdale County | 54031 | WV,Hardy County |
| 28077 | MS,Lawrence County | 54033 | WV,Harrison County |
| 28079 | MS,Leake County | 54035 | WV,Jackson County |
| 28081 | MS,Lee County | 54037 | WV,Jefferson County |
| 28083 | MS,Leflore County | 54039 | WV,Kanawha County |
| 28085 | MS,Lincoln County | 54041 | WV,Lewis County |
| 28087 | MS,Lowndes County | 54043 | WV,Lincoln County |
| 28089 | MS,Madison County | 54045 | WV,Logan County |
| 28091 | MS,Marion County | 54047 | WV,McDowell County |
| 28093 | MS,Marshall County | 54049 | WV,Marion County |
| 28095 | MS,Monroe County | 54051 | WV,Marshall County |
| 28097 | MS,Montgomery County | 54053 | WV,Mason County |
| 28099 | MS,Neshoba County | 54055 | WV,Mercer County |
| 28101 | MS,Newton County | 54057 | WV,Mineral County |
| 28103 | MS,Noxubee County | 54059 | WV,Mingo County |
| 28105 | MS,Oktibbeha County | 54061 | WV,Monongalia County |
| 28107 | MS,Panola County | 54063 | WV,Monroe County |
| 28109 | MS,Pearl River County | 54065 | WV,Morgan County |
| 28111 | MS,Perry County | 54067 | WV,Nicholas County |
| 28113 | MS,Pike County | 54069 | WV,Ohio County |
| 28115 | MS,Pontotoc County | 54071 | WV,Pendleton County |
| 28117 | MS,Prentiss County | 54073 | WV,Pleasants County |
| 28119 | MS,Quitman County | 54075 | WV,Pocahontas County |
| 28121 | MS,Rankin County | 54077 | WV,Preston County |
| 28123 | MS,Scott County | 54079 | WV,Putnam County |
| 28125 | MS,Sharkey County | 54081 | WV,Raleigh County |
| 28127 | MS,Simpson County | 54083 | WV,Randolph County |
| 28129 | MS,Smith County | 54085 | WV,Ritchie County |

| | | | |
|---|---|---|---|
| 28131 | MS,Stone County | 54087 | WV,Roane County |
| 28133 | MS,Sunflower County | 54089 | WV,Summers County |
| 28135 | MS,Tallahatchie County | 54091 | WV,Taylor County |
| 28137 | MS,Tate County | 54093 | WV,Tucker County |
| 28139 | MS,Tippah County | 54095 | WV,Tyler County |
| 28141 | MS,Tishomingo County | 54097 | WV,Upshur County |
| 28143 | MS,Tunica County | 54099 | WV,Wayne County |
| 28145 | MS,Union County | 54101 | WV,Webster County |
| 28147 | MS,Walthall County | 54103 | WV,Wetzel County |
| 28149 | MS,Warren County | 54105 | WV,Wirt County |
| 28151 | MS,Washington County | 54107 | WV,Wood County |
| 28153 | MS,Wayne County | 54109 | WV,Wyoming County |
| 28155 | MS,Webster County | 55001 | WI,Adams County |
| 28157 | MS,Wilkinson County | 55003 | WI,Ashland County |
| 28159 | MS,Winston County | 55005 | WI,Barron County |
| 28161 | MS,Yalobusha County | 55007 | WI,Bayfield County |
| 28163 | MS,Yazoo County | 55009 | WI,Brown County |
| 29001 | MO,Adair County | 55011 | WI,Buffalo County |
| 29003 | MO,Andrew County | 55013 | WI,Burnett County |
| 29005 | MO,Atchison County | 55015 | WI,Calumet County |
| 29007 | MO,Audrain County | 55017 | WI,Chippewa County |
| 29009 | MO,Barry County | 55019 | WI,Clark County |
| 29011 | MO,Barton County | 55021 | WI,Columbia County |
| 29013 | MO,Bates County | 55023 | WI,Crawford County |
| 29015 | MO,Benton County | 55025 | WI,Dane County |
| 29017 | MO,Bollinger County | 55027 | WI,Dodge County |
| 29019 | MO,Boone County | 55029 | WI,Door County |
| 29021 | MO,Buchanan County | 55031 | WI,Douglas County |
| 29023 | MO,Butler County | 55033 | WI,Dunn County |
| 29025 | MO,Caldwell County | 55035 | WI,Eau Claire County |
| 29027 | MO,Callaway County | 55037 | WI,Florence County |
| 29029 | MO,Camden County | 55039 | WI,Fond du Lac County |
| 29031 | MO,Cape Girardeau County | 55041 | WI,Forest County |
| 29033 | MO,Carroll County | 55043 | WI,Grant County |
| 29035 | MO,Carter County | 55045 | WI,Green County |
| 29037 | MO,Cass County | 55047 | WI,Green Lake County |
| 29039 | MO,Cedar County | 55049 | WI,Iowa County |
| 29041 | MO,Chariton County | 55051 | WI,Iron County |
| 29043 | MO,Christian County | 55053 | WI,Jackson County |
| 29045 | MO,Clark County | 55055 | WI,Jefferson County |
| 29047 | MO,Clay County | 55057 | WI,Juneau County |
| 29049 | MO,Clinton County | 55059 | WI,Kenosha County |
| 29051 | MO,Cole County | 55061 | WI,Kewaunee County |
| 29053 | MO,Cooper County | 55063 | WI,La Crosse County |
| 29055 | MO,Crawford County | 55065 | WI,Lafayette County |
| 29057 | MO,Dade County | 55067 | WI,Langlade County |
| 29059 | MO,Dallas County | 55069 | WI,Lincoln County |
| 29061 | MO,Daviess County | 55071 | WI,Manitowoc County |

| | | | |
|---|---|---|---|
| 29063 | MO,DeKalb County | 55073 | WI,Marathon County |
| 29065 | MO,Dent County | 55075 | WI,Marinette County |
| 29067 | MO,Douglas County | 55077 | WI,Marquette County |
| 29069 | MO,Dunklin County | 55078 | WI,Menominee County |
| 29071 | MO,Franklin County | 55079 | WI,Milwaukee County |
| 29073 | MO,Gasconade County | 55081 | WI,Monroe County |
| 29075 | MO,Gentry County | 55083 | WI,Oconto County |
| 29077 | MO,Greene County | 55085 | WI,Oneida County |
| 29079 | MO,Grundy County | 55087 | WI,Outagamie County |
| 29081 | MO,Harrison County | 55089 | WI,Ozaukee County |
| 29083 | MO,Henry County | 55091 | WI,Pepin County |
| 29085 | MO,Hickory County | 55093 | WI,Pierce County |
| 29087 | MO,Holt County | 55095 | WI,Polk County |
| 29089 | MO,Howard County | 55097 | WI,Portage County |
| 29091 | MO,Howell County | 55099 | WI,Price County |
| 29093 | MO,Iron County | 55101 | WI,Racine County |
| 29095 | MO,Jackson County | 55103 | WI,Richland County |
| 29097 | MO,Jasper County | 55105 | WI,Rock County |
| 29099 | MO,Jefferson County | 55107 | WI,Rusk County |
| 29101 | MO,Johnson County | 55109 | WI,St. Croix County |
| 29103 | MO,Knox County | 55111 | WI,Sauk County |
| 29105 | MO,Laclede County | 55113 | WI,Sawyer County |
| 29107 | MO,Lafayette County | 55115 | WI,Shawano County |
| 29109 | MO,Lawrence County | 55117 | WI,Sheboygan County |
| 29111 | MO,Lewis County | 55119 | WI,Taylor County |
| 29113 | MO,Lincoln County | 55121 | WI,Trempealeau County |
| 29115 | MO,Linn County | 55123 | WI,Vernon County |
| 29117 | MO,Livingston County | 55125 | WI,Vilas County |
| 29119 | MO,McDonald County | 55127 | WI,Walworth County |
| 29121 | MO,Macon County | 55129 | WI,Washburn County |
| 29123 | MO,Madison County | 55131 | WI,Washington County |
| 29125 | MO,Maries County | 55133 | WI,Waukesha County |
| 29127 | MO,Marion County | 55135 | WI,Waupaca County |
| 29129 | MO,Mercer County | 55137 | WI,Waushara County |
| 29131 | MO,Miller County | 55139 | WI,Winnebago County |
| 29133 | MO,Mississippi County | 55141 | WI,Wood County |
| 29135 | MO,Moniteau County | 56001 | WY,Albany County |
| 29137 | MO,Monroe County | 56003 | WY,Big Horn County |
| 29139 | MO,Montgomery County | 56005 | WY,Campbell County |
| 29141 | MO,Morgan County | 56007 | WY,Carbon County |
| 29143 | MO,New Madrid County | 56009 | WY,Converse County |
| 29145 | MO,Newton County | 56011 | WY,Crook County |
| 29147 | MO,Nodaway County | 56013 | WY,Fremont County |
| 29149 | MO,Oregon County | 56015 | WY,Goshen County |
| 29151 | MO,Osage County | 56017 | WY,Hot Springs County |
| 29153 | MO,Ozark County | 56019 | WY,Johnson County |
| 29155 | MO,Pemiscot County | 56021 | WY,Laramie County |
| 29157 | MO,Perry County | 56023 | WY,Lincoln County |

| | | | |
|---|---|---|---|
| 29159 | MO,Pettis County | 56025 | WY,Natrona County |
| 29161 | MO,Phelps County | 56027 | WY,Niobrara County |
| 29163 | MO,Pike County | 56029 | WY,Park County |
| 29165 | MO,Platte County | 56031 | WY,Platte County |
| 29167 | MO,Polk County | 56033 | WY,Sheridan County |
| 29169 | MO,Pulaski County | 56035 | WY,Sublette County |
| 29171 | MO,Putnam County | 56037 | WY,Sweetwater County |
| 29173 | MO,Ralls County | 56039 | WY,Teton County |
| 29175 | MO,Randolph County | 56041 | WY,Uinta County |
| 29177 | MO,Ray County | 56043 | WY,Washakie County |
| 29179 | MO,Reynolds County | 56045 | WY,Weston County |
| 29181 | MO,Ripley County | 56660 | WY,Big Horn National Forest |
| 29183 | MO,St. Charles County | 56661 | WY,Black Hills National Forest |
| 29185 | MO,St. Clair County | 56662 | WY,Medicine Bow National Forest |
| 29186 | MO,Ste. Genevieve County | 56663 | WY,Shoshone National Forest |
| 29187 | MO,St. Francois County | 56666 | WY,Bridger-Teton National Forest |
| 29189 | MO,St. Louis County | 56999 | WY,Undetermined County |
| 29195 | MO,Saline County | 999999 | All U.S. Counties |
| 29197 | MO,Schuyler County | | |
| 29199 | MO,Scotland County | | |
| 29201 | MO,Scott County | | |
| 29203 | MO,Shannon County | | |
| 29205 | MO,Shelby County | | |
| 29207 | MO,Stoddard County | | |
| 29209 | MO,Stone County | | |

7.  Subregion
    SUBREGION

The subregion code indicates geographic location (east or west) within four States (Alaska, Oregon, South Dakota, and Washington).

| Code | Subregion |
|---|---|
| -1 | Missing |
| 1 | No Subregion |
| 2 | East |
| 3 | West |

8.  RPA Assessment Region
    RPA_REGION

RPA region. Grouping of States into four regions for reporting purposes.

| Code | Region |
|---|---|
| 1 | North Assessment Region: Composed of the Northeast and North Central RPA Assessment Subregions. |
| 2 | South Assessment Region: Composed of the Southeast and South Central RPA Assessment Subregions. |
| 3 | Rocky Mountains Assessment Region: Composed of the Great Plains and Intermountain RPA Assessment Subregions. |
| 4 | Pacific Coast Assessment Region: Composed of the Pacific Northwest, Pacific Southwest, and Alaska RPA Assessment Subregions. |

| RPA Data Wiz Name<br>Access FIELD NAME | Definition |
|---|---|

9. RPA Assessment
   Subregion
   RPA_SUBREGION

RPA subregions. Grouping of States into nine subregions for reporting purposes. Subregions 1 and 2 belong in the Northern Region; subregions 3 and 4 belong in the Southern Region; subregions 5 and 6 belong in the Rocky Mountain Region; and subregions 7, 8, and 9 belong in the Pacific Coast Region.

| Code | RPA Subregion |
|---|---|
| 1 | Northeast Assessment Subregion: Composed of CT, DE, District of Columbia, MA, MD, ME, NH, NJ, NY, PA, RI, VT, and WV. |
| 2 | North Central Assessment Subregion: Composed of IA, IL, IN, MI, MN, MO, OH, and WI. |
| 3 | Southeast Assessment Subregion: Composed of FL, GA, NC, SC, and VA. |
| 4 | South Central Assessment Subregion: Composed of AL, AR, KY, LA, MS, OK, TN, and TX. |
| 5 | Great Plains Assessment Subregion: Composed of KS, NB, ND, and SD. |
| 6 | Intermountain Assessment Subregion: Composed of AZ, CO, ID, MT, NM, NV, UT, and WY. |
| 7 | Alaska Assessment Subregion: Composed of AK |
| 8 | Pacific Northwest Assessment Subregion: Composed of OR and WA. |
| 9 | Pacific Southwest Assessment Subregion: Composed of CA. |

10. *Administrative
    Forest
    ADMINFORU and
    ADMINFOR from
    RPA database
    modified to
    ADMINFORU in
    RPA Data Wiz
    database

A combined administrative unit-administrative forest code. The field name for the USDA Forest Service administrative unit code in the RPA database is ADMINFORU. In the RPA database, the field name for the administrative forest within a specific unit is ADMINFOR. The RPA Data Wiz field, ADMINFORU, is a combination of the two previous RPA database fields ((ADMINFORU * 100) + ADMINFOR). This code identifies the polygons in the usfs shapefile used in RPA Data Wiz to map lands administered by the USDA Forest Service. The usfs shapefile is a combination of the Automated Lands Project, Federal Lands and Indian Reservations of the United States (National Atlas Program), and the USFS Region 5 Administrative Boundaries maps. See the metadata associated with the usfs shapefile metadata (usfs.met or usfs.shp.xml located in the application directory) and the references directory on the installation CD for more information.

| Code | Administrative Forest |
|---|---|
| -1 | Missing |
| 102 | Beaverhead-Deerlodge |
| 103 | Bitterroot |
| 104 | Idaho Panhandle |
| 105 | Clearwater |
| 108 | Custer |
| 110 | Flathead |
| 111 | Gallatin |
| 112 | Helena |
| 114 | Kootenai |
| 115 | Lewis and Clark |
| 116 | Lolo |
| 117 | Nez Perce |
| 120 | Cedar River National Grassland |
| 121 | Little Missouri National Grassland |
| 122 | Sheyenne National Grassland |
| 124 | Grand River National Grassland |
| 199 | Other NFS Areas - Region 1 |
| 202 | Bighorn |
| 203 | Black Hills |

| | |
|---|---|
| 204 | Grand Mesa-Uncomp-Gunnison |
| 206 | Medicine Bow-Routt |
| 207 | Nebraska |
| 209 | Rio Grande |
| 210 | Arapaho-Roosevelt |
| 212 | Pike and San Isabel |
| 213 | San Juan |
| 214 | Shosone |
| 215 | White River |
| 217 | Cimarron National Grassland |
| 218 | Comanche National Grassland |
| 219 | Pawnee National Grassland |
| 220 | Oglala National Grassland |
| 221 | Buffalo Gap National Grassland |
| 222 | Fort Pierre National Grassland |
| 223 | Thunder Basin National Grassland |
| 299 | Other NFS Areas - Region 2 |
| 301 | Apache-Sitgreaves |
| 302 | Carson |
| 303 | Cibola |
| 304 | Coconino |
| 305 | Coronado |
| 306 | Gila |
| 307 | Kaibab |
| 308 | Lincoln |
| 309 | Prescott |
| 310 | Santa Fe |
| 312 | Tonto |
| 399 | Other NFS Areas - Region 3 |
| 401 | Ashley |
| 402 | Boise |
| 403 | Bridger-Teton |
| 405 | Caribou |
| 407 | Dixie |
| 408 | Fishlake |
| 409 | Humboldt-Toiyabe |
| 410 | Manti-LaSal |
| 412 | Payette |
| 413 | Salmon-Challis |
| 414 | Sawtooth |
| 415 | Targhee |
| 418 | Uinta |
| 419 | Wasatch-Cache |
| 420 | Desert Range Experiment Station |
| 499 | Other NFS Areas - Region 4 |
| 501 | Angeles |
| 502 | Cleveland |
| 503 | Eldorado |

| | |
|---|---|
| 504 | Inyo |
| 505 | Klamath |
| 506 | Lassen |
| 507 | Los Padres |
| 508 | Mendocino |
| 509 | Modoc |
| 510 | Six Rivers |
| 511 | Plumas |
| 512 | San Bernardino |
| 513 | Sequoia |
| 514 | Shasta-Trinity |
| 515 | Sierra |
| 516 | Stanislaus |
| 517 | Tahoe |
| 519 | Lake Tahoe Basin |
| 599 | Other NFS Areas - Region 5 |
| 601 | Deschutes |
| 602 | Fremont |
| 603 | Gifford Pinchot |
| 604 | Malheur |
| 605 | Mt. Baker-Snoqualmie |
| 606 | Mt. Hood |
| 607 | Ochoco |
| 608 | Okanogan |
| 609 | Olympic |
| 610 | Rogue River |
| 611 | Siskiyou |
| 612 | Siuslaw |
| 614 | Umatilla |
| 615 | Umpqua |
| 616 | Wallowa-Whitman |
| 617 | Wenatchee |
| 618 | Willamette |
| 620 | Winema |
| 621 | Colville |
| 699 | Other NFS Areas - Region 6 |
| 708 | Bureau of Land Management - 708 |
| 709 | Bureau of Land Management - 709 |
| 710 | Bureau of Land Management - 710 |
| 711 | Bureau of Land Management - 711 |
| 712 | Bureau of Land Management - 712 |
| 801 | NFS in Alabama |
| 802 | Daniel Boone |
| 803 | Chattahoochee-Oconee |
| 804 | Cherokee |
| 805 | NFS in Florida |
| 806 | Kisatchie |
| 807 | NFS in Mississippi |

| | |
|---|---|
| 808 | George Washington-Jefferson |
| 809 | Ouachita |
| 810 | Ozark-St. Francis |
| 811 | NFS in North Carolina |
| 812 | Francis Marion-Sumter |
| 813 | NFS in Texas |
| 816 | Caribbean |
| 899 | Other NFS Areas - Region 8 |
| 902 | Chequamegon-Nicolet |
| 903 | Chippewa |
| 904 | Huron-Manistee |
| 905 | Mark Twain |
| 907 | Ottawa |
| 908 | Shawnee |
| 909 | Superior |
| 910 | Hiawatha |
| 911 | Hoosier |
| 918 | Wayne |
| 919 | Allegheny |
| 920 | Green Mountain-Finger Lakes |
| 921 | Monongahela |
| 922 | White Mountain |
| 999 | Other NFS Areas - Region 9 |
| 1002 | Tongass |
| 1004 | Chugach |
| 1099 | Other NFS Areas - Region 10 |

11. Land Cover Class
   LANDCC

Land use code.

| Code | Land Use |
|---|---|
| -1 | Missing |
| 20 | Forest land: Land at least 10 percent stocked with forest trees of any size or formerly forested lands not currently developed for nonforest uses. These lands must be a minimum of 1 acre in area. Roadside, streamside, and shelterbelt strips of timber must have a crown width of at least 120 feet to qualify as forest land. Unimproved roads, trails, streams, and clearings within forest areas are classified as forest land if they are less than 120 feet wide. |
| 60 | Nonforest land: Land that has never supported forests or land formerly forested but now developed for other uses. If located within forest areas, then unimproved roads and nonforested strips must be more than 120 feet wide. Clearings must be more than 1 acre to qualify as nonforest land. Nonforest land includes areas used for crops, pasture, residential, commercial, industrial, city parks, improved roads, and adjoining clearings. |
| 91 | Census water: Streams, sloughs, estuaries, and canals more than 200 feet wide. Lakes, reservoirs, and ponds more than 4.5 acres in size. Exceptions occur for Alaska, Oregon, and Washington. The exceptions use the 1980 definition: Streams, sloughs, estuaries, and canals more than 1/8 of a statute mile (660 feet) in width. Lakes, reservoirs, and ponds more than 40 acres in size. |

92                    Noncensus water: Streams, sloughs, estuaries, and canals between 120 feet and 200 feet wide. Lakes, reservoirs, and ponds 1 to 4.5 acres in size. Exceptions occur for Alaska, Oregon, and Washington. The exceptions use the 1980 definition: Streams, sloughs, estuaries, and canals more than 120 feet and less than 1/8 of a mile (660 feet) in width. Lakes, reservoirs, and ponds 1 to 40 acres in size.

12. Reserved Class
    RESERCLASS                Reserved Class.

| Code | Reserve Class |
|------|---------------|
| -1 | Missing |
| 0 | Unknown |
| 1 | Unreserved forest land: All private forest lands and public forest lands where the harvest of trees is not prohibited by statute or administrative regulation. |
| 2 | Non-National Forest System reserved forest land: Lands that have statutory or administrative restrictions prohibiting the harvest of trees. Examples include forest land within national parks, monuments, National Wilderness Preservation System areas outside the national forests, and State parks. |
| 3 | National Forest System reserved forest land-nonwilderness: National Forest System forest lands that have restrictions prohibiting the harvest of trees. Examples include primitive areas, scenic research areas, scenic areas, wild and scenic rivers, recreation areas, game refuges, monument areas, and historic areas. In general, this code includes all reserved or withdrawn National Forest System forest lands not within the National Wilderness Preservation System. |
| 4 | National Forest System reserved forest land-wilderness: Public forest lands that have statutory or administrative restrictions prohibiting the harvest of trees. Examples include land within the National Wilderness Preservation System or State-designated wilderness areas. |

13. Site Productivity Class
    SPCLASS                Site productivity class. A classification of forest land in terms of inherent capacity to grow crops of industrial wood. The class identifies the average potential growth in cubic feet/acre/year (English) or in cubic meters/hectare/year (metric) and is based on the culmination of mean annual increment of fully stocked natural stands.

| English Version | | Metric Version | |
|------|-----------------|------|-----------------|
| Code | Site Productivity | Code | Site Productivity |
| -1 | Missing | -1 | Missing |
| 0 | Unknown | 0 | Unknown |
| 1 | 225-999 cubic feet/acre/year | 1 | 15.7+ cubic meters/hectare/year |
| 2 | 165-224 cubic feet/acre/year | 2 | 11.5-15.6 cubic meters/hectare/year |
| 3 | 120-164 cubic feet/acre/year | 3 | 8.4-11.4 cubic meters/hectare/year |
| 4 | 85-119 cubic feet/acre/year | 4 | 5.9-8.3 cubic meters/hectare/year |
| 5 | 50-84 cubic feet/acre/year | 5 | 3.5-5.8 cubic meters/hectare/year |
| 6 | 20-49 cubic feet/acre/year | 6 | 1.4-3.4 cubic meters/hectare/year |
| 7 | < 20 cubic feet/acre/year | 7 | < 1.4 cubic meters/hectare/year |
| 8 | Unproductive timberland | 8 | Unproductive timberland |

14. Forested Land Code   Forest land code. Differentiates between productive/unproductive and reserved/nonreserved forest land.
    FORCODE

| Code | Forest Land |
|------|-------------|
| -1 | Missing |
| 0 | Nonforest |
| 1 | Productive nonreserved forest land (timberland) |
| 2 | Productive reserved forest land |
| 3 | Unproductive nonreserved forest land |
| 4 | Unproductive reserved forest land |

15. *Owner Group   Ownership group. A broad grouping of ownership classes.
    OWNGROUP

| Code | Owner Group |
|------|-------------|
| -1 | Missing |
| 1 | National Forest land: Federal lands designated by executive order or statute as national forests or purchase units, and other lands under the administration of the U.S. Forest Service including experimental areas and Bankhead-Jones title III lands. |
| 2 | Other public land: publicly owned lands other than national forest lands. |
| 3 | Private land: All private lands. |
| 9 | Unknown ownership: Owner group not recorded. This code is legal for nonforest land and water cover classes only. |

16. *Owner   Owner class code. Indicates the class in which the landowner (at the time of the inventory) belongs.
    OWNER

| Code | Owner |
|------|-------|
| -1 | Missing |
| 11 | National Forest |
| 12 | Bureau of Land Management: Federal lands administered by the Bureau of Land Management, U.S. Department of the Interior. |
| 14 | Other Federal agencies: Federal lands other than lands administered by the USDA Forest Service or BLM. |
| 15 | State: Lands owned by State governments or lands leased by State governmental units for more than 50 years. |
| 16 | County and municipal: Lands owned by county or municipal agencies, or lands leased by these agencies for more than 50 years. |
| 20 | Private: All private lands. |
| 99 | Unknown: Ownership not recorded or unavailable. This code is legal for nonforest land and water. |

17. *Forest Type Group
    FORTYPE

Forest type group. The general forest-cover type of the inventoried stand based on the tree species forming a plurality of the stocking within the stand. This is a three-digit coded element where the first digit (1 or 2) represents either eastern or western type groups. The next 2 digits have been taken from a standard set of forest type codes.

| Code | Forest Type |
|---|---|
| -1 | Missing |
| 0 | Unknown |
| 100 | White - Red - Jack Pine |
| 110 | Spruce - Fir (East) |
| 120 | Longleaf - Slash Pine |
| 130 | Loblolly - Shortleaf Pine |
| 140 | Oak - Pine (East) |
| 150 | Oak - Hickory |
| 160 | Oak - Gum - Cypress |
| 170 | Elm - Ash - Cottonwood (East) |
| 180 | Maple - Beech - Birch |
| 190 | Aspen - Birch (East) |
| 198 | Other Forest Types (East) |
| 199 | Nonstocked (East) |
| 200 | Douglas-fir |
| 210 | Ponderosa Pine |
| 220 | Western White Pine |
| 230 | Fir - Spruce (West) |
| 240 | Hemlock - Sitka Spruce |
| 250 | Larch (West) |
| 260 | Lodgepole Pine |
| 270 | Redwood |
| 280 | Other Hardwoods (West) |
| 290 | Unclassified and Other Forest Types (West) |
| 293 | Pinyon - Juniper |
| 297 | Chaparral |
| 299 | Nonstocked (West) |

18. Local Forest Type
    LOCALTYPE

Local forest type. For the data derived from the Forest Inventory and Analysis Database (every State except Hawaii and interior Alaska; i.e., SUBREGION=3), local forest type is simply the value of FORTYPCD in the CONDITION record of the FIADB.

| Code | Local Forest Type |
|---|---|
| -1 | Missing |
| 0 | Unknown |
| 100 | White - Red - Jack Pine Group |
| 101 | Jack Pine |
| 102 | Red Pine |
| 103 | Eastern White Pine |
| 104 | Eastern White Pine - Hemlock |
| 105 | Eastern Hemlock |

| | |
|---|---|
| 106 | Scotch Pine |
| 110 | Spruce - Fir Group (East) |
| 111 | Balsam Fir |
| 112 | Black Spruce |
| 113 | Red Spruce - Balsam Fir |
| 114 | Northern White-cedar |
| 115 | Tamarack |
| 116 | White Spruce |
| 120 | Longleaf - Slash Pine Group |
| 121 | Longleaf Pine |
| 122 | Slash Pine |
| 130 | Loblolly - Shortleaf Pine Group |
| 131 | Loblolly Pine |
| 132 | Shortleaf Pine |
| 133 | Virginia Pine |
| 134 | Sand Pine |
| 135 | Eastern Redcedar |
| 136 | Pond Pine |
| 137 | Spruce Pine |
| 138 | Pitch Pine |
| 139 | Table-mountain Pine |
| 140 | Oak - Pine Group (East) |
| 141 | White Pine - Northern Red Oak - White Ash (East) |
| 142 | Eastern Redcedar - Hardwood |
| 143 | Longleaf Pine - Scrub Oak |
| 144 | Shortleaf Pine - Oak |
| 145 | Virginia Pine - Southern Red Oak |
| 146 | Loblolly Pine - Hardwood |
| 147 | Slash Pine - Hardwood |
| 149 | Other Oak - Pine (East) |
| 150 | Oak - Hickory Group |
| 151 | Post Oak, Black Oak, or Bear Oak |
| 152 | Chestnut Oak |
| 153 | White Oak - Red Oak - Hickory |
| 154 | White Oak |
| 155 | Northern Red Oak |
| 156 | Yellow Poplar - White Oak - Northern Red Oak |
| 157 | Southern Scrub Oak |
| 158 | Sweetgum - Yellow Poplar |
| 159 | Mixed Hardwoods (East) |
| 160 | Oak - Gum - Cypress Group |
| 161 | Swamp Chestnut Oak - Cherrybark Oak |
| 162 | Sweetgum - Nuttall Oak - Willow Oak |
| 163 | Sugarberry - American Elm - Green Ash |
| 165 | Overcup Oak - Water Hickory |
| 166 | Atlantic White-cedar |
| 167 | Baldcypress - Water Tupelo |
| 168 | Sweetbay - Swamp Tupelo - Red Maple |

| | |
|---|---|
| 169 | Palm - Mangrove - Other Tropical |
| 170 | Elm - Ash - Cottonwood Group (East) |
| 171 | Black Ash - American Elm - Red Maple (East) |
| 172 | River Birch - Sycamore |
| 173 | Cottonwood (East) |
| 174 | Willow (East) |
| 175 | Sycamore - Pecan - American Elm (East) |
| 176 | Red Maple - Lowland (East) |
| 179 | Mixed Lowland Hardwoods (East) |
| 180 | Maple - Beech - Birch Group |
| 181 | Sugar Maple - Beech - Yellow Birch |
| 182 | Black Cherry |
| 183 | Black Walnut |
| 184 | Red Maple - Northern Hardwoods |
| 187 | Red Maple - Upland (East) |
| 188 | Northern Hardwoods - Reverting Field |
| 189 | Mixed Northern Hardwoods |
| 190 | Aspen - Birch Group (East) |
| 191 | Aspen (East) |
| 192 | Paper Birch |
| 194 | Balsam Poplar |
| 198 | Other Forest Types (East) |
| 199 | Nonstocked (East) |
| 200 | Douglas-fir Group |
| 201 | Douglas-fir |
| 202 | Douglas-fir - Western Hemlock |
| 203 | Port Orford-cedar - Douglas-fir |
| 210 | Ponderosa Pine Group |
| 211 | Ponderosa Pine |
| 212 | Jeffrey Pine |
| 213 | Ponderosa Pine - Sugar Pine - Fir |
| 220 | Western White Pine Group |
| 221 | Western White Pine |
| 230 | Fir - Spruce Group (West) |
| 231 | White Fir - Grand Fir |
| 232 | Red Fir |
| 234 | Pacific Silver Fir - Hemlock |
| 235 | Engelmann Spruce |
| 236 | Engelmann Spruce - Subalpine Fir |
| 240 | Hemlock - Sitka Spruce Group |
| 241 | Western Redcedar |
| 242 | Sitka Spruce |
| 247 | Mountain Hemlock - Subalpine Fir |
| 248 | Western Hemlock |
| 249 | Alaska Cedar |
| 250 | Larch Group |
| 255 | Larch - Douglas-fir |
| 256 | Grand Fir - Larch - Douglas-fir |

| | |
|---|---|
| 257 | Ponderosa Pine - Larch - Douglas-fir |
| 260 | Lodgepole Pine Group |
| 261 | Lodgepole Pine |
| 270 | Redwood Group |
| 271 | Redwood |
| 280 | Other Hardwoods Group (West) |
| 281 | Red Alder |
| 282 | Poplar - Birch (West) |
| 283 | Aspen (West) |
| 284 | California Black Oak |
| 285 | Cottonwood - Willow (West) |
| 286 | Canyon Live Oak |
| 287 | Oak - Madrone |
| 288 | Other Oaks (West) |
| 289 | Ohia |
| 290 | Other Forest Types (Arizona cypress - western juniper) |
| 291 | Coulter Pine |
| 292 | Digger Pine - Oak |
| 293 | Pinyon - Juniper |
| 294 | Knobcone Pine |
| 295 | Bristlecone Pine |
| 296 | Whitebark Pine |
| 297 | Chaparral |
| 298 | Limber Pine |
| 299 | Nonstocked (West) |

19. Stand Origin
    STANDORIGIN

Stand origin code. Method of stand regeneration. An artificially regenerated stand is established by planting or artificial seeding.

| Code | Stand origin |
|---|---|
| -1 | Missing |
| 0 | Unknown |
| 1 | Natural stands |
| 2 | Clear evidence of artificial regeneration |

20. Stand-Size Class
    SSCLASS

Stand-size class code (derived by algorithm). A classification of the predominant (based on stocking) diameter class of live trees within the condition. Large-diameter trees are at least 11.0 inches (27.9 cm) diameter for hardwoods and at least 9.0 inches (22.9 cm) diameter for softwoods. Medium-diameter trees are at least 5.0 inches (12.7 cm) diameter but not as large as large-diameter trees. Small-diameter trees are less than 5.0 inches (12.7 cm) diameter.

| Code | Stand-size class |
|---|---|
| -1 | Missing |
| 0 | Unknown |
| 1 | Nonstocked: Forest land with all live stocking less than 10 percent |

| | |
|---|---|
| 2 | Small diameter: Stands with an all live stocking value of at least 10 percent (base 100) on which at least 50 percent of the stocking is in small-diameter trees |
| 3 | Medium diameter: Stands with an all live stocking of at least 10 percent (base 100) with more than 50 percent of the stocking in medium- and large-diameter trees and with the stocking of large-diameter trees less than the stocking of medium-diameter trees |
| 4 | Large diameter: Stands with an all live stocking of at least 10 percent (base 100) with more than 50 percent of the stocking in medium- and large-diameter trees and with the stocking of large-diameter trees equal to or greater than the stocking of medium-diameter trees |

21. *Ageclass
    AGECLASS

Stand age. In RPA Data Wiz, the average total age, to the nearest 5 years, of the trees (plurality of all live trees not overtopped) in the predominant stand-size class of the condition, determined using local procedures. Age is difficult to measure and therefore stand age may have large measurement errors. Nonstocked stands are recorded as 0. Any inventory dated 1995 or later contains stand ages recorded to the nearest year, but these were recoded to the nearest 5 years (required for RPA Data Wiz). For some older inventories, stand age was recorded using intervals of 10 or 20 years (CT, DE, KY, MD, NH, PA, RI, VT, and WV) for stands < 100 years old, 20-year age classes for stands between 100 and 200 years, and 100-year age classes if older than 200 years. The value recorded is the midpoint of the age class. Mixed age classes were allowed in older inventories (AR, CT, KY, LA, ME, MA, MS, NH, NY, OH, OK, PA, RI, TX, VT, and WV) and were assigned a coded value of -999.

22. Percent Stocking
    Class
    STOCKPC

Percent stocking class. A coded value indicating the percent stocking class for growing stock in the stand. The 10 percent interval classes range from nonstocked to 100 percent stocking, relative stocking basis. All 10 of these codes were used for Hawaii and interior Alaska. Only codes 1, 3, 5, 7, 9, and -1 were used for the other 48 States (the STOCKPC data for these States came from the GSSTKCD variable in the FIADB, which has fewer classes than STOCKPC). For the other 48 States, a code of 1 is equivalent to Nonstocked, 3 equals Poorly Stocked, 5 equals Medium Stocked, 7 equals Fully Stocked, 9 equals Overstocked, and -1 equals Missing.

| Code | Percent Stocking |
|---|---|
| -1 | Missing |
| 0 | Unknown |
| 1 | 0 - 9% or Nonstocked |
| 2 | 10 - 19% |
| 3 | 20 - 29% or Poorly Stocked |
| 4 | 30 - 39% |
| 5 | 40 - 49% or Medium Stocked |
| 6 | 50 - 59% |
| 7 | 60 - 69% or Fully Stocked |
| 8 | 70 - 79% |
| 9 | 80 - 89% or Overstocked |
| 10 | 90 - 100% |

23. Treatment Opportunity
    Class
    TREATOPP

Treatment opportunity class code. Identifies the physical opportunity to improve stand conditions by applying management practices. Determined only for timberland (SITECLCD 1-6). This variable is mandatory for nonindustrial private lands and may not be available for other ownerships.

| Code | Treatment Opportunity Class |
|------|------------------------------|
| -1 | Not available/unclassified |
| 0 | Unknown |
| 1 | Regeneration without site preparation: The area is characterized by the absence of a manageable stand because of inadequate stocking of growing stock. Growth will be much below the potential for the site if the area is left alone. Prospects are not good for natural regeneration. Artificial regeneration will require little or no site preparation. |
| 2 | Regeneration with site preparation: The area is characterized by the absence of a manageable stand because of inadequate stocking of growing stock. Growth will be much below the potential for the site if the area is left alone. Either natural or artificial regeneration will require site preparation. |
| 3 | Stand conversion: The area is characterized by stands of undesirable, chronically diseased, or off-site (found where not normally expected) species. Growth and quality will be much below the potential for the site if the area is left alone. The best prospect is for conversion to a different forest type or species. |
| 4 | Thinning seedlings and saplings: The stand is characterized by a dense stocking of growing stock. Stagnation appears likely if left alone. Stocking must be reduced to help crop trees attain dominance. |
| 5 | Thinning poletimber: The stand is characterized by a dense stocking of growing stock. Stocking must be reduced to prevent stagnation or to confine growth to selected, high-quality crop trees. |
| 6 | Other stocking control: The stand is characterized by an adequate stocking of seedlings, saplings, and poletimber growing stock, mixed with competing vegetation either overtopping or otherwise inhibiting the development of crop trees. The undesirable material must be removed to release overtopped trees, to prevent stagnation, or to improve composition, form, or growth of the residual stand. |
| 7 | Other intermediate treatments: The stand would benefit from other special treatments, such as fertilization, to improve the growth potential of the site, and pruning to improve the quality of individual crop trees. |
| 8 | Clearcut harvest: The area is characterized by a mature or over-mature sawtimber stand of sufficient volume to justify a commercial harvest. The best prospect is to harvest the stand and regenerate. |
| 9 | Partial cut harvest: The stand is characterized by poletimber- or sawtimber-size trees with sufficient merchantable volume for a commercial harvest that will meet intermediate stand treatment needs or prepare the stand for natural regeneration. The stand has a favored species composition and may be even- or uneven-aged. Included are such treatments as commercial thinning, seed tree, or shelterwood regeneration and use of the selection system to maintain an uneven-age stand. |
| 10 | Salvage harvest: The stand is characterized by excessive damage to merchantable timber because of fire, insects, disease, wind, ice, or other destructive agents. The best prospect is to remove damaged or threatened material. |
| 11 | No treatment: No silvicultural treatment is needed |

24. Observed - Modeled
    Data Source
    TSOURCE

Source of volume data. Identifies whether the data source for volume records (trees, stands, etc.) is based on observed or modeled tree d.b.h. ECOSUBCD is the code for ecosubsection (Miles and Vissage, In prep.).

| Code | Source |
|------|--------|
| -1 | Missing |
| 0 | Nonforestland. |
| 1 | Observed from tree data (all timberland plots are based on observed tree data). |
| 2 | Used for unproductive forest land and/or reserved forest land plots where no tree data are available. Plots with a value of 2 for TSOURCE have imputed values for the following variables: cubic, cubicsw, cubichw, cullsw, cullhw, cull, deadsw, deadhw, dead, biobolesw, biobolehw, biobole, biosapssw, biosapshw, biosaps. These variables were assigned the average values from similar plots (unproductive plots were matched with unproductive plots and reserved plots were matched with reserved plots where the plots had the same first two characters for the ECOSUBCD variable). A minimum of five plots having the same ECOSUBCD string through two characters was required for the plot to be assigned a TSOURCE code of 2. This plot failed the requirements to receive a TSOURCE code of 3. |
| 3 | Used for unproductive forest land and/or reserved forest land plots where no tree data are available. Plots with a value of 3 for TSOURCE have imputed values for the following variables: cubic, cubicsw, cubichw, cullsw, cullhw, cull, deadsw, deadhw, dead, bioboles w, biobolehw, biobole, biosapssw, biosapshw, biosaps. These variables were assigned the average values from similar plots (unproductive plots were matched with unproductive plots and reserved plots were matched with reserved plots where the plots had the same first three characters for the ECOSUBCD variable). A minimum of five plots having the same ECOSUBCD string through three characters was required for the plot to be assigned a TSOURCE code of 3. This plot failed the requirements to receive a TSOURCE code of 4. |
| 4 | Used for unproductive forest land and/or reserved forest land plots where no tree data are available. Plots with a value of 4 for TSOURCE have imputed values for the following variables: cubic, cubicsw, cubichw, cullsw, cullhw, cull, deadsw, deadhw, dead, bioboles w, biobolehw, biobole, biosapssw, biosapshw, biosaps. These variables were assigned the average values from similar plots (unproductive plots were matched with unproductive plots and reserved plots were matched with reserved plots where the plots had the same first four characters for the ECOSUBCD variable). A minimum of five plots having the same ECOSUBCD string through four characters was required for the plot to be assigned a TSOURCE code of 4. This plot failed the requirements to receive a TSOURCE code of 5. |
| 5 | Used for unproductive forest land and/or reserved forest land plots where no tree data are available. Plots with a value of 5 for TSOURCE have imputed values for the following variables: cubic, cubicsw, cubichw, cullsw, cullhw, cull, deadsw, deadhw, dead, bioboles w, biobolehw, biobole, biosapssw, biosapshw, biosaps. These variables were assigned the average values from similar plots (unproductive plots were matched with unproductive plots and reserved plots were matched with reserved plots where the plots had the same first five characters for the ECOSUBCD variable). A minimum of five plots having the same ECOSUBCD string through five characters was required for the plot to be assigned a TSOURCE code of 5. This plot failed the requirements to receive a TSOURCE code of 6. |
| 6 | Used for unproductive forest land and/or reserved forest land plots where no tree data are available. Plots with a value of 2 for TSOURCE have imputed values for the following variables: cubic, cubicsw, cubichw, cullsw, cullhw, cull, deadsw, deadhw, dead, bioboles w, biobolehw, biobole, biosapssw, biosapshw, biosaps. These variables were assigned the average values from similar plots (unproductive plots were matched with unproductive plots and reserved plots were matched with |

reserved plots where the plots had the same first six characters for the ECOSUBCD variable). A minimum of five plots having the same ECOSUBCD string through six characters was required for the plot to be assigned a TSOURCE code of 6.

96     Hawaii. Values for variables biosapssw, biosapshw, and biosaps were imputed based on the average ratio of biostumptop to biobole for the lower 48 States. Individual tree data were unavailable for computing trees per acre and basal area variables.

97     Interior Alaska. Values for variables cubic, cubicsw, cubichw, cullsw, cullhw, cull, deadsw, deadhw, dead, biobolesw, biobolehw, biobole, biosapssw, biosapshw, and biosaps, were imputed from information contained on six plots measured in the Northwest Territories.

98     Productive reserved plots that did not meet requirements for codes 1 through 6. They received the average values from all other productive reserved plots that were measured in their respective State and/or neighboring States (a minimum of five plots was required to develop the average).

99     Unproductive plots that did not meet requirements for codes 1 through 6. They received the average values from all other unproductive plots that were measured in their respective State and/or neighboring States (a minimum of five plots was required to develop the average). An exception occurs for Florida (332 plots). Information for these 332 plots was derived from a publication by Neal Cost on unproductive forest land.

25. *Mapped CONDPROP in RPA database modified to MAPPED in RPA Data Wiz database

This is a recoded version of CONDPROP (Miles and Vissage, In prep.). CONDPROP values less than 1 were recoded to 1 and indicate that the plot was mapped. CONDPROP values equal to 1 were recoded to 0 and indicate that the plot was not mapped.

| Code | Mapped |
|---|---|
| -1 | Missing |
| 0 | Not Mapped |
| 1 | Mapped |

26. *1983 Rural — Urban Continuum URCONT83

Rural/Urban Continuum Codes (updated 5/95) Stock #89021, Economic Research Service, United States Department of Agriculture.

References:
1.   Butler, Margaret A.; Beale, Calvin L. 1994. Rural-urban continuum codes for metro and nonmetro Counties, 1993. Staff Rep. 9425. Washington, DC: U.S. Department of Agriculture, Economic Research Service, Agriculture and Rural Economy Division.
2.   Butler, Margaret A. 1990. Rural-urban continuum codes for metro and nonmetro Counties. Staff Rep. 9028. Washington, DC: U.S. Department of Agriculture, Economic Research Service, Agriculture and Rural Economy Division.

27. *1993 Rural — Urban Continuum URCONT93

For RPA Data Wiz, plots were assigned continuum codes based upon the code associated with their county. The codes in the Economic Research Service database are assigned at the county scale.

| Code | Rural/Urban Continuum |
|---|---|
| 0 | Central counties of metropolitan areas of 1 million population or more |
| 1 | Fringe counties of metropolitan areas of 1 million population or more |
| 2 | Counties in metropolitan areas of 250,000 to 1 million population |
| 3 | Counties in metropolitan areas of less than 250,000 population |

| | |
| --- | --- |
| 4 | Urban population of 20,000 or more, adjacent to a metropolitan area |
| 5 | Urban population of 20,000 or more, not adjacent to a metropolitan area |
| 6 | Urban population of 2,500 to 19,999, adjacent to a metropolitan area |
| 7 | Urban population of 2,500 to 19,999, not adjacent to a metropolitan area |
| 8 | Completely rural or less than 2,500 urban population, adjacent to a metropolitan area |
| 9 | Completely rural or less than 2,500 urban population, not adjacent to a metropolitan area |

28. *Baileys' Ecosection
ECOSECTION

Baileys' ecoregions expressed as a six-digit number. It combines the domain, division, province, and section into one numeric code. The corresponding alphanumeric code exists in the field EcosectionTxt, only present in the database used with RPA Data Wiz. The translation from Baileys' alphanumeric ecocode to this integer value was taken from GTR SRS-36 (Rudis 1999) located in the references directory of the RPA Data Wiz CD. Plots were assigned an ecocode using an overlay analysis where plots with fuzzed (usually within a mile of the true location) locations were overlaid onto a Baileys' ecoregion polygon layer. Each plot was assigned the code of the ecoregion it contacted. If a plot did not intersect with a polygon, then it was assigned the ecoregion code of the polygon with the closest centroid. More information is available with the metadata (ecoregs.met or ecoregs.shp.xml in the application directory) of the ecoregs shapefile associated with RPA Data Wiz. Additional information can also be found in the references directory of the installation CD. Baileys' ecosection was not determined for HI or interior AK.

29. *107th Congressional division of District Code and 108th Congressional District Code CONGCD and CONGCD108

Congressional district codes for the 107th (CONGCD) and 108th (CONGCD108) Congress. A territorial a State from which a member of the U.S. House of Representatives is elected. There are 435 congressional districts in the United States apportioned to the States based on population. Each State receives at least one congressional district. The congressional district codes for the 107th and 108th Congress were assigned to each plot (regardless of when it was measured). CONGCD and CONGCD108 are four-digit numbers. The first two digits are the State FIPS code and the last two digits are the congressional district number. Plots were assigned congressional districts using an overlay analysis where plots with fuzzed (usually within a mile of the true location) locations were overlaid onto a congressional district polygon layer. Two overlay analyses were performed, one for the 107th and one for the 108th. Each plot was assigned the code of the congressional district it contacted. If a plot did not intersect with a polygon, then it was assigned the congressional district of the polygon with the closest centroid. If a plot was assigned a CONGCD or CONGCD108 that represented a congressional district from the incorrect State, then a visual inspection was used to assign the congressional district code of the closest polygon in the correct State (indicated by the State FIPS code associated with the plot). This situation occurred with plots near State borders due to the fact that the plot locations are fuzzed. More information is available with the metadata of the cgd107 and cgd108 shapefiles associated with RPA Data Wiz (cgd107.met or cgd107.shp.xml, cgd108.met or cgd108.shp.xml in the application directory). Additional information can also be found in the references directory of the installation CD. The 107th and 108th Congressional Districts were not determined for HI or interior AK.

30. *Hydrological Accounting Unit HUCACCUNIT

The hydrological accounting unit derived from USGS HUC (Hydrologic Unit Maps) attributes. (Region * 10000) + (Subregion * 100) + Accounting Unit is the formula for HUCACCUNIT. Plots were assigned a hydrological accounting unit using an overlay analysis where plots with fuzzed (usually within a mile of the true location) locations were overlaid onto a hydrological accounting unit polygon layer. Each plot was assigned the code of the hydrological accounting unit it contacted. If a plot did not intersect with a polygon, then it was assigned the hydrological accounting unit code of the polygon with the closest centroid. More information is available with the metadata (hucau.met or hucau.shp.xml in the application directory) of the hucau shapefile associated with RPA Data Wiz. Additional information can also be found in the references directory of the installation CD. The hydrological accounting unit was not determined for HI or AK.

31.  *Mean Stand DIA     Mean stand diameter class (2" increments) for all trees ≥ 1" d.b.h. Estimation is by calculating the quadratic
     2" Class or Larger    mean diameter (except HI and interior AK). Mean stand diameters ≥ 39" d.b.h. are classed as 40" d.b.h. This
     STDIAM2CLASS          field is used in the English version of RPA Data Wiz. See appendix D.

32.  *Mean Stand DIA     Mean stand diameter class (2" increments) for all trees ≥ 5" d.b.h. Estimation is by calculating the quadratic
     6" Class or Larger    mean diameter (except HI and interior AK). Mean stand diameters ≥ 39" d.b.h. are classed as 40" d.b.h. This
     STDIAM6CLASS          field is used in the English version of RPA Data Wiz. See appendix D.

33.  *Mean Stand DIA     Mean stand diameter class (5-cm increments) for all trees ≥ 3 cm (2.5 cm) d.b.h. Estimation is by calculating
     5 cm Class or Larger  the quadratic mean diameter (except HI and interior AK). Mean stand diameters ≥ 98 cm d.b.h. are classed
     STDIAM5CLASS          as 100 cm d.b.h. This field is used in the metric version of RPA Data Wiz. See appendix D.

34.  *Mean Stand DIA     Mean stand diameter class (5-cm increments) for all trees ≥ 13 cm (12.7 cm) d.b.h. Estimation is by
     15 cm Class or Larger calculating the quadratic mean diameter (except HI and interior AK). Mean stand diameters ≥ 98 cm d.b.h.
     STDIAM15CLASS         are classed as 100 cm d.b.h. This field is used in the metric version of RPA Data Wiz. See appendix D.

35.  108th Congressional  Defined with 107th Congressional District Code.
     District Code
     CONGCD108

# Appendix B
# Output Variables (English Version)

These are the definitions for the output variables in the English version of RPA Data Wiz. The corresponding field names in the RPA Data Wiz database, rpadb2002.mdb, are also provided. Most of the data in RPA Data Wiz (db2002.mdb, Access database) originally came from another database, the 2002 RPA Assessment database. Most of the definitions presented here are modified versions of those in *The 2002 RPA Plot Summary Database Users Manual Version 1.0* (Miles and Vissage, In prep.) associated with the 2002 RPA Assessment database. Field definitions have been modified to work in RPA Data Wiz. In the original 2002 RPA Assessment database, these output variables were expressed on a per acre basis. To speed up computations in RPA Data Wiz, these output variables, except area, were multiplied by their corresponding expansion factors (VEF) to come up with totals for each plot or record in the RPA Data Wiz database. The volume expansion factor, or VEF, is the number of acres the sample plot represents for making total estimates of volume, number of trees, and biomass. Sometimes other variables are mentioned in this appendix. Please refer to appendix A for definitions of selection variables like TSOURCE. Refer to appendix D for definitions of size classes. D.b.h. or diameter at breast height is mentioned in this appendix. It is defined as the stem diameter, outside bark, at a point 4.5 feet (137.16 cm) above ground. Any other variables mentioned but not defined in this appendix are defined by Miles and Vissage (In prep.).

| RPA Data Wiz Name Access FIELD NAME | Definition |
| --- | --- |
| 1. Area (acres) AEF | Area Expansion Factor. The number of acres the sample plot represents for making current estimates of area. The sum of AEF over all plot records for a particular State is the total land and water area of the State as calculated by the Bureau of Census. |
| 2. SW Board Foot Volume – International 1/4 BDFTSW | Softwood board foot volume (International 1/4" rule). The net volume (board feet) of softwood growing stock represented per plot. Trees must be ≥ 9 inches d.b.h. The minimum saw log top is 7" diameter outside bark. Available only for timberland plots(forcode = 1). |
| 3. HW Board Foot Volume – International 1/4 BDFTHW | Hardwood board foot volume (International 1/4" rule). The net volume (board feet) of hardwood growing stock represented per plot. Trees must be ≥ 11 inches d.b.h. The minimum saw log top is 9" diameter outside bark. Available only for timberland plots (forcode = 1). |
| 4. Board Foot Volume – International 1/4 BDFT | Board foot volume (International 1/4" rule). The net volume (board feet) of softwood and hardwood growing stock represented per plot. Available only for timberland plots (forcode = 1). |
| 5. SW Cubic Foot Volume CUBICSW | Softwood cubic foot volume. Net volume (cubic feet) of softwood growing stock represented per plot. Trees must be ≥ 5 inches d.b.h. The minimum top is 4" diameter outside bark. Available for all forest land plots. Values are imputed where the value of the variable TSOURCE is not equal to 1 (TSOURCE may not be equal to 1 for some reserved and unproductive forest land). |

6.  HW Cubic Foot Volume      Hardwood cubic foot volume. Net volume (cubic feet) of hardwood growing stock represented per plot. Trees
    CUBICHW                   must be ≥ 5 inches d.b.h. The minimum top is 4" diameter outside bark. Values are imputed where the value
                              of the variable TSOURCE is not equal to 1 (TSOURCE may not be equal to 1 for some reserved and unpro-
                              ductive forest land).

7.  Cubic Foot Volume        Cubic foot volume. Net volume (cubic feet) of hardwood growing stock represented per plot. Trees must be
    CUBIC                     ≥ 5 inches d.b.h. The minimum top is 4" diameter outside bark. Values are imputed where the value of the
                              variable TSOURCE is not equal to 1 (TSOURCE may not be equal to 1 for some reserved and unproductive
                              forest land).

8.  SW Live Cull Volume      Softwood live cull volume. Net volume (cubic feet) of live cull softwood trees represented per plot; trees must
    CULLSW                    be ≥ 5 inches d.b.h. Available for all forest land plots. Values are imputed where the value of the variable
                              TSOURCE is not equal to 1 (TSOURCE may not be equal to 1 for some reserved and unproductive forest
                              land).

9.  HW Live Cull Volume      Hardwood live cull volume. Net volume (cubic feet) of live cull hardwood trees represented per plot; trees
    CULLHW                    must be ≥ 5 inches d.b.h. Available for all forest land plots. Values are imputed where the value of the
                              variable TSOURCE is not equal to 1 (TSOURCE may not be equal to 1 for some reserved and unproductive
                              forest land).

10. Live Cull Volume         All live cull volume. Net volume (cubic feet) of all live cull trees represented per plot; trees must be ≥ 5
    CULL                      inches d.b.h. Available for all forest land plots. Values are imputed where the value of the variable TSOURCE
                              is not equal to 1 (TSOURCE may not be equal to 1 for some reserved and unproductive forest land).

11. SW Sound Dead            Salvable dead softwood. Net volume (cubic feet) of merchantable sound dead softwood trees represented per
    Volume                   plot. Merchantability is determined by regional standards. Available for all forest land plots. Values are
    DEADSW                   imputed where the value of the variable TSOURCE is not equal to 1 (TSOURCE may not be equal to 1 for
                              some reserved and unproductive forest land).

12. HW Sound Dead            Salvable dead hardwood. Net volume (cubic feet) of merchantable sound dead hardwood trees represented
    Volume                   per plot. Merchantability is determined by regional standards. Available for all forest land plots. Values are
    DEADHW                   imputed where the value of the variable TSOURCE is not equal to 1 (TSOURCE may not be equal to 1 for
                              some reserved and unproductive forest land).

13. Sound Dead Volume        Salvable dead. Net volume (cubic feet) of merchantable sound dead trees represented per plot. Merchantabil-
    DEAD                     ity is determined by regional standards. Available for all forest land plots. Values are imputed where the value
                              of the variable TSOURCE is not equal to 1 (TSOURCE may not be equal to 1 for some reserved and unpro-
                              ductive forest land).

| | |
| --- | --- |
| 14. SW Mortality<br>MORTSW | Softwood mortality. Volume (cubic feet) of annual mortality of softwood growing stock represented per plot; trees must be ≥ 5 inches d.b.h. Available only for timberland plots. |
| 15. HW Mortality<br>MORTHW | Hardwood mortality. Volume (cubic feet) of annual mortality of hardwood growing stock represented per plot; trees must be ≥ 5 inches d.b.h. Available only for timberland plots. |
| 16. Mortality<br>MORT | Mortality. Volume (cubic feet) of annual mortality of growing stock trees represented per plot; trees must be ≥ 5 inches d.b.h. Available only for timberland plots. |
| 17. SW Netgrowth<br>GROWTHSW | Net annual softwood growth. Net annual growth (cubic feet) of softwood growing stock represented per plot. Net growth is gross growth minus mortality and negative cull increment plus positive cull increment. Negative cull increment occurs when growing-stock trees at time zero are reclassified as cull trees at time one. Positive cull increment is when trees classified as cull at time zero are reclassified as growing stock at time one. Available only for timberland plots. |
| 18. HW Netgrowth<br>GROWTHHW | Net annual hardwood growth. Net annual growth (cubic feet) of hardwood growing stock represented per plot. Net growth is gross growth minus mortality and negative cull increment plus positive cull increment. Negative cull increment occurs when growing-stock trees at time zero are reclassified as cull trees at time one. Positive cull increment is when trees classified as cull at time zero are reclassified as growing stock at time one. Available only for timberland plots. |
| 19. Netgrowth<br>GROWTH | Net annual growth. Net annual growth (cubic feet) of softwood growing stock represented per plot. Net growth is gross growth minus mortality and negative cull increment plus positive cull increment. Negative cull increment occurs when growing-stock trees at time zero are reclassified as cull trees at time one. Positive cull increment is when trees classified as cull at time zero are reclassified as growing stock at time one. Available only for timberland plots. |
| 20. SW Gross Biomass 6"<br>Class or Larger<br>BIOBOLESW | Softwood biomass in the bole. Total gross biomass (including bark) represented per plot in dry pounds of all live softwood trees 5 inches d.b.h. or larger from a 1-foot stump to a minimum 4-inch top (diameter outside bark of the central stem). |
| 21. HW Gross Biomass 6"<br>Class or Larger<br>BIOBOLEHW | Hardwood biomass in the bole. Total gross biomass (including bark) represented per plot in dry pounds of all live hardwood trees 5 inches d.b.h. or larger from a 1-foot stump to a minimum 4-inch top (diameter outside bark of the central stem). |
| 22. Gross Biomass 6"<br>Class or Larger<br>BIOBOLE | Biomass in the bole. Total gross biomass (including bark) represented per plot in dry pounds of all live trees 5 inches d.b.h. or larger from a 1-foot stump to a minimum 4-inch top (diameter outside bark of the central stem). |

| RPA Data Wiz Name<br>Access FIELD NAME | Definition |
|---|---|
| 23. SW Gross Aboveground Biomass 2 to 6" Class<br>BIOSAPSSW | Softwood sapling biomass. Total gross aboveground biomass (including bark) represented per plot in dry pounds of all live softwood trees from 1 to 5 inches d.b.h., including tops and limbs. |
| 24. HW Gross Aboveground Biomass 2 to 6" Class<br>BIOSAPSHW | Hardwood sapling biomass. Total gross aboveground biomass (including bark) represented per plot in dry pounds of all live hardwood trees from 1 to 5 inches d.b.h., including tops and limbs. |
| 25. Gross Aboveground Biomass 2 to 6" Class<br>BIOSAPS | Sapling biomass. Total gross aboveground biomass (including bark) represented per plot in dry pounds of all live trees from 1 to 5 inches d.b.h., including tops and limbs. |
| 26. Number Live Trees 6" Class or Larger<br>TPA_5 | Number of live trees 5 inches in diameter and larger represented per plot. Only calculated for timberland plots (FORCODE = 1). Diameters are usually measured at d.b.h. except for certain woodland species where diameters are measured at the root collar. |
| 27. Number Live Trees 2" Class or Larger diameters<br>TPA_1 | Number of live trees 1 inch in diameter and larger represented per plot. Only calculated for timberland plots (FORCODE = 1). Diameters are usually measured at d.b.h. except for certain woodland species where<br><br>are measured at the root collar. |
| 28. SW Biomass-Stumps and Tops 6" Class or Larger<br>BIOSTUMPTOPSW | Biomass (pounds) in the stump and tops of live softwood trees 5 inches in diameter and larger represented per plot. Difference between total dry biomass and merchantable dry biomass on live trees 5 inches in diameter and larger. |
| 29. HW Biomass-Stumps and Tops 6" Class or Larger<br>BIOSTUMPTOPHW | Biomass (pounds) in the stump and tops of live hardwood trees 5 inches in diameter and larger represented per plot. Difference between total dry biomass and merchantable dry biomass on live trees 5 inches in diameter and larger. |
| 30. Biomass-Stumps and Tops 6" Class or Larger<br>BIOSTUMPTOP | Biomass (pounds) in the stump and tops of live trees 5 inches in diameter and larger represented per plot. Difference between total dry biomass and merchantable dry biomass on live trees 5 inches in diameter and larger. |
| 31. SW Salvable Dead Biomass 6" Class or Larger<br>BIOSALVDEADSW | Total gross biomass (dry weight in pounds) for salvable dead softwood trees represented per plot. The total aboveground biomass of trees 5 inches in diameter and larger, including all tops and limbs (but excluding foliage). |

| | |
|---|---|
| 32. HW Salvable Dead Biomass 6" Class or Larger BIOSALVDEADHW | Total gross biomass (dry weight in pounds) dry weight for salvable dead hardwood trees represented per plot. The total aboveground biomass of trees 5 inches in diameter and larger, including all tops and limbs (but excluding foliage). |
| 33. Salvable Dead Biomass 6" Class or Larger BIOSALVDEAD | Total gross biomass (dry weight in pounds) dry weight for salvable dead trees represented per plot. The total aboveground biomass of trees 5 inches in diameter and larger, including all tops and limbs (but excluding foliage). |

# Appendix C
# Output Variables (Metric Version)

These are the definitions for the output variables in the metric version of RPA Data Wiz. The corresponding field names in the RPA Data Wiz database, rpadb2002met.mdb, are also provided. Most of the data in RPA Data Wiz (rpadb2002met.mdb, Access database) originally came from another database, the 2002 RPA Assessment database. Most of the definitions presented here are modified versions of those in *The 2002 RPA Plot Summary Database Users Manual Version 1.0* (Miles and Vissage, In prep.) associated with the 2002 RPA Assessment database. Field definitions have been modified to work in RPA Data Wiz. In the original 2002 RPA Assessment database, these output variables were expressed on a per acre (not hectare) basis. To speed up computations in RPA Data Wiz, these output variables, except area, were multiplied by their corresponding expansion factors (VEF) to come up with totals for each plot or record in the RPA Data Wiz database. The volume expansion factor, or VEF, is the number of acres the sample plot represents for making total estimates of volume, number of trees, and biomass. After calculating the output variable totals per plot, a metric conversion factor was applied to the English units. Acres were converted to hectares (acres * 0.404686). Cubic-foot values were converted to cubic meters (cubic feet * 0.028317). Pounds were converted to metric tons (pounds * 0.000453592). Sometimes other variables are mentioned in this appendix. Please refer to appendix A for definitions of selection variables like TSOURCE. Refer to appendix D for definitions of size classes. Centimeters mentioned in the definitions below are rounded to the nearest integer. Inches were converted to centimeters using 2.54 as the conversion factor. D.b.h. or diameter at breast height is mentioned in this appendix. It is defined as the stem diameter, outside bark, at a point 4.5 feet (137.16 cm) above ground. Any other variables mentioned but not defined in this appendix are defined by Miles and Vissage (In prep.).

| RPA Data Wiz Name Access FIELD NAME | Definition |
| --- | --- |
| 1. Area (hectares) AEF | Area Expansion Factor. The number of hectares the sample plot represents for making current estimates of area. The sum of AEF over all plot records for a particular State is the total land and water area of the State as calculated by the Bureau of Census. |
| 2. SW Cubic Meter Volume CUBICSW | Softwood cubic foot volume. Net volume (cubic meters) of softwood growing stock represented per plot. Trees must be ≥ 13 cm d.b.h. The minimum top is 10 cm diameter outside bark. Available for all forest land plots. Values are imputed where the value of the variable TSOURCE is not equal to 1 (TSOURCE may not be equal to 1 for some reserved and unproductive forest land). |
| 3. HW Cubic Meter Volume CUBICHW | Hardwood cubic foot volume. Net volume (cubic meters) of hardwood growing stock represented per plot. Trees must be ≥ 13 cm d.b.h. The minimum top is 10 cm diameter outside bark. Values are imputed where the value of the variable TSOURCE is not equal to 1 (TSOURCE may not be equal to 1 for some reserved and unproductive forest land). |

| RPA Data Wiz Name<br>Access FIELD NAME | Definition |
|---|---|
| 4. Cubic Meter Volume<br>CUBIC | Cubic foot volume. Net volume (cubic meters) of hardwood growing stock represented per plot. Trees must be ≥ 13 cm d.b.h. The minimum top is 10 cm diameter outside bark. Values are imputed where the value of the variable TSOURCE is not equal to 1 (TSOURCE may not be equal to 1 for some reserved and unproductive forest land). |
| 5. SW Live Cull Volume<br>CULLSW | Softwood live cull volume. Net volume (cubic meters) of live cull softwood trees represented per plot; trees must be ≥ 13 cm d.b.h. Available for all forest land plots. Values are imputed where the value of the variable TSOURCE is not equal to 1 (TSOURCE may not be equal to 1 for some reserved and unproductive forest land). |
| 6. HW Live Cull Volume<br>CULLHW | Hardwood live cull volume. Net volume (cubic meters) of live cull hardwood trees represented per plot; trees must be ≥ 13 cm d.b.h. Available for all forest land plots. Values are imputed where the value of the variable TSOURCE is not equal to 1 (TSOURCE may not be equal to 1 for some reserved and unproductive forest land). |
| 7. Live Cull Volume<br>CULL | All live cull volume. Net volume (cubic meters) of all live cull trees represented per plot; trees must be ≥ 13 cm d.b.h. Available for all forest land plots. Values are imputed where the value of the variable TSOURCE is not equal to 1 (TSOURCE may not be equal to 1 for some reserved and unproductive forest land). |
| 8. SW Sound Dead Volume<br>DEADSW | Salvable dead softwood. Net volume (cubic meters) of merchantable sound dead softwood trees represented per plot. Merchantability is determined by regional standards. Available for all forest land plots. Values are imputed where the value of the variable TSOURCE is not equal to 1 (TSOURCE may not be equal to 1 for some reserved and unproductive forest land). |
| 9. HW Sound Dead Volume<br>DEADHW | Salvable dead hardwood. Net volume (cubic meters) of merchantable sound dead hardwood trees represented per plot. Merchantability is determined by regional standards. Available for all forest land plots. Values are imputed where the value of the variable TSOURCE is not equal to 1 (TSOURCE may not be equal to 1 for some reserved and unproductive forest land). |
| 10. Sound Dead Volume<br>DEAD | Salvable dead. Net volume (cubic meters) of merchantable sound dead trees represented per plot. Merchantability is determined by regional standards. Available for all forest land plots. Values are imputed where the value of the variable TSOURCE is not equal to 1 (TSOURCE may not be equal to 1 for some reserved and unproductive forest land). |
| 11. SW Mortality<br>MORTSW | Softwood mortality. Volume (cubic meters) of annual mortality of softwood growing stock represented per plot; trees must be ≥ 13 cm d.b.h. Available only for timberland plots. |
| 12. HW Mortality<br>MORTHW | Hardwood mortality. Volume (cubic meters) of annual mortality of hardwood growing stock represented per plot; trees must be ≥ 13 cm d.b.h. Available only for timberland plots. |

| RPA Data Wiz Name<br>Access FIELD NAME | Definition |
|---|---|
| 13. Mortality<br>MORT | Mortality. Volume (cubic meters) of annual mortality of growing-stock trees represented per plot; trees must be ≥ 13 cm d.b.h. Available only for timberland plots. |
| 14. SW Netgrowth<br>GROWTHSW | Net annual softwood growth. Net annual growth (cubic meters) of softwood growing stock represented per plot. Net growth is gross growth minus mortality and negative cull increment plus positive cull increment. Negative cull increment occurs when growing-stock trees at time zero are reclassified as cull trees at time one. Positive cull increment is when trees classified as cull at time zero are reclassified as growing stock at time one. Available only for timberland plots. |
| 15. HW Netgrowth<br>GROWTHHW | Net annual hardwood growth. Net annual growth (cubic meters) of hardwood growing stock represented per plot. Net growth is gross growth minus mortality and negative cull increment plus positive cull increment. Negative cull increment occurs when growing-stock trees at time zero are reclassified as cull trees at time one. Positive cull increment is when trees classified as cull at time zero are reclassified as growing stock at time one. Available only for timberland plots. |
| 16. Netgrowth<br>GROWTH | Net annual growth. Net annual growth (cubic meters) of softwood growing stock represented per plot. Net growth is gross growth minus mortality and negative cull increment plus positive cull increment. Negative cull increment occurs when growing-stock trees at time zero are reclassified as cull trees at time one. Positive cull increment is when trees classified as cull at time zero are reclassified as growing stock at time one. Available only for timberland plots. |
| 17. SW Gross Biomass<br>15 cm Class or Larger<br>BIOBOLESW | Softwood biomass in the bole. Total gross biomass (including bark) represented per plot in dry metric tons of all live softwood trees 13 cm d.b.h. or larger from a 30-cm stump to a minimum 10-cm top (diameter outside bark of the central stem). |
| 18. HW Gross Biomass<br>15 cm Class or Larger<br>BIOBOLEHW | Hardwood biomass in the bole. Total gross biomass (including bark) represented per plot in dry metric tons of all live hardwood trees 13 cm d.b.h. or larger from a 30-cm stump to a minimum 10-cm top (diameter outside bark of the central stem). |
| 19. Gross Biomass<br>15 cm Class or Larger<br>BIOBOLE | Biomass in the bole. Total gross biomass (including bark) represented per plot in dry metric tons of all live trees 13 cm d.b.h. or larger from a 30-cm stump to a minimum 10-cm top (diameter outside bark of the central stem). |
| 20. SW Gross Aboveground<br>Biomass 5 to 15 cm<br>Class<br>BIOSAPSSW | Softwood sapling biomass. Total gross aboveground biomass (including bark) represented per plot in dry metric tons of all live softwood trees from 3 to 13 cm d.b.h., including tops and limbs. |

| RPA Data Wiz Name<br>Access FIELD NAME | Definition |
|---|---|
| 21. HW Gross Aboveground Biomass 5 to 15 cm Class<br>BIOSAPSHW | Hardwood sapling biomass. Total gross aboveground biomass (including bark) represented per plot in dry metric tons of all live hardwood trees from 3 to 13 cm d.b.h., including tops and limbs. |
| 22. Gross Aboveground Biomass 5 to 15 cm Class<br>BIOSAPS | Sapling biomass. Total gross aboveground biomass (including bark) represented per plot in dry metric tons of all live trees from 3 to 13 cm d.b.h., including tops and limbs. |
| 23. Number Live Trees 15 cm Class or Larger<br>TPA_15 | Number of live trees 13 cm in diameter and larger represented per plot. Only calculated for timberland plots (forcode = 1). Diameters are usually measured at d.b.h. except for certain woodland species where diameters are measured at the root collar. |
| 24. Number Live Trees 5 cm Class or Larger<br>TPA_5 | Number of live trees 3 cm in diameter and larger represented per plot. Only calculated for timberland plots (forcode = 1). Diameters are usually measured at d.b.h. except for certain woodland species where diameters are measured at the root collar. |
| 25. SW Biomass-Stumps and Tops 15 cm Class or Larger<br>BIOSTUMPTOPSW | Biomass (metric tons) in the stump and tops of live softwood trees 13 cm in diameter and larger represented per plot. Difference between total dry biomass and merchantable dry biomass on live trees 13 cm in diameter and larger. |
| 26. HW Biomass-Stumps and Tops 15 cm Class or Larger<br>BIOSTUMPTOPHW | Biomass (metric tons) in the stump and tops of live hardwood trees 13 cm in diameter and larger represented per plot. Difference between total dry biomass and merchantable dry biomass on live trees 13 cm in diameter and larger. |
| 27. Biomass-Stumps and Tops 15 cm Class or Larger<br>BIOSTUMPTOP | Biomass (metric tons) in the stump and tops of live trees 13 cm in diameter and larger represented per plot. Difference between total dry biomass and merchantable dry biomass on live trees 13 cm in diameter and larger. |
| 28. SW Salvable Dead Biomass 15 cm Class or Larger<br>BIOSALVDEADSW | Total gross biomass (dry weight in metric tons) for salvable dead softwood trees represented per plot. The total aboveground biomass of trees 13 cm diameter or larger, including all tops and limbs (but excluding foliage). |

| | |
|---|---|
| 29. HW Salvable Dead Biomass 15 cm Class or Larger BIOSALVDEADHW | Total gross biomass (dry weight in metric tons) for salvable dead hardwood trees represented per plot. The total aboveground biomass of trees 13 cm diameter or larger, including all tops and limbs (but excluding foliage). |
| 30. Salvable Dead Biomass 15 cm Class or Larger BIOSALVDEAD | Total gross biomass (dry weight in metric tons) for salvable dead trees represented per plot. The total above-round biomass of trees 13 cm diameter or larger, including all tops and limbs (but excluding foliage). |

# Appendix D
# English and Metric Size Classes

These are the size classes as they appear in RPA Data Wiz. The numbers in the Metric Size Class Range column are rounded to the nearest integer.

| English size class | English size class range (inches) | Metric size class | Metric size class range (cm) |
|---|---|---|---|
| 0 | 0.0 | 0 | 0 |
| 2 | 1.0 - 2.9 | 5 | 3 - 7 |
| 4 | 3.0 - 4.9 | 10 | 8 - 12 |
| 6 | 5.0 - 6.9 | 15 | 13 - 17 |
| 8 | 7.0 - 8.9 | 20 | 18 - 22 |
| 10 | 9.0 - 10.9 | 25 | 23 - 27 |
| 12 | 11.0 - 12.9 | 30 | 28 - 32 |
| 14 | 13.0 - 14.9 | 35 | 33 - 37 |
| 16 | 15.0 - 16.9 | 40 | 38 - 42 |
| 18 | 17.0 - 18.9 | 45 | 43 - 47 |
| 20 | 19.0 - 20.9 | 50 | 48 - 52 |
| 22 | 21.0 - 22.9 | 55 | 53 - 57 |
| 24 | 23.0 - 24.9 | 60 | 58 - 62 |
| 26 | 25.0 - 26.9 | 65 | 63 - 67 |
| 28 | 27.0 - 28.9 | 70 | 68 - 72 |
| 30 | 29.0 - 30.9 | 75 | 73 - 77 |
| 32 | 31.0 - 32.9 | 80 | 78 - 82 |
| 34 | 33.0 - 34.9 | 85 | 83 - 87 |
| 36 | 35.0 - 36.9 | 90 | 88 - 92 |
| 38 | 37.0 - 38.9 | 95 | 93 - 97 |
| 40 | 39 + | 100 | 98 + |

www.ingramcontent.com/pod-product-compliance
Lightning Source LLC
Chambersburg PA
CBHW080258290526
45790CB00005B/1855